Living with Alzhiemers'

Living with Alzhiemers'

(A Conversation If You Will)

Joseph Potocny

Library of Congress Control Number:		2010915507
ISBN:	Hardcover	978-1-4535-9324-0
	Softcover	978-1-4535-9323-3
	Ebook	978-1-4535-9325-7

This book was printed in the United States of America.

To order additional copies of this book, contact:
Xlibris Corporation
1-888-795-4274
www.Xlibris.com
Orders@Xlibris.com
87750

Dedication

This narrative is dedicated to all those who traveled this road of Alzheimer's before me. Those that walk with me now and will in future times and to those who care for us Along The Way.

Acknowledgement

To all of you that have helped me along this journey that I am on to you I say Thank You.

You and my Loving Family have put up with me and my tirades' over the years, but have stuck by my side.

To the many organizations that have promoted my blog and to HBO for having the courage to put my mug in their documentary (that took courage) Thank You!

FOREWARD

This book if you will, is really a conversation between me and the over 43,000 people who have visited and contributed to my blog, with their comments and just their being there for me.

Together we have expressed our fears, hopes, dreams, tears, and personal pain. It has been our hope that others would benefit from our stories and journeys.

We want the reader to experience the frustration, anxiety, loneliness, hopelessness and fears that we who suffer from Alzheimer's experience on a daily basis in our lives.

Those who care for us, find themselves in a World of constant change and upheaval and many times have nowhere to turn. Hopefully that burden will be a little lighter for those who read this.

Those who travel this road with me, may you know that you are not alone.

WELCOME TO MY WORLD!

Contents

Monday, September 25, 2006

I truly hope those interested in those with AD and helping and sharing use this blog. It gets lonely out here in my own mind, which is rather confussed and frustrated. There are other sites that I go to such as Don Haydens' www.thetripover.com, alzg.org. It is hard to get people to respond to you, I think that they are afraid because they do not relate or do not want to offend. Please do not be either. Your contact helps keep my mind stimulated and aware which is something that one with Alzheimers' needs very much. Just knowing that others care and are willing to become aware of this disease is great. Many older and even younger folks suffer in silence with this disease, if nothing else come out for them and talk to me. Posted by Joseph Potocny at 08:20AM (-07:00)

Comments

—kenju   May 26, 2009

Joe, I saw your story on HBO and I wanted to tell you how pleased I am that you are writing your story. I am going to start at the beginning and read every post. Good luck from here on out and thank you for sharing.

—MelanieCarne   July 28, 2009

Joe,

Thank you for all that you do. I saw you on HBO, (the dvd just came on sale today and the Barnes and Nobles that carry media have limited numbers of it). My father has been recently diagnosed and is still somewhat in denial of his condition. I made him watch the show and you and your admission was monumentally helpful in breaking through some of the stigma and denial we are dealing with.

—Kathi   December 07, 2009

Thank you Joe! I am so grateful for your transparency, amazing honesty, and harsh truth—I need to learn from you (we ALL DO) and I HOPE your story on HBO will help BEGIN support for AD research!!! God bless you, your family, and especially your wife Lynn! . . . a daughter-in-law of the AD Thief

Monday, September 25, 2006

Living with Alzhiemers'

Posted by Joseph Potocny at 08:35AM (-07:00)

Saturday, December 02, 2006

Living with Alzhiemers'

As time goes on things get more difficult and frustrating, but now I am 62 and still breathing in and out. I enjoy hearing from others either through the blog or my email: jolynn1@cox.net, You all have a very Merry Holiday Season and God Bless You All.

Joe Posted by Joseph Potocny at 02:05PM (-08:00)

The Happy Momemts

Sunday, December 03, 2006

Last night the Wife, two daughters and my granddaughter (3yrs) started decorating the house for Christmas. My granddaughter was so proud that she got to put ornaments on the tree and point out with great pleasure each one to me. These are the moments I want her to remember, not the time that is coming when grandpa will not be very well shall we say with it. I cried most of the night in silence as I felt sorry for what my family is going through. I know my time will end of knowning anything, but they will be left with the wreckage. I have battled alcoholism, smoking, parkinson, my homosexuality and have stayed the course in these battles, but this is one that I am slowly loosing, Alzheimer's does not care who or what you are it just keeps eating away at your mind taking its' share each day. I know it sounds like I am very coherent, but it takes a great deal of concentration on each word and rechecking spelling. It hurts when my wife has to call me several times to acknowledge her, because I am somewhere else, God only knows where, because I sure the hell don't. But I am still here and still breathing. God Bless You All and This Great Country of Ours!

Posted by Joseph Potocny at 07:56AM (-08:00)

Monday, December 04, 2006

Howdy to you all today is not a good day for me. Been having problems forgetting what I am doing and where I am putting things. Getting to distracted today. Did have fun with grand daughter yesterday taking her for walks, good thing she remembered the way back, because I got confused. She wanted to go for a ride and I said ok I will drive. No Grandpa you cannot drive she said, you are not supposed to. Little bugger, God has Blessed me. Well that is all my brain can handle today.

God Bless You and This Great Country of Ours

Joe

Posted by Joseph Potocny at 01:53PM (-08:00)

Things Get Good and Go South

Wednesday, December 06, 2006

Spent the last few days with decorating the house for the holidays. Been chatting at alz.org with other folks suffering and caring for those with Alzheimers and have enjoyed the time. But the mind gets fuzzy after awhile and have to leave. It is nice to have a place to go and talk with others having and knowing others that have this disease. You do feel isolated and never know how it is going to progress, today your ok, tonight you have no idea what is going on. Well I am still breathing. Would like to hear from someone.

God Bless You and This Great Country of Ours

Joe

Posted by Joseph Potocny at 01:11PM (-08:00)

Comments

—Anonymous   December 06, 2006

Be patient people will find you.

The word has to get out that you are there.

—JosephPotocny   December 06, 2006

Thanks for caring and visiting.

Joe

I Took This From Don Hayden Posting at TheTripOver.com

Thursday, December 07, 2006

Visit Don's site and read his blogs he also is on the journey with AD and has alot of good postings.

Great words of advice out Mayo Clinic.

I'm going to paraphrase from an article I read today out of the Mayo Clinic. Dr. Eric Tangalos, an Alzheimer's specialist was interviewed.

When I tell people I have Alzheimer's but still drive and write and function normally, they tell me they didn't think AD could be diagnosed until autopsy. Dr. Tangalos affirms my belief that diagnosis can and should be made in early stages with examinations and other test. Despite the time and effort, there is no better investment in order to make an early diagnosis. Brief test in your primary care doctors can screen for the need for more thorough testing.

Early signs to lead you to the doctor to start with can be summed up simply: Change in behavior! Apply that to the following list:

1. Memory
2. Difficulty performing familiar tasks
3. Problems with language
4. Disorientation to time and place
5. Poor or decreased judgment
6. Problems with abstract thinking
7. Misplacing things
8. Changes in mood or behavior
9. Changes in personality
10. Loss of initiative

There are three stages in AD; cognitive decline, functional decline and behavioral decline. Most people are diagnosed in the second stage because they do not want to anticipate being told they have AD. Worst yet, doctors avoid the word as well. But that is going to change.

Early diagnosis allows the drugs now available to be most effective and gives time for the patient to prepare, socially and economically for what is to come. Dr. Tangalos points out the value of improving the home environment, perhaps downsizing to make the space more manageable or installing inexpensive devices like motion detector lights and big-button phones. Maintaining a routine is essential. If you are going to move or make a major change in your environment, do it in the early stage when the patient can adjust or in the late stage their function is already extremely impaired.

Dr. Tangalos ended the interview with this: "(People are coming in for diagnosis) much too late. That's easy to understand because Alzheimer's is such a devastating disease. But we'd like patients and families to run toward the diagnosis, rather than away from it."

From one who is living that reality, I say *Amen!*

Permalink: THETRIPOVER.COM/2006/12/06/great-words-of-advice-out-mayo-clinic.aspx

Posted by Joseph Potocny at 09:06AM (-08:00)

Feeling the Frustration

Friday, December 08, 2006

I just read a new post by Don Hayden on his site and I feel very much for him as he progresses along this path we are on. I understand his frustration and looking at who he is, but I say to him you are still there with us to talk so things are ok, we need you out here.

I am also thinking about my wife today who was bidding for an item for me on ebay and lost. I know how disappointed she will be, but I still love her for it. I have tears in my eyes as I am writing this and I think of what she still has to go through with me and it bothers me greatly. My family will feel the strain as well as will my friends. I can only hope that they find the strenghth inside themselves to know that they are loved by me and I care about their concerns. Someday this disease will be able to be fought and halted in its, tracks. Thanks to those who are working and giving of themselves to find the way.

God Bless You and This Great Country of Ours

Joe

Posted by Joseph Potocny at 09:14AM (-08:00)

Today is one of those days

Sunday, December 10, 2006

I just feel plain confussed and not connected today. I guess that is how this works. I am irritable and somewhat frustrated. They tell me this can go on for years. I sure hope not, this way of living with a mind that once was like a sponge, now drying up, just is not for me. I am sure those who suffer out there with Alzheimers must feel the same way and just want it to be over with. I am ready to move on now, I do not like this feeling. Yes I am on a pitty party right now. But I cannot change what is happening to me and that really ((***&&^&^%%%$ me off. I have been a fighter all my life and am so loosing this battle and really do not like it.

Well you all have a Great Holiday Season. God Bless You and This Great Country of Ours

Joe

Posted by Joseph Potocny at 08:49AM (-08:00)

A Different Day

Monday, December 11, 2006

Yesterday was just terrible for me. Trying to change things here, I not only lost the blog, but my profile for my browser, addresses book, bookmarks and the rest. Slowly getting back to normal now, whatever that is, meeting new friends in other Alzheimer chat rooms. Will be adding links to my blog for them. Hope the day gets better, if not right now is OK.

God Bless You and This Great Country of Ours

Joe

Posted by Joseph Potocny at 10:12AM (-08:00)

Alzheimers Newsletter I Subscribe Too

Tuesday, December 12, 2006

I subscribe to the following newsletter, you will find their link on the right side of this blog.

Alzheimer's Daily News A Publication of the Ageless Design Research Foundation Tuesday, December 12, 2006 in this issue

* Possible Fingerprint of Alzheimer's Found
* Pharmaceuticals Companies Enter Drug Alliance
* Early Diagnosis of Alzheimer's on the Rise
* More 'Creative and Responsible' Senior Care
* Cold-Weather Tips for Older Adults
* Richard's Views: I've Moved and I Didn't Know It
* Calendar of Events—Link to November Events

Dear Joseph, Editorial Note: Each day Ageless Design Research Foundation reviews the news wires, looking for press releases and current articles relating to dementia. We write a brief description of each article along with a link to the originally written story before including it in the Alzheimer's Daily News. For more information we strongly recommend that you read the full article and draw your own conclusions.

Mark & Ellen Warner

~~~~~~

Possible Fingerprint of Alzheimer's Found

(Source: AP)—Researchers at New York's Weill Cornell Medical College appear to have found a fingerprint of Alzheimer's disease lurking in patients' spinal fluid, a step toward a long-awaited diagnostic test.

The scientists discovered a pattern of 23 proteins floating in spinal fluid that, in very preliminary testing, seems to identify Alzheimer's not perfectly, but with pretty good accuracy.

The researchers then looked for that protein pattern in the spinal fluid of 28 more people—some with symptoms of Alzheimer's or other dementia, and some healthy. The test indicated Alzheimer's in nine of the 10 patients suspected of having the disease, and incorrectly fingered three people.

Dr. Norman Relkin, lead researcher in the project, has begun talks about testing his results, and preparing for larger studies to see if this is a potential "biomarker" of Alzheimer's.

Go to full story: lycos.com (*http://rs6.net/tn.jsp?t=yrmhx9bab.0.o4bfy9bab.oyf jcabab.10043&ts=S0218&p=http%3A %2F%2Fnews.lycos.com%2Fdynamic%2F stories%2FA%2FALZHEIMERS_SPINAL_FLU ID%3FSITE%3DLYCOS%26SECTION% 3DHEALTH%26TEMPLATE%3DDEFAULT%26 CTIME%3D2006-12-12-07-04-36*)

~~~~~~

Pharmaceuticals Companies Enter Drug Alliance

(Source: Business Wire)—GlaxoSmithKline and EPIX Pharmaceuticals announced a strategic collaboration to discover, develop and market novel medicines for the treatment of a number of diseases, including Alzheimer's.

EPIX will be responsible for the discovery and development of PRX-03140 for the treatment of Alzheimer's disease.

Go to full story: businesswire.com (*http://rs6.net/tn.jsp?t=yrmhx9bab.0.p4bfy9bab. oyfjcabab.10043&ts=S0218&p=http%3A %2F%2Fhome.businesswire.com%2Fpo rtal%2Fsite%2Fgoogle%2Findex.jsp%3FndmVie wld%3Dnews_view%26newsld% 3D20061212005330%26newsLang%3Den*)

~~~~~~

Early Diagnosis of Alzheimer's on the Rise

(Source: MSNBC)—James Smith remembers the shock of hearing his diagnosis. "I'm 45 years old, you know?" he recalls. "I can't have Alzheimer's."

But his doctor explained that this is not uncommon. The Alzheimer's Association says as many as 650, 000 Americans under age 65 have been diagnosed with the disease. Experts say the incidence of Alzheimer's is not increasing in younger people. Rather, doctors are better at diagnosing it and there is less of a stigma attached to the disease.

"Once I get to the point to where I've lost awareness and I can't recognize Juanita, I don't know who my children are, to me, that's a scary world because I don't know what that feels like," he says.

Researchers hope by studying young people with the disease they will find far better treatments.

Go to full story: msnbc.com (*http://rs6.net/tn.jsp?t=yrmhx9bab.0.q4bfy9bab. oyfjcabab.10043&ts=S0218&p=http%3A %2F%2Fwww.msnbc.msn. com%2Fid%2F16158987%2F*)

~~~~~~

More 'Creative and Responsible' Senior Care

(Source: LA Jewish Home for the Aging)—"The confluence of people living longer plus more people entering the senior age group sadly means that there will be a growing number of people afflicted with Alzheimer's disease," said Molly Forrest, president and chief executive officer at the Los Angeles Jewish Home for the Aging. "It is time that we start addressing their needs in a more visionary and aggressive way."

Forrest points to the Goldenberg-Ziman Special Care Center, opened in 2002, as an example of how "creative thinking" can have a dramatic impact on the care of Alzheimer's patients. The staff utilizes pioneering techniques on behalf of its residents. These include a "universal-worker" concept where all staff members are involved in all aspects of residents' care.

"It is time for us to start advocating on behalf of Alzheimer's victims and to do much more than we have done before," says Forrest. "It is a moral and ethical obligation we must face as a values-based society."

Go to full story: prnewswire.com (*http://rs6.net/tn.jsp?t=yrmhx9bab.0.r4bfy9bab. oyfjcabab.10043&ts=S0218&p=http%3A% 2F%2Fwww.prnewswire. com%2Fcgibin%2Fstories.pl%3FACCT%3D104%26STORY%3D%2Fwww%2Fstor y%2F12-112006%2F0004489031%26EDATE%3D*)

~~~~~~

Cold-Weather Tips for Older Adults

(Source: AMA)—A new booklet—Stay Safe in Cold Weather!—offers older adults tips on avoiding a dangerous condition called hypothermia. This free 12-page publication is now available from the National Institute on Aging.

"Older adults can lose body heat faster than when they were young, and some health problems and medicines can make it harder for them to stay warm," said NIA Director Richard J. Hodes. "This booklet describes hypothermia and offers simple steps seniors can take to lower their risk of this sometimes life-threatening health concern."

Hypothermia occurs when a person's body temperature drops below 95 degrees Fahrenheit because of exposure to cold, either indoors or outside. Low body temperature can cause heart attack, kidney problems, liver damage and sometimes death. According to the federal Centers for Disease Control and Prevention, about 600 people in the United States, half of them age 65 or older, die from hypothermia each year.

To order free copies or for more information about Stay Safe in Cold Weather! and other NIA publications, visit the NIA Web site at www.nia.nih.gov (*http:// rs6.net/tn.jsp?t=yrmhx9bab.0.s4bfy9bab.oyfjcabab.10043&ts=S0218&p=http% 3A %2F%2Fwww.nia.nih.gov*) or call (800)222.2225. Bulk orders are welcome.

Go to full story: nih.gov (*http://rs6.net/tn.jsp?t=yrmhx9bab.0.t4bfy9bab.oyfj cabab.10043&ts=S0218&p=http%3A% 2F%2Fwww.nia.nih.gov%2FHealthInfo rmation%2FPublications%2Fstaysafe%2F*)

~~~~~~

Richard's Views: I've Moved and I Didn't Know It

by Richard Taylor Not out of the house mind you. Just out of my current set of beliefs about myself. I thought I could do this, it turns out I can't. I thought I could figure that out, it turns out I can't. I don't know if I've moved on, or over, or up, or down; but

I know for sure I'm not the same person this afternoon that I thought I was when I woke up this morning. We are in the midst of a major re-do of our house. It started out with Granite Counter tops (I know, don't ask me either why we need them, we just do). It has grown into wood floors, new drapes, a complete house-wide paint job (Taupe for those of you who just had to know), new granite back splash for the kitchen, new plumbing, new this and new that. Everything will be new, except me! I still am living with dementia, probably of the Alzheimer's type. Well, who is going to install the under cabinet lighting? Not me. What about steaming the old wallpaper off in the dining room? Not me. Surely, someone will ask me to paint. No one else in the family likes to do it, except me. No one has asked! How about pulling up the rug, rolling it up and throwing it out? You guessed it, not me. Thus far, my job seems to be opening and closing the front door for the soon-to-be hired workers who are giving estimates to do MY work! This situation called for a family meeting. "Did you all forget I have, can and even like to work on home projects? Did you forget all the money I have saved us by figuring things out by trial and error, and if and when that doesn't work, consulting the directions for a number of highly complicated in-home projects?" I proudly asked. Silence from all others; stares at the table and out of the corners of their eyes at each other. I couldn't tell if they were mad or sad. I did know there was a common feeling holding back all their tongues from speaking. Then it hit me: "I have Alzheimer's disease! They don't trust me. They don't want me to do the work. Either they believe I can't do what needs to be done, or I will try and mess it up. Wow!" I confronted them directly and they offered half-assed excuses as to why I shouldn't do this or that. "Remember (15 years ago!) when you tried to fix the ceiling fans and when you turned them on they blew every fuse in the house?" "We thought you were too busy with your other projects and didn't want to take up your time" "How did we know you were interested when you didn't speak up?" And so the debate began. I won ALL the arguments, yet here I stand at the door waiting for the "floater" to walk in.

I suspect this experience is not unique to people who have a cognitive disease. Many families don't trust each other when it comes to doing things around the house because we are allegedly "sloppy, don't clean up after ourselves, do a half assed job," and so on. What turns this situation into a major downer for yours truly is the fact that I thought part of who I was, was being able to do these things. I thought other people loved and respected me because I could do all things, had done all these things, mostly successfully. Now the two key questions for me are: Do they still love me? and Why? Despite my claims to the contrary, I do define myself more or less by what I can do, not who I am. I'm no longer sure of who I am. I'm sometimes agitated, aggravating, insensitive (more that in the past), frustrated (much more than in the past), insecure (a great deal more than in the past), and simply unaware of what other people tell me. I have lost the definition of myself that I spent sixty plus years putting together. I don't trust my own self anymore! How many more times will I put my family through this personal rediscovery of the changes in my abilities to meet life's every day challenges? The other day I couldn't find the place to put gas in my lawn mower. I searched for more than half an hour before I asked a neighbor to come over and show me. I have started to use more and more pronouns because I can't recall people's names, even my own grandchildren! I know these things are true because others have told me I do this! I've been discovered. I've been exposed. Yet I still woke up this morning in my old self. Sometime, perhaps last night, I moved and didn't know it.

Richard

~~~~~~

Calendar of Events—Link to November Events

A list of education conferences is available at The Alzheimer's Daily News web site.

Click here to see a list of upcoming conferences click here (*http://rs6.net/ tn.jsp?t=yrmhx9bab.0.9tgo9ybab.oyfjcabab.10043&ts=S0218&p=http%3A*

%2F%2Falznews.org%2FFolderID%2F231%2FSessionID%2F%257B451658A
6-15F94 3 4 C—9 1 3 494045C1AEE1F%257D%2FPageVars%2FLibrary%2FInfoMa
nage%2FGuide.htm). To add your conference to our Calendar of Events c l i c k h e
r e (*http://rs6.net/tn.jsp?t=yrmhx9bab.0.mdmixybab.oyfjcabab.10043&ts=S021
8&p=http%3A %2F%2Falznews.org%2FInfoID%2F1484%2FRedirectPath%2FAdd
1%2FFolderID%2F231%2FSessionID%2F%257B451658A6-15F9-434C-91349404
5C1AEE1F%257D%2FInfoGroup%2FMain%2FInfoType%2FArticle%2FPageVars%
2FLibrary%2FInfoManage%2FZoom.htm*).

~~~~~~

Quick Links . . .

* Contribute to Alzheimer's Daily News
  *http://rs6.net/tn.jsp?t=yrmhx9bab.0.8i4whqbab.oyfjcabab.10043&ts
  =S0218&p=http%3A% 2F%2Fpartners.guidestar.org%2Fcontroller%2F
  searchResults.gs%3Faction_donateRepo* rt%3D1%26partner%3Dnetw
  orkforgood%26ein%3D03-0394452
* This Week's News
  *http://rs6.net/tn.jsp?t=yrmhx9bab.0.9bnblabab.oyfjcabab.10043&ts
  =S0218&p=http%3A% 2F%2Falznews.org*
* News from January, 2006
  *http://rs6.net/tn.jsp?t=yrmhx9bab.0.tvqqyrbab.oyfjcabab.10043&ts=
  S0218&p=http%3A% 2F%2Fagelessdesign.infoservecm.com%2FFolde
  rID%2F261%2FSessionID%2F%7BA8 A 3 F 1 9 5—5 A F 6—4 3 0 D—A
  A C 0752E0BAB1D0F%7D%2FPageVars%2FLibrary%2FInfoManage%2
  FGuide.htm*
* Share The News with a Friend
  *http://rs6.net/tn.jsp?t=yrmhx9bab.0.vpcwjdbab.oyfjcabab.10043&t
  s=S0218&p=http%3A% 2F%2Fui.constantcontact.com%2Fsa%2Ffwtf.
  jsp%3Fm%3D1100587767566%26ea%3D* ewarner%40agelessdesign.
  org%26a%3D1100691334065%26id%3Dpreview
* Visit the Alzheimer's Store
  http://rs6.net/tn.jsp?t=yrmhx9bab.0.rkksgkbab.oyfjcabab.10043&ts
  =S0218&p=http%3A% *2F%2Falzstore.com*

~~~~~~

email: ewarner@agelessdesign.org
phone: 800.752.3238
web: *http://alznews.org*
This email was sent to jolynn1@cox.net, by agelessd@aol.com Ageless Design
Research Foundation | 3197 Trout Place Road | Cumming | GA | 30041
Posted by Joseph Potocny at 10:51AM (-08:00)

Comments

—Lynn   December 13, 2006

Sounds like our house. I feel the same way sometimes.

—JosephPotocny   December 13, 2006

It is my house that is for sure. Joe

Thank God Today is Ok

Wednesday, December 13, 2006

Today has been a good day for me thus far. A far cry from the last couple of days filled with, frustration, confussion, anger and just not knowing what I was doing. But I guess that is to be expected with the damn disease. It is quiet in the house right now and that is wonderful, no noise, nothing, just peace and quiet. Truly wish I would hear from more of you out there without having to go to chat rooms, they type to fast at times for me, but what a great bunch of people. Well bye for now.

God Bless You and This Great Country of Ours!

Joe

Posted by Joseph Potocny at 01:13PM (-08:00)

What a Past 24 Hours

Thursday, December 14, 2006

I joined the DASN society yesterday and was greeted with such an overwhelming response that I am still responding to emails. Getting to slow. I am posting a new link today, that I think that if you are a child, parent, grandparent or just a person it will touch you. It was provided by a DASN user YoungHope.

http://parentswish.com/site01/big.html

Check it out it is awesome. It will be a permanent link on my blog until it is removed from the Internet which I hope is never. Today so far I feel rather connected, it is a good day, which I intend to enjoy while it lasts. Not all days are bad, but some a quite different. Searching and not knowing what you are searching for, or why you are searching. Thank God for my family and friends and newly found ones. It is nice not being alone.

God Bless You and This Great Country of Ours

Joe

Posted by Joseph Potocny at 08:35AM (-08:00)

Comments

—CyberCelt   January 26, 2007

Here from the Blog Village Carnival. Thanks for sharing! One thing I would suggest is you make a video about your life, as it is now, and whatever you want to remember in the past. When the shadows close in on your memory, you will be able to view the real you.

—JaneyLoree   January 27, 2007

Hi Joe, the video made me cry. I passed it on to my cousin. My Aunt is being touched by Alzheimer's.

I am visiting from the Blog Village Goes Gonzo Carnival!!!

—DirtyButter   January 31, 2007

WOW! I've reminded Daddy that we've all had our diapers changed as babies, so having to have help going to the bathroom is nothing new to any of us. It seemed to help him accept that this was something he could no longer be embarrassed by, as he really does need our help.

Thanks for posting this Joe. It means a lot to me, as a caregiver.

Lessons of A Day

Friday, December 15, 2006

Last night this disease taught me how it works on you. You think you have it all together and oops up pops the Devil. The wife asked me about several things from the week, that I had completely forgotten about doing that I did as I had been asked to do and about phone calls. This really gets to be worrisome. Still have to check my email today. Since I joined DANSI, the box is to full, takes forever to answer and read.

Bye for now. God Bless You and This Great Country of Ours

Joe

Posted by Joseph Potocny at 08:28AM (-08:00)

Poor Caregivers and Physicians

Sunday, December 17, 2006

Today I have read the seven stages of Alzheimer's and other dementia's and truly feel for the first time for those who try to diagnose and care for us. You just plain do not know for the most part. I have met a few who do. Imagine a test count back from 100 by 7s, what day is it, what is the date, who is the

President, draw these boxes, write a sentence. Hells bells, I know eight year old that can do that, so I progress from 62 years to 8 years, not a thing wrong. You do not see beyond your books, nor listen with your hearts to our tears and words. We feel the slow loss inside of us, we are aware more then you think. All we ask is talk to us, offer your hand and understanding when we need it, don't cast us off as we are creatures of the night. If I offend I intend tooooooo, I want others to join in the fight and try to understand us, just as those with AIDS have tried to do, but the ignorance of those out there is sometimes overwhelming. Great for spell check although sometimes words are mispelled for a reason. I was going to stop this blog, but not now, maybe one person will read and respond and start to understand and help pick up the torch.

God Bless You and This Great Country of Ours

Posted by Joseph Potocny at 05:58PM (-08:00)

My Mission

Tuesday, December 19, 2006

Dear Mr. Vice President,

I am writing to you rather than the President as I know I will ge the usually THANK YOU FOR YOUR SUGGESTION BS AS I HAVE FROM ALL 100 SENATORS OVER THE LAST DAY. I will include the message I sent each of them, except the President. I intend if able to, to contact all 435 Representatives as well. You all speak of helping to fix America, Family Values, Faith Based Programs, what about our PARENTS, GRANDPARENTS and a lesson to our Children of respect for them. I take no credit for the link that will be in the email I am 62 with Alzheimer's so maybe *you all think I am crazy.* But I CHALLENGE YOU all to put this in front of America and see how they feel. Thank goodness for spell check so I do not sound like a complete idiot, still getting the hang of grammar checker. I am a member of DANSI and AARP and have voted in every election State, Local and Federal since I was eighteen and proud of that right and fact.

I am a 62 year old American and a member of DANSI and I am writing individually this message to each and every Senator and hopefully all 435 Reps and the President. To see who has the tenacity to visit the the included web site. I suffer from Alzheimer's but that is not why I am writing I hope you and others visit the site with your speakers on and pass it on to others, maybe one person at a time will help bring back the respect among ourselves there once was.

http://parentswish.com/site01/big.html

Cordially, Joseph Potocny 5435 Lariat Way Oceanside, CA 92057 760-758-5699 my blogs:

http://blog.360.yahoo.com/blog-7yVoyXs7dLV6bGvI9qFQUgS4oJvA http://living-with-alzhiemers.blogspot.com/

Posted by Joseph Potocny at 08:49AM (-08:00)

Here I am Again

Wednesday, December 20, 2006

Yesterday I wrote to you about my mission that I am on, even though I have Alzheimer's I am not yet lost to this world. Here are some of the responses:

Mr. VP: Thank you for e-mailing Vice President Cheney. Your comments, suggestions and concerns are important to him. Unfortunately, because of the large volume of e-mail received, the Vice President cannot personally respond to each message. However, members of the Vice President's staff consider and report citizen ideas and concerns. Please visit the White House website for the most up-to-date information on Presidential initiatives, current events, and topics of interest to you.

Thank you again for taking the time to write. (Real concern here)

My two Senators Fienstein and Boxer:

Dear Mr. Potocny:

<> Thank you for taking the time to send information to my office. One of the most important aspects of my job is keeping informed about the views of my constituents, and I welcome your comments so that I may continue to represent California to the best of my ability. Should I have the opportunity to consider legislation on this issue, I will keep your views in mind. </> <> For additional information about my activities in the U.S. Senate, please visit my website, *http://boxer.senate.gov*. >From this site, you can access statements and press releases that I have issued about current events and pending legislation, request copies of legislation and government reports, and receive detailed information about the many services that I am privileged to provide for my constituents. You may also wish to visit *http://thomas.loc.gov* to track current and past legislation. </>

Again, thank you for taking the time to share your thoughts with me. I appreciate hearing from you.

Barbara Boxer

United States Senator

Please visit my website at *http://boxer.senate.gov* (next time I remember who you are)

December 18, 2006

Joseph Potocny

5435 Lariat Way

Oceanside, California 92057

Dear Joseph:

Thank you for writing to me with your thoughts regarding the 2007 Labor, Health and Human Services, Education Appropriations bill. I appreciate hearing your thoughts on this issue and welcome the opportunity to respond.

I share your concerns regarding funding for vital health and social services programs. Be assured, I have been supportive of efforts to increase funding for programs, such as Community Health Centers, Health Professions, and the National Institutes of Health, and will continue to work with my Senate colleagues to ensure these programs received appropriate funding.

Unfortunately, the 109th Congress adjourned on December 9, 2006 having only completed the Department of Defense and Department of Homeland Security spending bills for Fiscal Year 2007. Senator Robert Byrd (D-WV) and Representative Dave Obey (D-WI)—the incoming chairmen of the Senate and House Appropriations Committees—announced that they intend to pass a year-long joint resolution to fund Fiscal Year 2007 government programs at the same level as 2006 when Congress reconvenes next year. Please be assured that I will keep your views in mind during funding consideration for Fiscal Year 2008.

Again, thank you for writing. Should you have any further questions or comments, please feel free to contact my Washington, D.C. office at (202) 224-3841. Best regards.

Sincerely yours,

Dianne Feinstein United States Senator

http://feinstein.senate.gov

Further information about my position on issues of concern to California and the Nation are available at my website *http://feinstein.senate.gov*. You can also receive electronic e-mail updates by subscribing to my e-mail list at *http://feinstein.senate.gov/issue.html.* (Shares my concerns, doesn't even know them)

I could list what Seantors, Kennedy, Larry Craig, Frist, Clinton (I want to be President) said and the rest of the 100 but you got the gist. No concern and do not give a hoot or a howler. Just a nut in the wind, BUT I VOTE AND SO DO MILLIONS OF OTHER SENIORS AND THOSE WITH ALZHEIMER'S, maybe then they will hear!

God Bless You and This Country of Ours

Joe

Posted by Joseph Potocny at 09:56AM (-08:00)

Wednesday, December 20, 2006

Please sign petition titled Fighting for Our Parents and Grandparents, through our Children hosted with free Petition hosting site. Posted by Joseph Potocny at 01:28PM (-08:00)

Another Day in Hazy land

Thursday, December 21, 2006

Sometimes I feel like, I am lost and do not know what I am doing. Maybe that is normal for the condition, but it sure frustrates me. As some of you have read I am on a mission and have posted a news article at: *http://www.younewz. com/article/health-news-20*

Maybe waisting my time, but that is all I have now. I read others blogs and pages, some of which I have on my blog. But I want to leave something other than just an old person with Alzheimer's that was nut to you. I want you to know that we care and we want you to know that this affects, yes affects people in their 20's, 30's, 40's, 50's and older, it is not just an old folks disease. Finally research and professionals are waking up to the fact and leaving their little boxes that they diagnose in and coming to grips with reality. Thank God this has spell checker. Well leave a comment. At the little box on the bottom of this message. It would be nice, say I nuts, you agree, go away at least acknowledge I exist.

God Bless You All and this Great Country of Ours

Joe Posted by Joseph Potocny at 09:44AM (-08:00)

Comments

—Anonymous   February 09, 2007

i don't think you're nuts. ;o) ~shannon

Stages of Alzheimer's

Friday, December 22, 2006

Today I am going to start to help you understand the disease simply as possible and will start with the first through third stages and continue next time with 4 and so on. Remember this is not my list, but I agree I got from others.

First Stage: No cognitive impairment *Unimpaired individuals experience no memory problems and none are evident to a health care professional during a medical interview.

Second Stage: Very mild cognitive decline *Individuals at this stage feel as if they have memory lapses, especially in forgetting familiar words or names or the location of keys, eyeglasses or other everyday objects. But these problems are not evident during a medical examination or apparent to Friends, family's (at times) or coworkers.

Third Stage: Mild cognitive decline (Early stage Alzheimer's can be diagnosed in some, but not all, individuals with these symptoms) *Friends, family or co-workers begin to notice deficiencies. Problems with memory or concentration may be measurable in clinical testing or discernible during a detailed medical interview. Common difficulties include:

1: Word or name finding problems noticeable to family or close associates.
2: Decreased ability to remember names when introduced to new people.
3: Performance issues in social or work settings noticeable to family, friends or coworkers.
4: Reading a passage and retaining little material.
5: Losing or misplacing a valuable object.
6: Decline in ability to plan or organize.

Great spell checker. More to follow tomorrow. Now maybe my world and others is starting to sink in and you know how we feel. I can imagine how you must feel.

God Bless You and This Great Country of Ours

Joe

Posted by Joseph Potocny at 10:52AM (-08:00)

As Promised The Next Stages 4 & 5

Saturday, December 23, 2006

But First my horoscope for the day how fitting: You feel like Alice, tumbling down the rabbit hole. Unlike her, you land in your own wonderland that makes perfect sense. After all, isn't your reality what you wished and hoped for so long ago?

Stage 4: Moderate cognitive decline (what really does moderate mean to you?) (Mild or early-stage Alzheimer's disease) At this stage, a CAREFUL MEDICAL REVIEW (Doc pay attention please) detects clear—cut deficiencies in the following areas:

1:   Decreased knowledge of recent occasions or current events.
2:   Impaired ability to perform challenging mental arithmetic-for example, to count backward from 100 by 7s (I know eight year old who can do this, so I guess I can I am eight)
3:   Decreased capacity to perform complex tasks, such as marketing, planning dinner for guests or paying bills and managing finances. (I screw up the check book, did computers for a living and now have trouble doing email, although allot of people will say no he doesn't.)
4:   Reduced memory of personal history.
5:   The affected individual may seem subdued and withdrawn, especially in socially or mentally challenging situations. (too many people over two cause me confusion) (had to stop and spell check I sound smarter)

Stage 5: Moderately severe cognitive decline (Moderate or mild-stage Alzheimer's disease) Major gaps in memory and deficits in cognitive function emerge. Some assistance with day-to-day activities becomes essential. At this stage, individuals may:

1:   Be unable during a medical interview to recall such import details as their current address, their telephone number or the name of the college or high school from which they graduated.
2:   Become confused about where they are or about the date, Day of the week, or season. (I do that all the time now, good thing for calenders and my family to keep me on course).
3:   Have trouble with less challenging mental arithmetic: for example counting backward fro 40 by 4s or from 20 by 2s.
4:   Need help choosing proper clothing for the season or occasion. (my work around wear the same thing, until told different.)
5:   Usually retain substantial knowledge about themselves and know their own name and the names of their spouse or children. (I guess that is why I have to point to their rooms so my wife knows who I am talking about or play 20 questions, but we get there.)
6:   Usually require no assistance with eating or using the toilet. (Yeah I can still do that all by myself, I am a big boy now).

Well tomorrow six and seven. Till then: God Bless You and this Great Country of Ours

Joe

Posted by Joseph Potocny at 09:14AM (-08:00)

The Final Two Stages 6 & 7

Sunday, December 24, 2006

Before I begin I want to wish you all the Happiest of Holiday Season and a Great New Year.

Stage 6: Severe Cognitive Decline (Moderately severe or mid-stage Alzheimer's disease) Memory difficulties continue to worsen, significant personality changes may emerge and affected individuals need extensive help with customary daily activities. With this stage, individuals may:

1: Lose most awareness of recent experiences and events as well as of their surroundings.
2: Recollect their personal history imperfectly, although they generally recall their own name.
3: Occasionally forget the name of their spouse or primary caregiver but generally can distinguish familiar from unfamiliar faces.
4: Need help getting dressed properly; without supervision, may make such errors as putting pajamas over daytime clothes or shoes on wrong feet.
5: Experience disruption of their normal sleep and waking cycle.
6: Need help with handling details of toileting (flushing toilet, wiping and disposing of tissue properly).
7: Have increasing episodes of urinary or fecal incontinence.
8: Experience significant personality changes and behavioral symptoms, including suspiciousness and delusions (for example, believing that their caregiver or spouse or family are impostors); hallucinations (seeing or hearing things that are not really there); or compulsive, repetitive behaviors such as hand-wringing or tissue shredding.
9: Tender to wander and become lost.

Stage 7: Very Severe Cognitive Decline (Severe or late-stage Alzheimer's Disease) This is the final stage of the disease when individuals lose the ability to respond to their environment, the ability to speak and, ultimately, the ability to control movement.

1: Frequently individuals lose their capacity for recognizable speech, although words or phrases may occasionally be uttered.

2: Individuals need help with eating and toileting and there is general incontinence of urine (most health care issues are problematic).

3: Individuals lose the ability to walk without assistance, then the ability to sit without support, the ability to smile, and the ability to hold their head up. Reflexes become abnormal and muscles grow rigid. Swallowing is impaired.

Generally by this time many are put in nursing homes and the like because family's cannot deal with or want to deal with the person. Many people with Alzheimer's die from infection, this disease kills. One of the problems is it can take fro2-3 years to 20 years for all of this to happen. How would you like to live like this it is estimated that over 4.5 million Americans do, I believe that number is higher because we are often diagnosed as just being depressed and cannot get through to others what is really happening to us inside. Many times until meds won't help us at all. Watch those you love, even people as young as 20, 30, 40 more now in the 50's not only 65 and older are being diagnosed. There is no cure at this time. Researchers are working, but looking at so many things, I personally wonder if they are on the right track. As much as is known about the brain, they know more about the moon than the brain. Right now the only confirmation is opening the BRAIN after death.

So be patient with us and try to understand, I hope these blogs and articles have brought you some in site into our world, remember we once lived in yours.

watch this: *http://parentswish.com/site01/big.html*

God Bless You and This Great Country of Ours

Posted by Joseph Potocny at 08:38AM (-08:00)

Happy Greeting for the Day

Monday, December 25, 2006

Merry Merry Christmas and Happy New Year I am sending you good wishes filled with cheer May your day be pleasant and filled with good friends Santa has come and gone leaving your with glad tidings For the rest of the Year He hopes you remember to spread them around And keep the spirit strong and abound So MERRY CHIRSTMAY AND HAPPY NEW YEAR You have help to make my life happier with all your good tidings.

God Bless You and This Great Country of Ours

Joe

Posted by Joseph Potocny at 09:14AM (-08:00)

I am back

Wednesday, December 27, 2006

I hope your holidays were fine and brought you the joy and happiness you deserve. I took the time off to be with my family, I have been lost on this beast of modern technology and have forgotten them. Part of the disease. I hope to start posting on other forms of Dementia starting tomorrow. Most of it will be copied and pasted from various sites that will be credited and their links given. I am finding it harder to remember and concentrate on things. I know I sound fine, but you should see all the yellow marked words when I do spell check. Message looks like a patch work quilt. Well until tomorrow.

God Bless You and This Great County of Ours!

Joe

Posted by Joseph Potocny at 10:55AM (-08:00)

Entry for December 29, 2006 — Lewy BodyDementia

Friday, December 29, 2006

As Promised First in a series on Lewy Body Dementia

Before I begin I would like you to visit the following site:

http://www.inspiringthots.net/movie/alzheimer-prayer.php

The following comes from Lewy Body site. Thank goodness for cut and paste it sure helps someone like me.

http://www.lewybodydementia.org

What is Lewy Body Dementia? Facts

Lewy body dementia (LBD) is a progressive brain disease and the second leading cause of degenerative dementia in the elderly. The clinical name, "dementia with Lewy bodies" (DLB), accounts for up to 20% of all dementia cases, or 800, 000 patients in the US. Over 50% of Parkinson's disease patients develop "Parkinson's disease dementia" (PDD), which accounts for at least 750, 000 patients. (PDD is also a Lewy body dementia.)

Other names for the Lewy body dementias are:

* Lewy body disease (LBD)
* Diffuse lewy body disease (DLBD)
* Cortical Lewy body disease (CLBD)
* Lewy body Variant of Alzheimer's (LBV)(LBVA)
* Parkinson's disease with dementia (PDD)

In the early 1900's, while researching Parkinson's disease, the scientist Friederich H. Lewy discovered abnormal protein deposits that disrupt the brain's normal functioning. These Lewy body proteins are found in an area of the brain stem where they deplete the neurotransmitter dopamine, causing Parkinsonian symptoms. In Lewy body dementia, these abnormal proteins are diffuse throughout other areas of the brain, including the cerebral cortex. The brain chemical acetylcholine is depleted, causing disruption of perception, thinking, and behavior. Lewy body dementia exists either in pure form, or in conjunction with other brain changes, including those typically seen in Alzheimer's disease and Parkinson's disease.

© 2006 Lewy Body Dementia Association, Inc. Posted by Joseph Potocny at 04:59PM (-08:00)

Lewy Body Dementia — Symptoms

Saturday, December 30, 2006

Due to length will only publish part the rest will follow tomorrow remember credit is: *http://www.lewybodydementia.org* visit them.

LBD Symptoms Lewy body dementia symptoms and diagnostic criteria

Every person with LBD is different and will manifest different degrees of the following symptoms. Some will show no signs of certain features, especially in the early stages of the disease. Symptoms may fluctuate as often as moment-to-moment, hour-to-hour or day-to-day. NOTE: Some patients meet the criteria for LBD yet score in the normal range of some cognitive assessment tools. The Mini-Mental State Examination (MMSE), for example, cannot be relied upon to distinguish LBD from other common syndromes.

The latest clinical diagnostic criteria for LBD groups symptoms into three types: Central feature Progressive dementia

Deficits in attention and executive function are typical. Prominent memory impairment may not be evident in the early stages. Core features:

* Fluctuating cognition with pronounced variations in attention and alertness.
* Recurrent complex visual hallucinations, typically well formed and detailed.
* Spontaneous features of parkinsonism.

Suggestive features:

* REM sleep behavior disorder (RBD), which can appear years before the onset of dementia and parkinsonism.

41

* Severe sensitivity to neuroleptics occurs in up to 50% of LBD patients who take them.
* Low dopamine transporter uptake in the brain's basal ganglia as seen on SPECT and PET imaging scans. (These scans are not yet available outside of research settings.)

Supportive features:

* Repeated falls and syncope (fainting).
* Transient, unexplained loss of consciousness.
* Autonomic dysfunction.
* Hallucinations of other modalities.
* Visuospatial abnormalities.
* Other psychiatric disturbances.

A clinical diagnosis of LBD can be probable or possible based on different symptom combinations.

A probable LBD diagnosis requires either:

* Dementia plus two or more core features, or
* Dementia plus one core feature and one or more suggestive features.

A possible LBD diagnosis requires:

* Dementia plus one core feature, or
* Dementia plus one or more suggestive features.

Posted by Joseph Potocny at 09:46AM (-08:00)

Continuation of Lewy Body Symptoms

Sunday, December 31, 2006

Entry for December 31, 2006—Lewy Body Symptons Please remember this comes from link below and visit them as well as the other links.

http://www.lewybodydementia.org
http://www.alz.org
http://www.dansinternational.org

Tomorrow Diagnosing LBD

Symptoms Explained

In this section we'll discuss each of the symptoms, starting with the key word: dementia. Dementia is a process whereby the person becomes progressively confused. The earliest signs are usually memory problems, changes in their way of speaking, such as forgetting words, and personality problems. Cognitive symptoms of dementia include poor problem solving, difficulty with learning new skills and impaired decision making.

Other causes of dementia should be ruled out first, such as alcoholism, overuse of medication, thyroid or metabolic problems. Strokes can also cause dementia. If these reasons are ruled out then the person is said to have a degenerative dementia. Lewy Body Dementia is second only to Alzheimer's disease as the most common form of dementia.

Fluctuations in cognition will be noticeable to those who are close to the person with LBD, such as their partner. At times the person will be alert and then suddenly have acute episodes of confusion. These may last hours or days. Because of these fluctuations, it is not uncommon for it to be thought that the person is "faking". This fluctuation is not related to the well-known "sundowning" of Alzheimer's. In other words, there is no specific time of day when confusion can be seen to occur.

Hallucinations are usually, but not always, visual and often are more pronounced when the person is most confused. They are not necessarily frightening to the person. Other modalities of hallucinations include sound, taste, smell, and touch.

Parkinsonism or Parkinson's Disease symptoms, take the form of changes in gait; the person may shuffle or walk stiffly. There may also be frequent falls. Body stiffness in the arms or legs, or tremors may also occur. Parkinson's mask (blank stare, emotionless look on face), stooped posture, drooling and runny nose may be present.

REM Sleep Behavior Disorder (RBD) is often noted in persons with Lewy Body Dementia. During periods of REM sleep, the person wi Posted by Joseph Potocny at 09:26AM (-08:00)

Final Posting On Lewy Body Dementia

Monday, January 01, 2007

Happy New Year and Remember this is directly from: http:\www.lewy bodydementia. org What is LBD? Symptoms Diagnosis Glossary Educational Publications Events Helpline Support Groups Newsletter Other LBD Resources Articles Related Organizations Scientific Advisory Council Diagnosing LBD Diagnosis

An experienced clinician within the medical community should perform a diagnostic evaluation. If one is not available, the neurology department of the nearest medical university should be able to recommend appropriate resources or may even provide an experienced diagnostic team skilled in Lewy body dementia.

A thorough dementia diagnostic evaluation includes physical and neurological examinations, patient and family interviews (including a detailed lifestyle and medical history), and neuro-psychological and mental status tests. The patient's functional ability, attention, language, visuospatial skills, memory and executive functioning are assessed. In addition, brain imaging (CT or MRI scans), blood tests and other laboratory studies may be performed. The evaluation will provide a clinical diagnosis. Currently, a conclusive diagnosis of LBD can be obtained only from a postmortem autopsy for which arrangements should be made in advance. Some research studies may offer brain autopsies as part of their protocols. Participating in research studies is a good way to benefit others with Lewy body dementia.

Medications

Medications are one of the most controversial subjects in dealing with LBD. A medication that doesn't work for one person may work for another person.

Prescribing should only be done by a physician who is thoroughly knowledgeable about LBD. With new medications and even "over-the-counter," the patient should be closely monitored. At the first sign of an adverse reaction, consult with the patient's physician. Consider joining the online caregiver support groups to see what others have observed with prescription and over-the-counter medicines.

Risk Factors

Advanced age is considered to be the greatest risk factor for Lewy body dementia, with onset typically, but not always, between the ages of 50 and 85. Some cases have been reported much earlier. It appears to affect slightly more men than women. Having a family member with Lewy body dementia may increase a person's risk. Observational studies suggest that adopting a healthy lifestyle (exercise, mental stimulation, nutrition) might delay age-associated dementias.

Clinical Trials

The recruitment of LBD patients for participation in clinical trials for studies on LBD, other dementias and Parkinsonian studies is now steadily increasing. For those interested in participating in LBD research, consider enrolling in a medical school clinical patient program, and review ongoing clinical trials here (search on 'Lewy')

The Treatment of Agitation/Psychosis in Dementia/Parkinsonism (TAP/DAP) clinical trial is currently accepting LBD participants.

Prognosis and Stages

No cure or definitive treatment for Lewy body dementia has been discovered as yet. The disease has an average duration of 5 to 7 years. It is possible, though, for the time span to be anywhere from 2 to 20 years, depending on several factors, including the person's overall health, age and severity of symptoms.

Defining the stages of disease progression for LBD is difficult. The symptoms, medicine management and duration of LBD vary greatly from person to person. To further complicate the stages assessment, LBD has a progressive but vacillating clinical course. It is typical to observe a significance progression, followed by regression back to a higher functioning level. Downward fluctuations are often caused by medications, infections or other compromises to the immune system, but may also be due to the natural course of the disease.

Home | What is LBD? | Services | Resources | About Us | Contact Us | LBDA Blog | Forums | Volunteer | Donate | Site Terms and Policies

God Bless You All and This Great Country of Ours

Posted by Joseph Potocny at 09:58AM (-08:00)

Comments

—DirtyButter   January 01, 2007

Hi Joe!

I've just found your blog, and I'm glad I did. I was diagnosed with Parkinson's Disease in 2006, and I have a blog of my own where I journal what's happening with me. I'm going to add you to my list of links, and I'd love to have you stop by sometime.

http://parkinsons.dirtybutter.com

—DirtyButter   January 01, 2007

Sorry for the incomplete link. It should be http://parkinsons.dirtybutter/blog/ ! I have another blog that doesn't have the /blog/ part at the end, and I'm forever getting them mixed up. LOL

—JosephPotocny   January 04, 2007

Thanks for finding me. Hope you come back. God Bless Joe

—Lisa December   03, 2009

With organizations such as yourself, and champions in the media such as, Micheal J. Fox and Muhammad Ali, Parkinson's Disease has finally gained the notoriety it deserves. Due to the extensive research and awareness your organization spreads, medical advancements and Parkinson's symptom remedies have been created. Here, at Disease.com (a website dedicated to disease preventions and treatments) we not only appreciate your success, but we are dedicated to your future. If you could, please list us as a resource or host our social book mark button, it would be much appreciated. Let us spread the awareness, while fight the cause.If you want more information on that please email me back with the subject line as your URL

—Anna   February 03, 2010

Hi,

I am The editor/writer with physician.com. I really liked your site and i am interested in building a relationship with your site. We want to spread public awareness. I hope you can help me out. Your site is a very useful resource.

Please email me back with your URl in subject line to take a step ahead and also to avoid spam.

Thank you, Anna Huges editorial.physician@gmail.com www.physician.com

—GWhite   June 01, 2010

I've never had braces, my teeth have always been straight and I didn't get my first cavity til I was 17. I should've had my wisdom teeth pulled years ago but I'm scared so I have a tiny gap between 2 teeth on the bottom:(My middle and oldest sons have perfect teeth but my youngest sons were a mess and he had a horrible underbite. He had a palate expander put in first and then braces which he's had in for almost 2 years now.

—Health September   21, 2010

The early stages of Alzheimer's and other causes of dementia can be difficult to spot, but there are some signs that are useful in spotting the disease.

A Little Levity for the New Year

Tuesday, January 02, 2007

I wanted to start the New Year off with a little levity, what follows is a message I got from a dear friend, how true and enjoy. Our disease needs humor in it.

Subject: Seniors, you can't replace experience with anything.

A 98 year old woman wrote this to her bank. The bank manager thought it amusing enough to have it published in the New York Times.

Dear Sir:

I am writing to thank you for bouncing my check with which I endeavored to pay my plumber last month.

By my calculations, three 'nanoseconds' must have elapsed between his presenting the check and the arrival in my account of the funds needed to honor it. I refer, of course, to the automatic monthly deposit of my Social Security check, an arrangement which, I admit, has been in place for only eight years.

You are to be commended for seizing that brief window of opportunity, and also for debiting my account $30 by way of penalty for the inconvenience caused to your bank. My thankfulness springs from the manner in which this incident has caused me to rethink my errant financial ways.

I noticed that whereas I personally attend to your telephone calls and letters, but when I try to contact you, I am confronted by the impersonal, overcharging, pre-recorded, faceless entity which your bank has become.

From now on, I, like you, choose only to deal with a flesh-and-blood person. My mortgage and loan payments will therefore and hereafter no longer be automatic, but will arrive at your bank by check, addressed personally and confidentially to an employee at your bank whom you must nominate.

Be aware that it is an offense under the Postal Act for any other person to open such an envelope. Please find attached an Application Contact Status which I require your chosen employee to complete. I am sorry it runs to eight pages, but in order that I know as much about him or her as your bank knows about me, there is no alternative.

Please note that all copies of his or her medical history must be countersigned by a Notary Public, and the mandatory details of his/her financial situation (income, debts, assets and liabilities) must be accompanied by documented proof.

In due course, I will issue to your employee a PIN number which he/she must quote in dealings with me.

I regret that it cannot be shorter than 28 digits but, again, I have modeled it on the number of button presses required of me to access my account balance on your phone bank service. As they say, imitation is the sincerest form of flattery.

Let me level the playing field even further. When you call me, press buttons as follows:

1—To make an appointment to see me.

2—To query a missing payment.

3—To transfer the call to my living room in case I am there.

4—To transfer the call to my bedroom in case I am sleeping.

5—To transfer the call to my toilet in case I am attending to nature.

6—To transfer the call to my mobile phone if I am not at home.

7—To leave a message on my computer (a password to access my computer is required. A password will be communicated to you at a later date to the Authorized Contact.)

8—To return to the main menu and to listen to options 1 through 7.

9—To make a general complaint or inquiry, the contact will then be put on hold, pending the attention of my automated answering service. While this may, on occasion, involve a lengthy wait, uplifting music will play for the duration of the call.

Regrettably, but again following your example, I must also levy an establishment fee to cover the setting up of this new arrangement.

May I wish you a happy, if ever so slightly less prosperous, New Year.

Your Humble Client

(Remember: This was written by a 98 year old woman)

JUST GOTTA LOVE SENIORS!

God Bless You All and This Great County of Ours! Posted by Joseph Potocny at 09:34AM (-08:00)

Comments

—DirtyButter   January 04, 2007

Thanks for a good laugh, even though the point of the letter is serious business. At least the bank saw themselves in it enough to have it published. And kudos to the 98 year old lady for composing such a witty letter!

—DirtyButter   January 04, 2007

Hi Joe!

I'd like to invite you to join our family friendly BLOG VILLAGE TopList. We have 245 members, and we're striving for a diverse group of blogs. I think your blog would be a great addition.

You can find out more about it at the Blog Village blog.

—Anonymous   January 04, 2007

Yes we can be buggers, but how true it is.

—JaneyLoree   January 04, 2007

This post was great! Joseph, welcome to BLOG VILLAGE!!!

We are GrandParents Once More

Friday, January 05, 2007

Today is filled with happiness and sadness. This morning our newest Grandchild burst upon the scene MS. Lillian Patterson standing 21" Tall and weighing 8lbs 2oz, brown with some blond full head of hair. The joy is because she is here. The sadness is that I was unable to be in Port Angeles, WA to greet her. You see I missed the birth of my first son, was at my mothers' funeral sitting and my son was born that night. I knew I belong with him at his birth today, my priorities were wrong. So since then I have been in the labor and delivery for my next four children and my first three grandchildren. You see family comes first and foremost with me, that is mine, other relatives, friends and siblings may not like that, but they have to deal with it not me. Strong statement I know but with this disease my family is even more important to me, while I still remember at times who they are. So share in my happiness this day, because at 12 Am and some seconds 1/05/2007 Lillian let the world know that God placed her upon his earth to be loved.

God Bless You and This Great Country of Ours!

Joe

Posted by Joseph Potocny at 02:09PM (-08:00)

Comments

—DirtyButter   January 06, 2007

Congratulations, GRANDPA!!! You are right. Enjoy your family while you can. None of us knows how long that may be, so ENJOY!!!!!!

For Those Who Remember The Boys as TheyWere Called

Saturday, January 06, 2007

My very dear old friend Dick Laird sent me this, since I love Abbott&Costello, have all 36 movies of their's

You have to be old enough to remember Abbott and Costello, and too old to REALLY understand computers, to fully appreciate this. For those of us (you) who sometimes get flustered by our computers, please read on . . .

If Bud Abbott and Lou Costello were alive today, their infamous sketch, "Who's on First?" might have turned out something like this:

COSTELLO CALLS TO BUY A COMPUTER FROM ABBOTT

ABBOTT: Super Duper Computer Store. Can I help you?
COSTELLO: Thanks. I'm setting up an office in my den and I'm thinking about buying a computer.
ABBOTT: Mac?
COSTELLO: No, the name's Lou.
ABBOTT: Your computer?
COSTELLO: I don't own a computer. I want to buy one.
ABBOTT: Mac?
COSTELLO: I told you, my name's Lou.
ABBOTT: What about Windows?
COSTELLO: Why? Will it get stuffy in here?
ABBOTT: Do you want a computer with Windows?
COSTELLO: I don't know. What will I see when I look at the windows?
ABBOTT: Wallpaper.
COSTELLO: Never mind the windows. I need a computer and software.
ABBOTT: Software for Windows?
COSTELLO: No. On the computer! I need something I can use to write proposals, track expenses and run my business. What do you have?
ABBOTT: Office.
COSTELLO: Yeah, for my office. Can you recommend anything?
ABBOTT: I just did.
COSTELLO: You just did what?
ABBOTT: Recommend something.
COSTELLO: You recommended something?
ABBOTT: Yes.
COSTELLO: For my office?
ABBOTT: Yes.
COSTELLO: OK, what did you recommend for my office?
ABBOTT: Office.
COSTELLO: Yes, for my office!
ABBOTT: I recommend Office with Windows.
COSTELLO: I already have an office with windows! OK, let's just say I'm sitting at my computer and I want to type a proposal. What do I need?
ABBOTT: Word.

COSTELLO: What word?

ABBOTT: Word in Office.

COSTELLO: The only word in office is office.

ABBOTT: The Word in Office for Windows.

COSTELLO: Which word in office for windows?

ABBOTT: The Word you get when you click the blue "W".

COSTELLO: I'm going to click your blue "w" if you don't start with some straight answers. What about financial bookkeeping? You have anything I can track my money with?

ABBOTT: Money.

COSTELLO: That's right. What do you have?

ABBOTT: Money.

COSTELLO: I need money to track my money?

ABBOTT: It comes bundled with your computer.

COSTELLO: What's bundled with my computer?

ABBOTT: Money.

COSTELLO: Money comes with my computer?

ABBOTT: Yes. No extra charge.

COSTELLO: I get a bundle of money with my computer? How much?

ABBOTT: One copy.

COSTELLO: Isn't it illegal to copy money?

ABBOTT: Microsoft gave us a license to copy Money.

COSTELLO: They can give you a license to copy money?

ABBOTT: Why not? THEY OWN IT!

A few days later:

ABBOTT: Super Duper computer store. Can I help you?

COSTELLO: How do I turn my computer off?

ABBOTT: Click on "START

Got to love it, even with Alzheimer's they make me laugh. God Bless You and This Great Country of Ours!

Joe

Posted by Joseph Potocny at 10:49AM (-08:00)

Comments

—DirtyButter   January 06, 2007

This is great. I worked with computers and for years taught the other teachers and my 4th and 5th graders how to use them!!

I love it, and I'm still chuckling LOL!!

—DirtyButter   January 07, 2007

I've just posted a Stick-to-it-tiveness Award for you on our BLOG VILLAGE News blog.

You earned it the hard way, Joe!!

Who The Hell Cares

Tuesday, January 09, 2007

It has taken me all day to get to this and thry to think through it and I am snot going to use spell checker. I have to look at the keys now andaa sitll things do not come out right. I started this to educate and inform and let people out there know who this disease nown as AD works. I have given all my friends and family the site logation with the links to other blogs and my home pape. Thanks for the lack of support and comments and signing my guest book. Maybe you cannot deal with this, just guess how the frick it feels inside of my head. Had a debate over this with my closetla friend the other night and told him fine don't deal with me then, it is going to get worse so deal with it, I have to, if you cann't move one and take my love with you. I grow angrier and more frustrated each day as one mome slice of me goes away. I have not drive but 2 times I think in the last year, surrendering my license isa; like giving up the last of my freedoms. No where to go and everyone has to take me. This life sucks and I look forward to the end of it. Joe Posted by Joseph Potocny at 03:09PM (-08:00)

Comments

—Lynn   January 10, 2007

I'm sorry that you are so frustrated. I see the changes and wish that I could help stop them. Please don't lose faith in us who find it so difficult to see the changes in you and can only hold on.

—DirtyButter   January 11, 2007

Your frustration and anger are understandable, Joe, but not all family members are going to be able to deal with the "new you." They probably can't deal with it emotionally. I doubt seriously if it's because they don't care about you. Seeing a close loved one change like this is very difficult. As you know, I watched my mother go through it, as well as my father in law.

As for reading or commenting on your blog—I've been blogging now for about a year and a half, and my hubby has never read a thing I've written, as he can't stand computers. Our daughters have read just a few posts that I know of, and then only because I made a point of saying something about it.

—Marion   January 11, 2007

I'm sorry, Joe.

That doesn't help you, I know, but I do understand some of what you are going through, as my mother has fallen prey to a similar disease. She thinks we don't care, either. But we do, so much. As much as I know your friends and family care about you.

—Marsha   January 11, 2007

Hi Joe, I too am a member of blog village. My family and real life friends don't take the time to read or comment on my blog much either. I have made some lovely friends through blogging and get a lot of support from the strangers on the Internet. I hope the same thing happens for you.

—DirtyButter   January 12, 2007

I hope you've had a better day today, Joe, and that the new medicine is making you feel more like your old self.

Take care ;)

Ben Away For A Few Days

Saturday, January 13, 2007

I know my last positing was rather harsh. But it is how I feel. I know others care and have a hard time with this damn Disease. But they need to know, how much hell it is for me inside. To look ant their faces and not know who they are and not know what I am doing. They need to know a word a smile from them means more to me then anything else in this world. Got somle new meds and they knocked me on my, well you get the picture and I had no idea where I was nothing new, little humor there. I have joined a number of advocay groups for those who suffer, but more importantly to help those who are to follow soon after me. Maybe they will not have to go through this, I thought living as an alcoholic 33½ years ago was bad, but this beats it hands down, because I have no defense or tools to use to fight it. Just the support of family friends and professionals, who really do not know what to do. I do feel sorry for them. But their words of encoouragement are needed. No spell check anymore the real me will be here from now on. Once a brillliannt person now being humbled.

God Bless You and This Great Countyr of Ours!

Joe

Posted by Joseph Potocny at 09:36AM (-08:00)

Comments

—DirtyButter   anuary 13, 2007

I'm glad to see you have "calmed down" a bit. Not that your anger and even rage aren't understandable, mind you. But at least this post shows that you know you have family that do care and love you. It's odd to me in a way that you are so very aware of how much you are changing. My Mama and my hubby's Pop weren't at all aware of what was happening to them. Maybe the difference was their age, or maybe it's because the diagnosis is made sooner nowadays.

You're a brave soul to do without spellcheck. My typing has deteriorated so much in the last 3 or 4 months that it's pathetic. Sometime, when I get up the nerve, I'll have to leave you a comment without correcting anything LOL. Do they still prescribe Aricept? That's what both of our parents were on.

This is What I Hold on To Each Day

Monday, January 15, 2007

Whaat follows has beeen cut and pasted and is what helps me try to deall with my disease daily. I no loolnger use speel check so that you know tha==t thiss thing does affect me. I am no longer proud enough toto try to sound intelligent when it is fading this is me now. Hope you can us this:

Serenity Prayer

God grant me the serenity to accept the things I cannot change; courage to change the things I can; and wisdom to know the difference.

Living one day at a time; Enjoying one moment at a time; Accepting hardships as the pathway to peace; Taking, as He did, this sinful world as it is, not as I would have it; Trusting that He will make all things right if I surrender to His Will; That I may be reasonably happy in this life and supremely happy with Him Forever in the next. Amen.

—Attributed to Reinhold Niebuhr

Posted by Joseph Potocny at 08:28AM (-08:00)

Comments

—DirtyButter   January 17, 2007

I don't think I've ever read the second part of this prayer. Thank you fro spoting it!!

I decided not to use speel check either, my friend. I reverse letter s a lot in my tying now. I hope you can read this!!

—Marion   January 19, 2007

I've never read the second part of this prayer, thank you!

My thoughts are with you, my friend . . . I so appreciate your blog!

Some Levity Today

Tuesday, January 16, 2007

CONGRATULATIONS TO ALL THE KIDS WHO WERE BORN IN THE 1930's 40's, 50's, 60's and 70's !!

First, we survived being born to mothers who smoked and/or drank while they carried us.

They took aspirin, ate blue cheese dressing, tuna from a can, and didn't get tested for diabetes.

Then after that trauma, our baby cribs were covered with bright colored lead-based paints.

We had no childproof lids on medicine bottles, doors or cabinets and when we rode our bikes, we had no helmets, not to mention, the risks we took hitchhiking. As children, we would ride in cars with no seat belts or air bags. Riding in the back of a pick up on a warm day was always a special treat.

We drank water from the garden hose and NOT from a bottle. We shared one soft drink with four friends, from one bottle and NO ONE actually died from this.

We ate cupcakes, white bread and real butter and drank soda pop with sugar in it, but we weren't overweight because . . .

WE WERE ALWAYS OUTSIDE PLAYING!! We would leave home in the morning and play all day, as long as we were back when the streetlights came on.

No one was able to reach us all day. And we were O.K. We would spend hours building our go-carts out of scraps and then ride down the hill, only to find out we forgot the brakes. After running into the bushes a few times, we learned to solve the problem. We did not have Playstations, Nintendo's, X-boxes, no video games at all, no 99 channels on cable, no video tape movies, no surround sound, no cell phones, no text messaging, no personal computers, no Internet or Internet chat rooms . . . WE HAD FRIENDS and we went outside and found them!

We fell out of trees, got cut, broke bones and teeth and there were no lawsuits from these accidents. We played with worms and mud pies made from dirt, and the worms did not live in us forever.

We were given BB guns for our 10th birthdays, made up games with sticks and tennis balls and although we were told it would happen, we did not put out very many eyes. We rode bikes or walked to a friend's house and knocked on the door or rang the bell, or just yelled for them!

Little League had tryouts and not everyone made the team. Those who didn't had to learn to deal with disappointment. Imagine that!! The idea of a parent bailing us out if we broke the law was unheard of. They actually sided with the law!

This generation has produced some of the best risk-takers, problem solvers and inventors ever!

The past 50 years have been an explosion of innovation and new ideas. We had freedom, failure, success and responsibility, and we learned HOW TO DEAL WITH IT ALL! And YOU are one of them! CONGRATULATIONS! You might want to share this with others who have had the luck to grow up as kids, before the lawyers and the government regulated our lives for our own good. and while you are at it, forward it to your kids so they will know how brave their parents were. Kind of makes you want to run through the house with scissors, doesn't it?! Joe

Posted by Joseph Potocny at 11:08AM (-08:00)

Comments

—DirtyButter   January 17, 2007

So much truth and humor there, all rolled up into a great post. Thanks for sharing it, Joe.qxjc

This Is My Wish Tto You Also

Friday, January 19, 2007

The foollowing was sent by a friend and cut and paasted that is why it will sound ok.

After serious & cautious consideration . . . your contract of friendship has been renewed for the New Year 2007! It was a very hard decision to make. So try not to screw it up!!!

My Wish for You in 2007

May peace break into your house and may thieves come to steal your debts. May the pockets of your jeans become a magnet of $100 bills. May love stick to your face like Vaseline and May laughter assault your lips! May your clothes smell of success like smoking tires and May happiness slap you across the face and May your tears be that of joy. May the problems you had forget your home address!

In simple words . . .

May 2007 be the best year of your life!!!

HAVE A HAPPY 2007! Posted by Joseph Potocny at 04:41PM (-08:00)

Comments

—Tomas   January 21, 2007

Dear Joseph Potocny, heartily thank you for the wonderful wishes on 2007. Let heavy clouds never will come even close your house but the sunbeams play on your joyful eyes.

—DirtyButter   January 21, 2007

Smell of success like smoking tires?? Well, I get what he means, anywya, but that's not my idea of a good simile!!!!!!

I see you fixed the Carnival banner to fit. Good for you!!

—DirtyButter   January 22, 2007

I sent Matt from Sharing our Days your link, Joe. He amay email you about doing an interview. I told him I didnt' know if you'd want to, but I figured it ouldn't hurt to ask, anywya.

I can rally tell I'm tires toight. I don't knwo if you will even be able to read this!!

I figured if you could wirth without speel checker, the least I could do was show my ture self and answer you without spell chaeker!!

Picks or Frontal Lobe Dementia

Wednesday, January 24, 2007

This information came from: www.mydr.com.au

FRONTAL LOBE DEMENTIA AND PICK'S DISEASE

Like Alzheimer's disease, Pick's disease and frontal lobe dementias cause a progressive and irreversible decline in a person's abilities over a number of years. Frontal lobe dementia and Pick's disease are the cause of less than 10 per cent of all dementias and may usually be distinguished from Alzheimer's disease early in the course of the illness.

Arnold Pick first described Pick's disease in a 71-year-old man in 1892. Pick's disease affects the temporal lobes of the brain in 25 per cent of cases, frontal lobes in 25 per cent and both frontal and temporal lobes in 50 per cent. Frontal lobe dementia affects the frontal lobes initially. Damage to the frontal lobes leads to alterations in personality and behaviour, changes in the way a person feels and expresses emotion, and loss of judgement.

The following information about Pick's disease is also appropriate for other frontal lobe dementias.

Common symptoms of Pick's disease

Personality and behavioural problems The first symptoms of Pick's disease are typically psychological and behavioural problems. Initially, the diagnosis may be suspected to be a mental illness. People may show symptoms of a change in their character and in their social behaviour. They may have a diminished drive and often their expression is vacant.

A person with Pick's disease may show insensitivity, which is especially noticeable in a person who previously showed consideration to others. There may be a lack of restraint and the person may be caught up in the criminal justice system because of stealing or behaviour which lands him/her in trouble.

Another sign of Pick's disease is that the person often becomes quite obsessional during the early stages, insisting that everything is absolutely neat and in order, or repeatedly washing his hands or observing little rituals each time a certain task is carried out.

There may be sexual misadventures, social graces may deteriorate, the person may talk to strangers, make inappropriate comments in public and indulge in practical jokes. Unfortunately, people with Pick's disease often suffer from significant absence of insight into the effects of their behaviour.

Language problems Language problems also occur early in the disease: limited speech output, lack of speech spontaneity, stereotyping of phrases (e.g. use of pat phrases repeatedly and excessively), perseveration (a meaningless persistence of verbal activity), a decreased vocabulary, and a considerable amount of repetition, especially of brief words and phrases.

Often there is jargon and instead of being able to find the word to describe an object, the person with this disease will give a description of it instead (e.g a watch referred to as 'something you tell the time with'). This means that the person may not be able to name objects early in the disease.

Eventually the person becomes mute for periods and then completely mute by the end of the disease.

Kluver-Bucy syndrome This refers to a group of problems which are relatively common in Pick's disease. These are hypersexuality, gluttony, and an obsession to touch and seize any objects in the person's field of vision. Overeating may lead to considerable weight gain.

Who can get the disease? Anybody can get the disease, although there may be geographical differences in the incidence of Pick's disease. Some studies suggest the disease to be more common in women while others suggest a greater risk in men. The most severe cases of Pick's disease occur before the age of 60 years. The highest incidence is between 50 and 60, but people may develop the disease earlier or up to 80 years.

What is the cause? As with Alzheimer's disease, in most cases, the cause cannot yet be determined. However, there are strong genetic components in certain families. When there is a genetic element, it is autosomal dominant, (on average, half of the children of an affected parent will develop the disease, but half will not) but is clearly modified by a number of environmental factors as yet to be discovered. The genetic component has been variously described as affecting 20 to 50 per cent of people with Pick's disease.

Diagnosis Although Pick's disease can only be conclusively diagnosed after a person's death by a post mortem examination of the brain, there are several techniques, such as brain scans and EEGs, which can be used during the person's lifetime to give a probable diagnosis. These techniques can help in determining whether the dementia is likely to be Pick's disease or a closely related disorder, for example, Alzheimer's disease.

Prognosis and treatment As yet, there is no cure for Pick's disease and neither can the progression be slowed down with any medication treatment. Probably because Pick's disease is much less common than Alzheimer's disease, there is less research into Pick's, and there are currently no drug trials taking place in relation to treating Pick's disease.

The course of Pick's disease is an inevitable progressive deterioration. From the onset of the disease, life expectancy is 2-15 years, with an average of 6-12 years. Death is usually caused by infection.

Some of the symptoms of the disease can be treated effectively. For example, certain medications can reduce some of the behavioural problems. Also knowing more about the disease and why the person is behaving as they are can in itself be an effective means of helping people to cope with the disease. (The Alzheimer's Association NSW has an extensive dementia library, education and counselling services).

What are the differences between Pick's disease and Alzheimer's disease? The main difference between Pick's disease and Alzheimer's disease is that the damage occurs in different areas of the brain, at least in the early stages. In most cases of Pick's disease, the frontal and temporal lobes of the brain are the areas affected and with Alzheimer's disease, the temporal and parietal lobes are affected.

Mendez and co-workers (1993) found, even in the absence of temporal or frontal lobe atrophy on CT brain scans, that Pick's disease can be distinguished from Alzheimer's disease if 3 of the following 5 characteristics are present early in the disease:

* presenile onset (under 65 years old);
* initial personality change;
* hyperorality (loss of normal controls, e.g. excessive eating, indiscriminate putting things in one's mouth);
* disinhibition; and
* roaming behaviour.

Compared with Alzheimer's disease, impairment of intellect and memory occur later. As well, epilepsy is uncommon, delusions and hallucinations are rare, and apraxia (inability to perform, command, or imitate a familiar action) and agnosia (inability to recognise objects) are less common. Gait and muscle tone are less affected. In the late stages, Parkinsonism symptoms, immobility, incontinence and mutism occur. In the terminal stage, the different dementias are clinically indistinguishable.

Carers Being a family carer of a person with dementia, regardless of whether it's Alzheimer's disease, Pick's disease or another type, can be physically and emotionally exhausting. However, Pick's disease can often be even harder on families because:

* of the personality changes and behavioural quirks which are very distressing;
* often there is a delay in diagnosis of the disease;
* it receives less publicity than Alzheimer's disease and therefore, is even less understood by the public, friends, etc;
* often, persons affected with Pick's disease are younger; and language problems develop earlier.

Families of people with Pick's disease and other frontal lobe dementias need support in their caring role.

myDr, 2001. Reproduced with kind permission from the Alzheimer's Association of NSW.

Reviewed : 9/3/2001 myDr Health Information

myDr Health Centres

* myDr Seniors' Health Centre
* A-Z list of myDr articles about brain health
* Health support groups for Alzheimer's disease

Additional Health Resources

* Alzheimer's Association NSW Posted by Joseph Potocny at 11:41AM (-08:00)

myDr Articles
myDr Health Support Group Information

Comments

—DirtyButter   January 25, 2007

My Mama kept her own sweet personality with some exeptions, right up until close to her death. Pop, on the ther hand, became very angry and aggressive for awhile. i really feel for those whose love dones chang into strangers right n front of their eyeys.

BLOG VILLAGE Community NEWS

Friday, January 26, 2007

BLOG VILLAGE Community NEWS Posted by Joseph Potocny at 08:54PM (-08:00)

Comments

—DirtyButter   January 27, 2007

Thanks for the announcement, Joe. I haven't had time to read very many fo the entries yet, but th eones I have read are very weell dont!!

I haven't gotten to yours et, but I'm looking forward to reading it.

—JosephPotocny   January 27, 2007

I truly hope the carnival was a great success. I know that You, Kilroy and the rest put your hearts into it. I am proud to have played a very small part in it and look forward to the next one. Stay Well In Gods' Mighty Arms. With Love, Joe

To Clear Up Some Possible Confussion

Monday, January 29, 2007

If you read this blog you willll notice that you can click on comment and leave one. But I have listed a form on teh side for those who want comments private and not published. Comments left at the pottom of the post are made public, those sent to me are not and I will answer them in time. This so called DISEASE i suffer srom really has a way of screwwing up my mind. No spell checker this is me. I frustate those I love and care for. I find my self wandering in the house and the corrridors of mly mind wich are all messed up. Days go bye and I do not remember them. This is my life and it will only get worse until my circle is closed. Which I truly hope is soon. I do not like living this way. Play the Alzheimers Prayer located on the side bar, maybe you will understand.

God Bless Joe Posted by Joseph Potocny at 10:52AM (-08:00)

Comments

—DirtyButter   January 29, 2007

Do you really wish to have a short life Joe? I can tell you for sure that my Mama still had pleasure in her life for a long time, even after she broke her hip. It was a different kind of pleasure, that's true, but for the most part she was happy. When she did become agitated, we had medicines to help her calm down.

Her quality of life was not horribly diminished until after the hip surgery at 90!

—DirtyButter   February 01, 2007

I just wanted to stop by and tell you I was thinking of you this morning, Joe.

—Marion   February 01, 2007

I bet you feel differently on some days, Joe, when things go well. Take those days and live life to the fullest, as I know you already do . . . my prayers are with you.

—Anonymous   February 01, 2007

Dear Joe,

I'm writing from Portugal and I sincerely wish you all the best you can get. My mum suffers from the same disease but she doesn't know, and I will always believe that she's blessed for that. Sometimes she knows there's something wrong but we've been able to avoid the confrontation with reality trying to make her life happier.

Pardon me if I believe I understand your fears but from the bottom of my heart hope you will be able to live with them. I would feel the same, I'm sure . . .

I know I can't change your feelings, but accept a huge hug from this side of the Atlantic.

Sincerely

Helena

Sometime Since Last Post

Saturday, February 03, 2007

I have been awya for ahwile but here I am again. Have been in a days and hve been answering email comming out the old, well you know. Life is getting a little hareder each day. Spelling stinks, but this is how the disease affects me at least. If you see wohm I really am, you may begain to understand how my life, what I use to know of it, slips away litlle by little each day. I see the frustration and confusioon and pain in my falyms eyse and how they trey ther best to bollster me up. It is difficult to relate to someone without this damn disease what it is really lkie as it progresses. A big word. One time a knew a great deal of them and even new how to spel and what they meant. I am looking forward to running a series on Parkinsons for my very dear friedn Dirty Butter, don't you just love the name, she has Parkinsons. Also am considering getting an ebook site and try and I mean try to write my story from the start, not in a chatper way, but as a conversation between me and the person who reads it, if anyone. Well the day is getting harder and less clear so time to go.

God Bless You and This County of Ours!

Joe

Posted by Joseph Potocny at 02:36PM (-08:00)

Comments

—DirtyButter   February 03, 2007

Hving dealt with it twice as a care giver, plus known several people with it at church, I can tell you that no two people act the same with Alzheimer's. If you've seen one Alzheimer's patient—you've seen one Alzheimer's patient.

I think I do know just a little of what your'e going through Joe, if that helps any.

—DirtyButter   February 05, 2007

Thinking of you this morning, Joe. I hope you have a clear day today, and not a foggy one.

To Moms & Fathers and their kids.

Monday, February 05, 2007

Because my site is jsut not for sufers of dementia, but humor and famliy values, here is something my seconded eldest daughter sent me.

Mean Moms Someday when my children are old enough to understand the logic that motivates a parent, I will tell them, as my Mean Mom told me: I loved

63

you enough . . . to ask where you were going, with whom, and what time you would be home.

I loved you enough to be silent and let you discover that your new best friend was a creep. I loved you enough to stand over you for two hours while you cleaned your room, a job that should have taken 15 minutes.

I loved you enough to let you see anger, disappointment, and tears in my eyes. Children must learn that their parents aren't perfect. I loved you enough to let you assume the responsibility for your actions even when the penalties were so harsh they almost broke my heart.

But most of all, I loved you enough . . . to say NO when I knew you would hate me for it.

Those were the most difficult battles of all. I'm glad I won them, because in the end you won, too. And someday when your children are old enough to understand the logic that motivates parents, you will tell them.

Was your Mom mean? I know mine was. We had the meanest mother in the whole world! While other kids ate candy for breakfast, we had to have cereal, eggs, and toast. When others had a Pepsi and a Twinkie for lunch, we had to eat sandwiches.

And you can guess our mother fixed us a dinner that was different from what other kids had, too.

Mother insisted on knowing where we were at all times. You'd think we were convicts in a prison. She had to know who our friends were, and what we were doing with them. She insisted that if we said we would be gone for an hour, we would be gone for an hour or less.

We were ashamed to admit it, but she had the nerve to break the Child Labor Laws by making us work. We had to wash the dishes, make the beds, learn to cook, vacuum the floor, do laundry, empty the trash and all sorts of cruel jobs. I think she would lie awake at night thinking of more things for us to do.

She always insisted on us telling the truth, the whole truth, and nothing but the truth. By the time we were teenagers, she could read our minds and had eyes in the back of her head. Then, life was really tough!

Mother wouldn't let our friends just honk the horn when they drove up. They had to come up to the door so she could meet them. While everyone else could date when they were 12 or 13, we had to wait until we were 16.

Because of our mother we missed out on lots of things other kids experienced. None of us have ever been caught shoplifting, vandalizing other's property or ever arrested for any crime. It was all her fault.

Now that we have left home, we are all educated, honest adults. We are doing our best to be mean parents just like Mom was.

I think that is what's wrong with the world today. It just doesn't have enough mean moms!

PASS THIS ON TO ALL THE MEAN MOTHERS YOU KNOW. And Their Kids!!!)

God Bless You and This Great Country of Ours!

Joe

Posted by Joseph Potocny at 10:03AM (-08:00)

Comments

—DirtyButter   February 05, 2007

I'll be sending a copy of this to both our daughters!! I'm sure our grandchildren already think they have a mean mom!!

A Sad Day for Dementia Suffers

Tuesday, February 06, 2007

Yesterday we who suffer from Alzheimers and other forms of dementia, lost the world most foremost aat=utority and leader in the field for fighting and working on Alzheimers, unfortunately I cannot reamber his name and the news i have looked at has not mentitoned. Only shows how they care about us. Hopefully they will be one of us soon and suffer the ravages that it brings and then will know. The following link shows how much our govenment gives a damn about us. Let them remember 2008 is coming and we are millions strong and vote. If you think there was a change in 2006, just wait, hopefully the millions like me and the tens of millions of seniors who vote, will toss this govenment on its head and vote out eveyone possibleand showwwww them we are no longer going to take there BS.

http://www.alz.org/news_and_events_5220.asp

God Bless You All and Keep This Coutry of Ours The Greatest! Joe Posted by Joseph Potocny at 10:15AM (-08:00)

Comments

—DirtyButter

February 06, 2007

Cutting back on Alzheimer's research is like turning off the water hose when a wild fire is coming, so you can save on your water bill.

When the Baby Boomer generation becomes disabled with this disease, our economy is in for big trouble. And, to make matters worse, as a broad generalization, the Boomers brought up their children to not have to lack for anything or struggle to get anything, so they will not be as inclined to take care of their demented parents.

I am breaking a promise, I think you will understand.

Wednesday, February 07, 2007

Yesterday I received an Email from an individual who will remain anonymous, since they sent it through the email form on the side of my page. I responded to this individual, but I think her statement needs to be shown and addressed publicly. I truly thank this person for contacting me. Content of message:

Message = why does everyone try to make it sound so loving and cozy. It is a horrible horrible disease. I'm here to help but not a family member and not a professional. Is there a way to do this perfectly? NO! The stress is unbearable some days, called disgusting names by a woman who doesn't even know i feed her every single day. There is nothing loving or sweet about this situation. And to top it all off, having these feelings makes me feel like a bad person. So cut the crap about. we're going through this with loving kindness. You must still be in stage 1.

First I say to you, that you are not a BAD PERSON, you are a loving and caring individual, who is seeing the ravages of this disease. The person you love and care for is not capable of controlling their words, thoughts, deeds and actions. Trust me they know you are there. On my site is the Alzheimer's prayer, watch it, maybe it may help you. You see my family goes through this daily with me. I am not in stage one, not by along shot. I cannot even remember who they are at times when talking and looking at them. I have days that go by that I cannot remember anything of. My site is to tell of my life, but also to bring some humor to the world as much as I can, because it helps ME. If you read all of my entries, you will see that I have ran stuff of Lew Body's and the Seven Stages of Alzheimer's and plan to run a series on Parkinson's for a dear friend of mind. DEMENTIA kills plain and simple, but first it robs you of yourself and physical functions before it lets you go. That is not any fun from THIS side or yours. I truly feel for you, but understand your friend is sick and not responsible for their actions. I hope you do not feel betrayed by me, but continue to contact me. I will do the best I can to help you understand our side of this disease and maybe in doing so show you the great worth and service you are giving. I will go back to not using spell checker, so you know who I am. If you should write me again, you will see me as I am. Till Then,

God Bless You and This Great Country of Ours!

Joe

Posted by Joseph Potocny at 07:59AM (-08:00)

Comments

—Marion   February 07, 2007

Well expressed reply, Joe!

I watch my Mom losing touch and forgetting . . . some days she's who I know and other day's she's someone completely different . . . on no day is it ever easy, for her or for me.

—DirtyButter   February 08, 2007

The stress of being a care giver is tremedous, whether the person has dementia or not. Mama was easy to handle most of the time, but even she became mean toward the end. Pop, on the other hand, was so agitated and aggressive that we could not keep him at home any longer, but moved him to a nearby Assisted Living home.

It IS a horrible disease, and I think your pain as one who has it comes through your writing loud and clear. It's just that we see you on your lucid days, when you're able to post and make sense. You family seels you on your worst days, too.

—DirtyButter   February 08, 2007

Speaking of spell checker, have you noticed that my typing has improved? I certainly have. The Zelepar is working!!

—Meesha   February 16, 2007

Hello sweet joe, My name is shawnna I saw your sites on parent's wish I cried like a baby over this video. I think one of your visitors that made the post . . .

Message = why does everyone try to make it sound so loving and cozy.It is a horrible horrible disease. I'm here to help but not afamilymember and not a professional. Is there a way to do this perfectly? NO! The stress is unbearable some days, called disgusting names by a woman who doesn't even know i feed her every single day. There is nothing loving or sweet about this situation. And to top it all off, having these feelings makes me feel like a bad person.So cut the crap about. we're going through this with loving kindness.You must still be in stage 1.

she needs to be slapped side ways and her privalege of caring for some one revoked as it is a privalege! I watched both my aunt nancy slip away as well as my grandmother I cherished every waking moment I remembered who they were it only made me sad when they did not remember me not angry just sad . . . yes it can be scary, and hard but we all need to remember they are still the same loving beautiful caring giving person they were they just don't always remember what is happening around them. I used to hide in my friends garage as his grandad had severe altimers and he would think he was back in the war and chase us down trying to kill the enemy it was extreamly scary but after a while he would cry on his hands and knees because he could not remember where he was why he was there or if he had hurt any one. tears wheled up in my eyes every time I was only 12 then but I still remember and what it was like to see some one go through this. they never took him to a home as back then they would not accept him. so they had to watch him very close the mother quit her job to care for him but even she got scared at times. I know that some day I too will be in this situation and I have seven beautiful children and I can only hope that they grow up to be compasionate caring giving and paitient. I am 29years old now but know that If you raise your children to love god more than all and any thing they will do what is right with happy hearts I am living proof of that! I love my parents dearly my sister is very materialistic, and does not have time for any of us I guess that is my blood fathers genes coming through . . . But for me I look to the lord in all that I do He is lord over my life and all that I say. God has taken care of me since before I was born. He helped me with my grand mother, my children my once abusive husband and keeping me alive and sain. He will be there for me when My parents need me as I WILL NOT let them be in a home! my husband worked in a home and told me of great horror stories I will never let happen to any of my family! i PRAY THAT gOD WILL KEPP YOU AND WATCH OVER YOU i PRAY THAT HE WILL BLESS YOU IN ALL THAT YOU DO. yOU ARE A BEAUTIFUL MAN AND YOU INSPIRE ME. tHANK YOU FOR HAVING THESE POST AND PLEASE DO NOT EVER think of doing any thing horrible to your self Your grand children are not sad cause you get lost or can't play they are sad because you are sad and can not remember things as they know you want to and can't so they are sad for you not beacause of the things you do or an't do. Always remember God has a plan for you and right now you are doing his plan by having this site and doing what you can for your family and others going through hard times. when God is ready and your work is done you will be able to go home and the love you will feel is emense It is like nothing you have ever felt you will beg God to keep you and never send you back . . . I almost died 3 times during delivery and once I swear I was before God I could not see his face but I knew. I fell to my knees and cried for him not to send me back over and over and over I felt the love so powerful I fell flat on my face. it was God people can call me crazy if they want but I am not ashamed to say I was before God! I obviously still had work to do as He gave me an image of my yet to be born son and my two daughters and in that same instant I was awake bleeding all over the place. God has a plan for us all when and if you feel sad or down lonely or just need to talk Email me I am glad to be a shoulder to cry on or an ear to listen or some one to pray with we are all brothers and sisters in christ! Love hugs and prayers always Shawnna.

—LaraBelonogoff February 27, 2007

I think Marion and you, Joe, make good points as the disease affects both the one with it and his/her caregiver. The bittersweet irony becomes that both the person with dementia and the primary caregiver need "care," but in very different ways. I just finished writing a blog post a few days ago about caregiver burnout, which is a very common and real problem. (I work for a company that write reviews of long-term care options along with covering many senior issues.) Keeping the needs of two people in balance is difficult.

(Marriage is a good example of this.) And if it is polarized by something like a life-threatening disease then life can feel more about surviving the minutes than enjoying them. Keeping up your spirits—and trying to raise those of others—is one of the best remedies I have found for almost any illness along with keeping realistic expectations of yourself and others.

A Day Gone To Hell

Thursday, February 08, 2007

Todya srated out fine, got up took my meds, did the normall stuff. Fed the kity, let the dog out and fed and wtered hr, fed the bird had it on my shoulder whlie I was working on the beast of humanity. Took my granddauhgter to the park to paly and walk and enjoy her company and due what grandpas do, whatever that is. Leaving thngs went to hell in a =hand basket, I forgot where we were, luckily she took my hand and new where to go, I was clumbsy and feeling quite unstable both upstairs and bodily sies. Got home took I thing some orange juice, laid down and cried bgecause I has lost par to fo my day and may my granddaughter sad. This fricken disease really sucks. I waitn on My Lord to take my hand willing to go with him. I have tought serouisly oabout doing something, but wor=uld screw that up. Be paraliiized and not know it or who I was. Wahat a bitch. This is my life now. One day at a time, it leaves me further behind and I catn catch it. Keep those cards and letters coming in, I due answer them, the best I can, normalllly the first time with spel ckr, after that you get me.

God Bless You and This Great Country of Ours!

Joe

Posted by Joseph Potocny at 04:45PM (-08:00)

Comments

—DirtyButter   February 08, 2007

God Bless U, Joe!! I would imagine that was very hard to share. Such a scary thing to watch yourself disappear. But you can still love and be loved until God is ready to take you home, Joe. Cleng to that!!!

—Anonymous   February 08, 2007

I LOVE. Lynn

—DirtyButter   February 15, 2007

You're on my mind today, Joe. I've been having computer problems, plus very busy with Daddy, so I haven't been able to write, but I think and pray about you and Lynn every day.

—DirtyButter   February 19, 2007

Are you OK, Joe? Well, as OK as you can be under the circumstances?? Missing your posts!!

—Marion   February 19, 2007

You leave me at a loss for words, Joe, I thank you so much for giving me such insight into your illness.

You have helped me immeasurably with my Mother, who is very quickly forgetting so much. It is hard for her, she gets very frustrated.

I am able to help her with the info that is available here. Thank you.

—MercysMaid   March 01, 2007

I can't imagine how scared and frustrated you must be. My aunt suffered from AD and it was so difficult to watch her struggle with it.

I think you sound like a great grandfather. I know your grandkids must really appreciate the time you spend with them.

God bless.

It Has been some tiem

Wednesday, February 21, 2007

I did not relize how long it has been since I last posted anything. Been a little lost in time. Right now I am in Port Angeles, WA, visiting my daughter and two grandkids and finally met my son thaaat I have note seen in over 30 years. What is nice I have not had to think about anything but relaxing, taking my two thousands meds each day, eating and sleeping. No remembering what I am to do each day at home. Hate to see my email. May take days to go through it and answer. I believe we head home sometime tin the next couple of days. Will be glad to get to my safe place. But am enjoying myself. Still cannt talk right or get thinks to come out the way I want them, but what the heck. I am still alive and breathing. Doc says as long as I keep breathing I am ok, once I stop I may have a problem. Well tinl i remember again.

God Bless You All and This Country of Ours!

Joe

Posted by Joseph Potocny at 10:38AM (-08:00)

Comments

—DirtyButter   February 22, 2007

Sounds like you've had a great time, and I'm glad for you. Don't stress over the email pile. The people who wrote you would be upset if they thought they were making things hard on you. Just do a few more than usual each day, and you'll get to all of them in time.

{{{{HUGS}}}}

—Marion   February 25, 2007

Sounds like you're having fun . . . that's so great! By the way, I love Port Angeles!

—Anonymous   February 26, 2007

I hope you guys had a great time! *Shannon*

Back Home Again

Thursday, March 01, 2007

Well we are back from Washingto and things are getting to normal. Still forgetting who the heck I am talking to and not able to remembeer conversations. But life goes on each day a little less than the last one, but I can still commmmmunicate to some degree with others. Seem to P$#@ off alot of people more than usual. But that is their problem. They do not know what the corrrridors of my mind are like. I really cannot explain it to them. I know it is hard for them, but it sure is not easy on this side of the fence. Thre grass is not green it is getting brown. I have becomee somewhat disencahanted with those taughting how wonderful they are with this disease. And they can write books and their blogs are art this point or another. I sometimes think the have there heads ups their ass. I had to have mine surgicallly removed, to see the light of day. They write so eloquantly and do not show others how this disease and other forms of dementia really are. It is know wonder peopel and practioners just do not get it. I am real, I profess no secret knowledge of this disease, all I know is i suffer its relentless ravages. Imagine sitting accross from your family as they talke to you and you have no idea who the hell the are or what they are saying. That is the reality of it. Yes I can recall days gone by, but yesterday or this morning forget it. Enough from me this day.

71

God Bless You All and This Great Country of Ours!

Joe

Posted by Joseph Potocny at 01:20PM (-08:00)

While I still Can Think

Monday, March 05, 2007

Today has knowt been wone of mey better days. Have been angry and frustratied. Some have felt that today, even my granddaughter. Soon my optometrist will feeel it, taking over 5 week for lenses. I have no patient left with waht if feel in incompentency or out right stupidness. I should talk, cant even spel right or thing straing anymore. But take your meds you will be okd BS. These tiny slices are killing me, mly emotions, I have no controolll over anymore, no matter how hard I try. This disease sucks big time. The hell of it is our people in congress and the white house give a shit. It isn't a minority issue. WElll soon it will be a vast majority issue as they and theirs begein to suffer the ravages. As nasty as this sounds, I can hardly wait for them to join me. When it is to late to do anything, and alll they can do is say "If only I had listened". Posted by Joseph Potocny at 01:56PM (-08:00)

A BIT OF TRUTH TODAY

Thursday, March 08, 2007

As is set here having my grandddauhters bird on my shoulder eating what is leftt of my ears, I was going thtoouh some old emails and came accross this and thought you migh find the humor buth the real thruth in it.

Gates vs. GM

For all of us who feel only the deepest love and affection for the way computers have enhanced our lives, read on.

At a recent computer expo (COMDEX), Bill Gates reportedly compared the computer industry with the auto industry and stated,

"If GM had kept up with technology like the computer industry has, we would all be driving $25.00 cars that got 1, 000 miles to the gallon."

In response to Bill's comments, General Motors issued a press release stating:

If GM had developed technology like Microsoft, we would all be driving cars with the following characteristics (and I just love this part):

1. For no reason whatsoever, your car would crash . . . Twice a day.
2. Every time they repainted the lines in the road, you would have to buy a new car.

3. Occasionally your car would die on the freeway for no reason. You would have to pull to the side of the road, close all of the windows, shut off the car, restart it, and reopen the windows before you could continue. For some reason you would simply accept this.
4. Occasionally, executing a maneuver such as a left turn would cause your car to shut down and refuse to restart, in which case you would have to reinstall the engine.
5. Macintosh would make a car that was powered by the sun, was reliable, five times as fast and twice as easy to drive—but would run on only five percent of the roads.
6. The oil, water temperature, and alternator warning lights would all be replaced by a single "This Car Has Performed An Illegal Operation" warning light.

I love the next one!!!

7. The airbag system would ask "Are you sure?" before deploying.
8. Occasionally, for no reason whatsoever, your car would lock you out and refuse to let you in until you simultaneously lifted the door handle, turned the key and grabbed hold of the radio antenna.
9. Every time a new car was introduced car buyers would have to learn how to drive all over again because none of the controls would operate in the same manner as the old car.
10. You'd have to press the "Start" button to turn the engine off.

Please share this with your friends who love—but sometimes hate—their computer! Posted by Joseph Potocny at 01:27PM (-08:00)

Comments

—Anonymous   March 08, 2007

I love it! I'm going to send it to my dad, cuz he gets really frustrated when things happen to his computer "for no reason" lol who knows what he actually does to it? Thanks for sharing! *Shannon*

My Warpped Sense of Humor I'm Allowed

Tuesday, March 13, 2007

(From a Dear Friend—God Bless Her) Test for Dementia Below are four (4) questions and a bonus question. You have to answer them instantly. You can't take your time, answer all of them immediately. OK?

Let's find out just how clever you really are . . .

Ready? GO!!! First Question: You are participating in a race. You overtake the second person. What position are you in?

Answer: If you answered that you are first, then you are absolutely wrong! If you overtake the second person and you take his place, you are second!

Try not to screw up next time. Now answer the second question, but don't take as much time as you took for the first question, OK?

Second Question: IF you overtake the last person, then you are . . . ?

Answer: If you answered that you are second to last, then you are wrong again. Tell me, how can you overtake the LAST Person?

You're not very good at this, are you?

Third Question:

Very tricky arithmetic! Note: This must be done in your head only.

Do NOT use paper and pencil or a calculator. Try it. Take 1000 and add 40 to it. Now add another 1000. Now add 30. Add another 1000. Now add 20. Now add another 1000. Now add 10. What is the total?

Did you get 5000? The correct answer is actually 4100. If you don't believe it, check it with a calculator! Today is definitely not your day, is it?

Maybe you'll get the last question right . . . Maybe. Fourth Question: Mary's father has five daughters: 1 Nana, 2. Nene, 3. Nini, 4. Nono. What is the name of the fifth daughter?

Did you Answer Nunu? NO! Of course it isn't. Her name is Mary. Read the question again! Okay, now the bonus round: A mute person goes into a shop and wants to buy a toothbrush. By imitating the action of brushing his teeth he successfully expresses himself to the shopkeeper and the purchase is done. Next, a blind man comes into the shop who wants to buy a pair of sunglasses; how does HE indicate what he wants?

He just has to open his mouth and ask . . . It's really very simple . . . Like you! PASS THIS ON TO FRUSTRATE THE SMART PEOPLE IN YOUR LIFE! God Bless You and This Country of Ours!

Posted by Joseph Potocny at 12:26PM (-07:00)

Comments

—DirtyButter   March 18, 2007

Hi JOe, thanks for the good laugh!! And my DD and I both did horribly!!

Haha! I tripped up on the second question . . . silly me. But it did make me laugh out loud (and get strange looks from people walking by.) ;o) *Shannon*

To All Who Care

Wednesday, March 14, 2007

as you know I suffer for AD and very seldom use spell checker, I lack the wisdom to have made this up. I do not know who did, but they are held close in my prayers.

Lord, hold our troops in your loving hands. Protect them as they protect us. Bless them and their families for the selfless acts they perform for us in our time of need. Amen. When you view this, please stop for a moment and say a prayer for our ground troops in Afghanistan, saliors on ships, and airmen in the sky, and for those in Iraq. Of all the gifts you could give a US Soldier, Sailor, Marine, Coastguardsman or Airman, prayer is the very best one. Our Military Personnel Described: The average age of the U.S. military man is 19 years of age. He is a short haired, tight—muscled kid who, under normal circumstances is considered by society as half man, half boy. Not yet dry behind the ears, not old enough to buy a beer, but old enough to die for HIS COUNTRY. He never really cared much for work and he would rathe wax his own car than wash his father's; but he has never collected unemployment either. He is a recent High School graduate, he was probably an average student, pursued some form of sport; activites, dives a ten year old jalopy, and has a steady girlfriend that either broke up with him when he left, or swears to be waitng when he returns fro half a world away. He listens to rock and roll or hip-hop or rap or jazz or swing and 155mm holwitzers. He is 10 to 15 pounds lighter now than when hew was at home because he is working or fighting from before dawn to well after dusk. He has trouble spellin, thus letter writing is a pain for him, but he can field strip a rile in 30 seoconds and reassemble it in less time in the dark. He can recite to you the nomenclature of a machine gun or grenade launcher and use either one effectively if he must. He digs foxholes and latrines and can apply first aid like a professional. He can march until he is told to stop or stop until he is told to march. He obeys orders instantly and without hesitation, but he is not without spirit or individual dignity. He is self sufficient. He has two sets of fatiques: he washes one and wears the other. He keeps his canteens full and his feet dry. He sometimes forgets to brush his teeth, but never to clean his rifle.He can cook his own meals, mend his own clothes, and fix his own hurts. If you're thirst, he'll share his water with you; if you are hungry his food. He'll even split his ammunition with you in the midst of battle when you run low. He has learned to use his hands like weapons and weapons like they were his hands. He can save your life or take it, because that is his job. He will often do twice the work of a civillian, draw half the pay and still find ironic humor in it all. He has seen more suffering and death then he should have in his short lifetime. Hes has stood atop mountains of dead bodies, and helped to create them. He has wept in public and private, for friends who have fallen in combat an is UNASHAMED. He feels every note of the Nathional Anthem vibrate through his body while at rigid attention, while tempering the burning desire to 'square away' those around him who haven't bothered to stand, remove their hat, or even stop talking. In an odd twist, day in and day out, far from home, he defends their right to be disrespectul. Just as did his Father, Grandfather, and Great Grandfather, he is paying the price for our freedom. Beardless or not, he is not a boy. He is the American Fighting Man that has kept this Country Free for over 200 years. He has asked nothing in return, except our friendship and understanding. Remember him, always, for he has earned our respect and admiration with his blood. And now we even have women over there in danger, doing their part in this tradition of going to War when our nation calls us to to so. As you go to bed tonignt, remember this shot. A short lull, a little shade and a picture of loved ones in their helmets. SAY A PRAYER FOR THEM TONIGHT. If only I could have truly written these words. God Bless You and This Country of Ours!

Joe

Posted by Joseph Potocny at 09:25AM (-07:00)

Comments

—Lynn	March 19, 2007

It hits a little closer to home these days with the loved ones in our family and possibly coming into it fighting the wars here on the home front and overseas. Very nice Joseph. Lynn

—DirtyButter	April 22, 2007

Thanks for sharing this, Joe.

Lost In My World

Tuesday, March 20, 2007

I started this blog for those with theis disease (A) and other forms of demeeentia. My goal was to keep up daily, but that does not seem tooo work to wel anymore. I have received over 1100 emails in the last, I donot no several weeks and am at a lost to get to mem all. It took me over 3 hours to put a new facet in the kitchen yesterday, had to rest betwwen steps and went off and did other things and forgot what I was doing, but alll ened well, no leaks, what a suprise. I find walking for any length of time with my grandddaughter and playing at the park is causing me great tiredness and loss of where I am at. Good she knows the way home. For some unknown reaason I have even opened an online business, like I have hte time and energy anymore. Oh well, was never considerrred the brightest light bulb in the lamp. Thought before the day disappears I would make this post. Welcom to my world.

God Bless, Joe Posted by Joseph Potocny at 12:33PM (-07:00)

Comments

—Lynn   March 22, 2007

You are lucky it did not leak. I wouldn't let you do any more plumbing. And that has nothing to do with the AD but past history.

—Anonymous   March 27, 2007

hey joe . . . just wanted to say hi! and that i was thinking of you. Also, my friends mom has AD and i guess she is pretty bad so i told him about your blog and he really liked it. Take care . . . *shannon*

—Anonymous   March 27, 2007

hey daddy!!! i love you and i miss you. i am always here for you whenever you need to talk. **muah***

morgan

—DirtyButter   April 22, 2007

Sounds like it's time to get one of those GPS things that locates you if you get lost, Joe.

I'll see if I can find out more about how to get one.

Try to celebrate what you do accomplish . . . instead of how long it took you to do it, OK?

Advice I need for myself, too. LOL

It Has Been Awhile

Tuesday, April 03, 2007

I have not posted is ome time now. I keep forgetting two. One of my dearest friends recently losst her farther and I forgot to send her my sympathies. I stop one of my meds and that was a big mistake, thoought I was dying, but apparently God nor the Devil want me at this time. Life is geetting a little more confusing and frustrating for me, I don't even answer my emails the way I used to. I feel like a captive in my own mind, body and home. The need to lash out grows stonger each day and is becoming a little harder to manage day by day. Part of this is the disease part of it is myoun defects of my character. Do not know which is becomeing the more dominate part. I have been alone in life, but never felt lonely, I now do. There is sadness in my sould and being and the tears and emotions come more easily. It seems being loved and cared for does not matter all thaaat muc anymore, because I am solwy starting not to care for me or this life anylonger. Well enough of my pitty party, life goes on, until.

God Bless You and This Country of Ours

Posted by Joseph Potocny at 09:17AM (-07:00)

Comments

—Anonymous   April 05, 2007

I LOVE YOU!!!

MORGAN:)

—ErwinErhard   April 05, 2007

Hi Joe,

My name is Erwin, I used to work with Lynn at Ricoh. My mom suffers from Alzhiemers too and is in stage 5, nick named, "The Long Goodbye" I just wanted to say, "thank you" for putting out this blog. Your blog has helped me understand what my mom could never communicate to me or anyone else in my family. I hope you'll still keep writing because I will be reading every entry you make. Don't give up hope, it's all we have.

Take care, Erwin

—Lynn   April 06, 2007

God or the Devil may not want you at this time but your wife and family do. We all love you. And when the time is right God will welcome you home.

Today Is Here

Saturday, April 21, 2007

Well here I am today, thought I would post early before I once again forget and the day is gone and so are the next couple of days. Tried removing my self from meds again but at a slower pace this time, that did not work either. With a ½ brain cell left not real brilliant anymore. Juts dont like living this way anymore. Tireed of all the crap goinginto my body, but it keeps me going, for what I dont know. I have been slowlly deleting my email add book and removing myself from things on the web, no time to respondd or get no will or energy. It is exttremely frustrating in the mind of mine and world. Never quite sure what is oing on in it, just waiting to go home and hope it is soon. Well enough of my rattling.

God Bless You and This Country of Ours.

Joe

Posted by Joseph Potocny at 09:58AM (-07:00)

Comments

—Mauigirl   April 21, 2007

Just found your blog and am very impressed with it. You are doing a great service by telling us your experiences and how this terrible disease affects you. My father had AD in the last few years of his life and my mother-in-law has it now. Best wishes to you and let's all hope they find a cure. Many of us will be in the same situation as you are in the coming years.

—DirtyButter   April 22, 2007

When I get behind with email, like I did when Daddy died, I get brutal with the delete key, or I send a copy/paste of a quick apology for no time to respond email.

A Gentle Day

Tuesday, April 24, 2007

Those of you thatt visit my blog will start to notice changes on the side as I atttempt to clean it up. I have been tryingg al morning to get through my emails to no avail. More immmportatly I have spent time reading Bible Stories to my Granddaughter, this is an exxperience believe me, trying to explain what things are to a four year old is not exactly my mental forteee. But these are the times she will remember and I will forget, in the not to distant future. But that is ok, I can enjoy the moment, even though my nose runs, my voice quivers and my eyes run. This will pass and soon won't even be a memory to me as my mind goes else where. So much for today. Catch Ya on the other side.

God Bless You and This Country of Ours!

Joe

Posted by Joseph Potocny at 01:01PM (-07:00)

Comments

—Anonymous   April 24, 2007

Hey Joe . . . Just wanted to say HI and that I was thinking of you! *Shannon*

—Lynn   April 24, 2007

Thank you for giving our grandchildren memories and our children memories that will carry on. I'm glad today is a gentle day for you.

—Anonymous   April 27, 2007

Dad I'm so happy that at least Emma and M.J. are able to grow up with you during this time. I wish we could be there with you so Chase and Lilly could share those same memories as the other two. I love you so much and I hate this time right now. I can't stand to know what the future holds for our family. It's not fair and I am not ready to loose you. I am so greatful that you are my father and always will be. I love you with all my heart.

Morgan

My Friend Tracy Wrote This

Wednesday, May 02, 2007

What follows is a post written by a friend on a different board, I think that I have never heard this disease more eliquently stated than this and how to handle us. The wisdom that follows is not mine, I entirely give Tracey full credit and hope she does not mind my usage of it.

This has been my mission of education and very well may be my last post. Read, learn and listen to her, she suffers from this rotten mind robbing disease herself.

On 5/1/07, YoungHope wrote: > > There are ALL kinds of books that have been written clinically and > scientifically from professionals of all walks of life about > Alzheimer's Disease. These books profoundly state what the symptoms > are? How old you HAVE to be to be diagnosed. Books that describe the > different stages. Books that tell about the different medications > that are available to treat the symptoms of the disease. These books > also tell us how we should treat our loved ones with > Alzheimer's/dementia, how we should take care of them, what we > should do, what we shouldn't do. The books also tell us how we > should feed them, what we should feed them, how we should dress them > and keep them potty trained, what type of a routine they need to be > on, how to keep them awake during the daytime, how to make them > sleep at night. These books even tell us how to keep your loved one > happy and active, when to get your POA and Guardianship papers drawn > up. These books give all of these answers and more but these books > do not tell HOW OUR LOVED ONES WANT TO BE TREATED only what they > think should be. What they are forgetting is that one day they could > be this person with Alzheimer's Disease and then would they want all > of these demands put upon them? Probably not. > > The answers that are not in the book are the important things such > as, if we are in the final stages and do not want to eat, do not > force feed us. Don't grind our meat up to look like something that > the cat just spit up. Would you want it? probably not. > > Don't force us take our clothes off and take a shower, but be > patient and treat us with dignity and respect. Help us to bathe from > our chair, help us brush our teeth or our gums and to put on clean > clothes, but please don't scold us for a fear of the unknown. > > Don't force us to get up in the morning, help us turn from one side > to another to keep our skin healthy. Open the curtains to let the > sunshine in, read us a story or just sit and talk with us. Remember, > we are still human. > > Don't force us to go places that we no longer remember. Show us a > picture and tell us about this long forgotten place and maybe, just > maybe, we will decide on our own to go with you, but if we don't, > don't be angry, remember that you were that way many years ago. > > Don't force us to go to bed, tell us that it is time. Help us change > into our night clothes, dim the lights, turn some music on from our > day years ago, soft and low and sit near us, let us know once again > that we are not alone.

> > Encourage us to take our medicine. There will come a time that no > matter what we take, the medicine will no longer work and the > disease will have won its battle with us. Don't yell at us or curse > at us, remember we have fought long and hard, now we just need to > rest at our own pace not at the pace of medical technology. > > These are some of the answers that you won't find in a book but only > from the eyes and heart of a person with dementia. > > Tracy Reposted here by Joe. Posted by Joseph Potocny at 12:05PM (-07:00)

Comments

—Anonymous   May 03, 2007

Thank you Joe, for reposting and sharing this . . . Hopefully it will help my dad when he is with my grandma.

shannon

As The Storm Clouds Gather

Friday, May 04, 2007

Today is one of those daaays that my head is filled with thunder and grey clouds. I am having a hard time conccentrating and paying atttention to what it is that

I am doing. My head is filled with pain that asprin and such will not relieve. It is the total frustration of what is happending and I have no fricken control over it. It makes sit and cry whrn I am alone and even others are around. My only ansswer is that everything is ok, when it is not. It is becoming more difficult to express my self and feelings. All I know is that my house is in order and I await. So each day I slowly slip off to some unknown adventure and listen to all those whoo think that they know what is best and have no idea. There will come a time that this is nolonger holding me.

God Bles

Joe

Posted by Joseph Potocny at 01:37PM (-07:00)

Comments

—Anonymous   May 05, 2007

i know i have no idea what you are going through but you are not alone. even though i live far away i am always here for you t otry to talk too. i love you

morgan

—Anonymous   May 13, 2007

hi dad!!! i want you to know that i appriate everything you have done and do for me. your a wounderful and thoughtful person. i look for those qualities in other people. i am sorry that i do not know how to exactly help you but as long as i keep asking God to give me patiants and being able to help you, then i think i am doing good. and as you can see i can not spell at all!!!! We are here for you dad and although i do not know what is best for you i will still ask you every day "HOW ARE YOU FEELING!!!" i love you and so does everybody else. love sabrina

In The Mornings Quietness

Monday, May 14, 2007

I am sitting heree this morning trying to think of how I feel and really am not sure. I am slowly starting to feel that neither me, my friends, loved onees ore even those who do not care one way or the other give much of a damn anymore. The confusion creaps in a little deeper each day, the harder I try the worssse it seems to get. Interest in things is leaving me, I am looking through different eyes then what I used to have and they don't see much light anymore, and I accept that as ok. I guess it is what it is whatever that means. Why I do this makes no sense in my ½ brain cell, then much of how I feel or thinkkk anymore does not seen to make any sense. I keep trying to help and control myself but I know ai I am doing is slowly loosing it and probably making people not so comfortable in my presence. All I know is that my so called friends and good part of my family no longer communicate with me. Maybe they are afraid, well fuck welcome to the crowd. So much for my ramblings, but this is my only outlet, words do not come out of my protective shell to others very easily at all. Beaten to many times as a kid and left unloved to give up of me very much. Now when I want to my wonderful brain (the pink matter) doesn't graps the concept very welll. anymore. God Bess Joe Posted by Joseph Potocny at 08:23AM (-07:00)

Comments

—Anonymous   May 18, 2007

You may think we're afraid and you know you might be right to an extent. I lost my brother 5 years ago, now I have a new brother. And I am finally starting to fully except that. I lost my sister when she got married both times. And that was okay. We developed a new relationship. I never had my other sister. She has always been like a stranger to me, and thats not okay. But we have started to get our relationship on a track. It may not be the best one, but at least we have one. I have yet to lose my mother and I am thankful for that. But I know I am losing my father and that scars the shit out of me! I am not ready to lose you yet!!!! But I know it is happening and I will lose you forever in a short time. I know you want to go, but you have to know we aren't ready to let you go. And wether or not you want to hear it I am tiered of reading about how were aren't here for you and how you want to go! I love you and I am not ready for you to leave.

To My Daughter—My Terror

Friday, May 18, 2007

Dear Daughter, I can only imagine your fear and how scarred you must be. You see, the brother you lost 5 years ago was my son and I lost him to. I have had to learn to accept and love the new person he is because of the acccident. But I can still remember having to teach him to wipe his ass all over again at 17, how to walk, to talk, to spelll (me of all people), you were not there the first day they sat him up in bed and he just ddroped over and drulled and I had to leave the room because I could not stand it and had to go back in and help, that is what parents do. I lost your sister twice when she got married both times also, I was sad but was filled with hope and joy for her future, which seems to be coming together. Your other sister, yes you guys never really had her, but neither did mom and I, she put us through hell, such as I wanted to beat her sense, but that would not have helped becauuuse she already was senseless. I remember carring her in

83

my arms bleeding to death because of her canceer and now she has given us two really beutiful grandchildren, your niece and nephew. You I will be loosing soon to someone you love dearly and I will be hurt but happy for the adventure that awaits you and the wonder that can be yours. I climb a mountain from time to time to survey as far back as I can see to the present to look for the rays of hope for each of you and I have seen them. Maybe you need to due the same with your older sister and get awaaay from the trees so you can see the ever so small changes and the attempts she is making and open your heart. I have learned not to morn over losses of those we love, but to cherrish the time that we have had with them. Scarry step into my brain where the storm continually rages and I cannot find my way. Shit I can not even hold your mother anymore and love her as I did once, becuase I forget how to. Don't cry for me or pitty me, this is the way it is period. Don't have to like it, but loved one we cannot change it. The doctors are changing my meds the time I take them and the doses to try and slow things down. Will it help, who knows? But I do what I have to. I have always loved you guys and will even when I no longer can remember who you are. I have tried and probably failed miserabllly at times to be the best I could for you guys and do the best and right thing. But I am only a person with faults and now a failing brain. It may scar you, but try to listen to the Alzheimers Prayer on my site. Plays best unfortunately in IE and maybe it may help. But remember you I love and am proud of as I am all of my family.

With Gods Love, Your Dad Posted by Joseph Potocny at 08:27PM (-07:00)

Comments

—Anonymous   May 19, 2007

Dad you never lost me when i got married either time, gosh that sounds horrible. The only time anyone has ever lost me is when i let everyone down with my drug and alchol problems. I am just greatful that everyone welcomed me back and didn't have to see me in those conditions. I am with Kat on this and so is everyone. We aren't ready to lose you. I know I want my kids to be bale to grow up with you and to be able to have good memorie of the times they have spent with their grandfather. They are too little to remmeber anything now unlike Emma who is lucky to have these times with you. We all love you and we will all be here for you through times. I LOVE YOU Morgan

Where Am I?????

Wednesday, May 23, 2007

This is a question that I was always asking myself and slooowly seem not to anymore. I does not seem to matter. I fall and stumble more and it bothers

others, but it is like I almost don't notice it or it is gone from my mind in seconds. I sit and stare at this beast of humanity and family think I am dooing somthing, but reallly I do not have the faintist idea what is going on. It is becoming more difficult for me tho pull my mental tissue together to focus on what I am doing or talking about. Blankness is becoming more normal to me. Dr. has increased meds to help, I take more vitamins. Physically Ifeel fine, but the head and body seem to not like each other anymore, go in different directions. Look at new reasearch and they say it is promising, but dig furher and find reasearch that says the opposite. It seems no one is talking with those of us with AD on a daily basis to really see what happens. There are 100s like me that have blogs and websites, that try to tell the world what we are like and the tortures that take place in our brains. But unless you are drulling at the mouth, pissing in your closthes, not eating at all, wearing the saame clothers for months and need nearly 24 hour care, you cannot possibly have this disease and should not beaware of what is happening to you. News People, we know. Ask Nancy Regan about our President Ronald and listen to her and what she and him together went throug. Some of us hang on, because of physical condition others go quickly, we don't know where our own step over the edge point is. Try living that way and see how you feeeel.

God Bless You and This Country of Ours!

Joe

Posted by Joseph Potocny at 12:40PM (-07:00)

Today Is Mine — Welcome To My World

Wednesday, May 30, 2007

Yes today is mine, tomorrow may not be. This road that i now travel has exit rammps, but who knowws where they lead so I stay on it. One may be the one I take that ends in a few steps and I am gone, not in a physical sense, but me who I am will be gone. That is the nature of this fricken disease, you never know when that moment is going to arrive. I belong to a 12 step program for 34 years that hass done its best to teach me to live one day at a time, that now has an entire different meaning to me today, for now it is hour to hour. Went shopping with the Mrs. last night, got some soda, candy (i am a push over for that), paper towels and a bunch of toliet paper. You see we keep the sanitaaation departmentt working. Probably took all of 45 minutes, I was totally exhausted from it. So there you have it, a day with Alzheimers you never know when you are going to disappear into the realm of whatever, not knowing anyone or anything, pretty damn scarry isn't it. In the words of Elvis Presley (The King), WELCOME TO MY WORLD, WON'T YOU COME ON IN. Posted by Joseph Potocny at 09:44AM (-07:00)

Comments

—Anonymous   June 01, 2007

I hope you had a little fun on our outing and seeing other people. It was nice to get out of the house with you.(Without everybody else) Love

A DISABLED MANIFESTO—WE STAND TALL

Thursday, May 31, 2007

A DISABLED MANIFESTO We proclaim that we are born free and equal human beings; that our disabilities are limitations only, and that our identity does not derive from being disabled. We proclaim that we have the same value as people who are not disabled, and we reject any scheme of labeling or classifying us that encourages people to think of us as having diminished value. We reject the idea that institutions must be created to "care" for us, and proclaim that these institutions have been used to "manage" us in ways that non-disabled people are not expected to accept. We particularly denounce institutions whose purpose is to punish us for being disabled, or to confine us for the convenience of others.

We reject the notion that we need "experts," to tell us how to live, especially experts from the able-bodied world. We are not diagnoses in need of a cure or cases to be closed. We are human, with human dreams and ambitions. We deny that images of disability are appropriate metaphors for incompetence, stupidity, ugliness or weakness. We are aware that as people with disabilities, we have been considered objects of charity and we have been considered commodities. We are neither. We reject charitable enterprises that exploit our lifestyle to titillate others, and which propose to establish the rules by which we must live without our participation.

We also reject businesses that use us as "warm bodies" to provide a passive market for their services, again laying down rules by which we must live for their profit. We recognize that the lines between charities and businesses are blurred in the disability industry, and we do not accept services from either if their essential function is to exploit us. We assert our rights of self-determination in the face of rules, eligibility criteria, regulations, customs, laws or other barriers, and we pledge not to allow any authority or institution to deprive us of our freedom of choice.

Finally, we assert that any service we need, from specialized teaching to personal care, can be provided to us in the community among our non-disabled peers. Segregated institutions are not necessary to serve us, and they have been the greatest source of our oppression, especially when they have been run by able-bodied people without our participation. All human beings are more alike than we are different.

We recognize that when we assert this belief we will find ourselves in conflict with regressive institutions and their supporters, some of whom may be disabled themselves. We do not expect thousands of years of stereotyping to dissipate quickly. We commit ourselves and those who come after us to challenge our oppression on every level until we are allowed to be fully human and assert our individuality ahead of our disability.

By John R. Woodward, M.S.W. Center for Independent Living of North Florida, Inc.

Posted by Joseph Potocny at 02:40PM (-07:00)

Comments

—Anonymous   June 01, 2007

Yes you do stand tall. You are trying to educate those around you about what is happening and you still get involved in causes. You are still a thinking body. Sometimes it gets jumbled but in the end it works out. Love

MY WISH TO YOU THIS DAY!

Friday, June 01, 2007

A woman came out of her house and saw! 3 old m en with long white beards sitting in her front yard. She did not recognize them. She said "I don't think I know you, but you must be hungry. Please come in and have something to eat."

Is the man of the house home?", they asked. "No", she replied. "He's out." "Then we cannot come in", they replied. In the evening when her husband came home, she told him what had happened. "Go tell them I am home and invite them in!" The woman went out and invited the men in" "We do not go into a House together," they replied. "Why is that?" she asked. One of the old men explained: "His name is Wealth," he said pointing to one of his friends, and said pointing to another one, "He is Success, and I am Love." Then he added, "Now go in and discuss with your husband which one of us you want in your home." The woman went in and told her husband what was said. Her husband was overjoyed. "How nice!!", he said. "Since that is the case, let us invite Wealth. Let him come and fill our home with wealth!" His wife disagreed. "My dear, why don't we invite Success?" Their daughter-in-law was listening from the other corner of the house. She jumped in with her own suggestion: "Would it not be better to invite Love? Our home will then be filled with love!" "Let us heed our daughter-in-law's advice," said the husband to his wife. "Go out and invite Love to be our guest." The woman went out and asked the 3 old men, "Which one of you is Love? Please come in and be our guest." Love got up and started walking toward the house. The other 2 also got up and followed him.

Surprised, the lady asked Wealth and Success: "I only invited Love, Why are you coming in?" The old men replied together: "If you had invited Wealth or Success, the other two of us would've stayed out, but since you invited Love, wherever He goes, we go with him. Wherever there is Love, there is also Wealth and Success!!!!!!" MY WISH FOR YOU . . .

Where there is pain, I wish you peace and mercy. Where there is self-doubting, I wish you a renewed confidence in your ability to work through it. Where there is tiredness, or exhaustion, I wish you understanding, patience, and renewed strength. Where there is fear, I wish you love, and courage. You have two choices right now:

1. Click this off
2. Invite love by sharing this story with all the people you care about.

I hope you will choose #2. I did.

A dozen angels r sent 2 u! God Bless, Joe Posted by Joseph Potocny at 12:33PM (-07:00)

Comments

—gkcowell	June 03, 2007

What a beautiful story!

—gkcowell	June 03, 2007

What a wonderful post!

My Mind Is Overwhelmed

Wednesday, June 06, 2007

About a week ago, I think, I goined a group of peopp;e on the internest, to talk with otheer normal mental people. I was never welcomed openly by the other dementia groups I joined and really got tired of their living ing the problem, of course we do not have much of a solution except meds and that crap for us. But I know each day I loose a very small slice of who and what I once was. I starrred out at things and donot even know where the hell I am or have been, until something or someone brings me back to this shitty reality I call life. But this group has welccomed me with such open arms and encouragement that my heart, soul and eyes remain filled with tears. I have even met people with the disease and have gotten comments from others who have had parents, friends and others with it, and they say my writting has given them a neweer understanding of our side and helped them to cope with the frustration and pain theyyy have unfortunately experienced. I been call courageous, good, outstanding and ben thanked. I am neither courag. or outstanding, good ?, I am just trying to let people know what this hell is really like f=rom the inside, watching yourself disappear. Yes I will die from this, complications they call it, mostly infections. I forget to eat take meds go to the restroom to the point that this screen inf front of me gets jaundice, then I know your in trouble. I have promised myself that before I have stepped over the edge into oblivion, unless it happens and I do not know it, but sense it at the tip of my toes, that my agony and that of my family further agony with me as a useless individual will cease. Do not get all bent out of shape, if you were here, I am sure you would feel the same, on the side of my blog listen to the Alzheimers Prayer, Parents Wish, you will need speakers and power point for(A Parents Wish) and you just may understand.

God Bless

Joe

Posted by Joseph Potocny at 09:19AM (-07:00)

Been Away For A Couple of Days

Wednesday, June 13, 2007

Sorry thaat I have not keept up with you folks but. The grou I joined I quit. 6000+ emails a day was more than I could even begin to handle, leat alone read or answer. So you are stuck with me. Each day getts a little worse then the day befoe, i sit talking with mmy family and wonder who the hell are these people and why are they arrround me. Then suddenly it dawns on me who they are.= This is becoming a nightmare. I am tire now so will check in with you all later.
Posted by Joseph Potocny at 02:40PM (-07:00)

My Farwell

Sunday, July 15, 2007

The one thing I have tried to say to those I love and care about, my frineds, family, whoever they maybe, I no longer know for sure is not to cry for me when I am gone, both mentally and physically. Hopefully my ashes will be spread in Gods' Country, YellowStone National Park, where I want to be. Whether this blog remains or not only time will tell. You can see I do not post as often, things are begining to mean less to me than they did befor. So while I can say it and have the will to, I bid all those I have known a found farwell and hope I have left something good in your lives. I am not going today, but I need this to get out of me before I forget and do not have the time to do so. Some of my family will read this others won't the same as friends and so on, because they are just caught up in their own lives and mine is not that important in the Grand Scheme of things. Only to me and my Lord.

God Bless You and This Country of Ours!

Joe

Posted by Joseph Potocny at 01:34PM (-07:00)

Comments

—Anonymous   July 15, 2007

well to this one family member your life does matter to me. you are the best dad anyone could have ever asked foe. i love you

—Anonymous   October 30, 2007

Daddy your life matters to all of us. Its not nesaverally that were too busy to read your blogs, but more that its hard to read. Not because of the spelling or grammar, but the content of what you are saying. I love you Daddy!!! Kat

The 2008 Democratic Convention

Monday, July 16, 2007

I got this from a friend and could not resist—it echos my feelings politically: Schedule of Events

7:00 pm ~ Opening flag burning
7:15 pm ~ Pledge of Allegiance to the U. N.
7:20 pm ~ Ted Kennedy proposes a toast
7:25 pm ~ Nonreligious prayer and worship with Jesse Jackson and Al Sharpton
7:45 pm ~ Ceremonial tree hugging
7:55 pm ~ Ted Kennedy proposes a toast
8:00 pm ~ How I Invented the Internet—Al Gore
8:15 pm ~ Gay Wedding Planning—Barney Frank presiding
8:35 pm ~ Ted Kennedy proposes a toast
8:40 pm ~ Our Troops are War Criminals—John Kerry
9.00 pm ~ Memorial service for Saddam and his sons Cindy Sheehan and Susan Sarandon
10:00 pm ~ "Answering Machine Etiquette"—Alec Baldwin
11:00 pm ~ Ted Kennedy proposes a toast
11:05 pm ~ Collection for the Osama Bin Laden kidney transplant fund B arbra Streisand
11:15 pm ~ Free the Freedom Fighters from Guantanamo Bay—Sean Penn
11:30 pm ~ Oval Office Affairs—William Jefferson Clinton

11:45 pm ~ Ted Kennedy proposes a toast
11:50 pm ~ How George Bush Brought Down the World Trade Towers—Howard Dean
12:15 am ~ "Truth in Broadcasting Award"—Presented to Dan Rather by Michael Moore
12:25 am ~ Ted Kennedy proposes a toast
12:30 am ~ Satellite address by Mahmoud Ahmadinejad
12:45 am ~ Nomination of Hillary Rodham Clinton by Nancy Pelosi
1:00 am ~ Ted Kennedy proposes a toast
1:05 am ~ Coronation of Hillary Rodham Clinton
1:30 am ~ Ted Kennedy proposes a toast
1:35 am ~ Bill Clinton asks Ted Kennedy to drive Hillary home
Posted by Joseph Potocny at 01:12PM (-07:00)

Comments

—Elanor   July 21, 2007
hello, and thanks for the good laugh to start the day! I am a releatively new reader of your blog and I really like it, thankyou for sharing your journey.

Well Today Is Monday

Monday, July 23, 2007

The staart of another week at home with most everyone gone. My brain must be cleuless at 62 and a half I am digging out juniper bushes and leveling the ground to build a wall. Most I can handle is an hour or so. Body stops and brains quits. Not to smart theses days. I get a PET scan sometime this week I think. Had lungs and coratic ateries checked, called me today and said everything is ok there. Sounds other then normal aging aches and pains, physically I am ok. Upstaitts is a difereent story.It is peaceful and quite in the house right now and I am alone and really like it. My brain isn't really doing anything either. Been closing up my on line businesses, one left to go, in fight with credit chard companies and FTC over all of this but what the heck. It helps my my mind hold on to somethinging rather then going off to whereeever it goes. Half my doctors believe it is Alzheimers especially the one who lost his father to it, the others say maybe but you do not fit in theis fricken box. Askw what the heck is wrong and well you might as well look a a wall for nothing comes back nor is ist said. Well heaven doesn't want me, the devil could care less and death turns a cold shoulder, what is a guy to do. so much for the pitty me side to day. May your life be filled with love, happiness, health and peace.

God Bless, Joe Posted by Joseph Potocny at 01:00PM (-07:00)

Comments

—Elanor	August 14, 2007

Hi Joe,

how are you going? any results yet from the tests? It must be every frustrating to be getting different opinions from the drs.

Well Another Day

Tuesday, August 14, 2007

Had annual physical two weeeks ago, funny thing they say my lungs are ok, but two years ago x-rays said had emphazema, I questioned how that could be, I am not the brightest light bulb in the pack, but I do know that shit does not go away it works till it kills you. So it appears after I had the doc (himself) look at the xrays and not take the radiologists word for things, the original x-rays were so bad he could not make any kind of a diagnosis, but the current ones are good. Two years on meds that I did not need because some idiot cannot do their job right. So to help with the old brain, we had a PET Scan and it shows that half of my frontal lobes are, well in Peru. That means the rest will follow. Have read some recent studies that AD is thought to start as other dementias in the frontal lobes. WEll we are off to see one of the two best neurologists in the state on 9/4, that ought to be fun. Can hardly wait for this diagnosis. All I know for sure is my life is slowly disapating and I get lost in a world I do not know where and my youngest now tells me I am mixing of the sexes when I talk hes are shes and so on. Life is still ok I am breathing, I can still do that right at least.

God Bless You and this Country of Ours!

Joe

Posted by Joseph Potocny at 01:59PM (-07:00)

Comments

—Anonymous	August 14, 2007

Hey Joe . . . I haven't written in a while but I wanted to say Hi and that I was thinking of you.

Shannon

—DirtyButter	August 19, 2007

I've been remiss in visitnins and wanted to say Hi, too!! Glad your loungs are OK, but sorry it took them so long to figure that out. It's ban endouth to be taking meds that youhave to have without taking some you didn't need!!

I know you feel like you're disappearing, but you r posts still sound like you're HERE. Keep at it, dear firend!!

PS As you see, my uncorrected writing continues to deteriorate. You're the only one I send to un editted. LOL!

—DirtyButter   August 30, 2007

Thinking of you this orning, Joe. I'm doing a little better than I was last time I posted as my typing whos. Well, I still make mistakes, but we all do that when we tpe, right?

Have a great day today, Joe!!

Farwell To My Old Friend Pain

Saturday, September 29, 2007

The letter that follows has never been sent this is all done in spell check so that it makes some sense. At long last I need to close what is the next to final chapter of my life. I know the individual will never see this but it serves to finish my part and clean my side of the street. It has been awhile since I have posted or written anything, that is because things are well taking their toll or scheckles if you will.

August 24, 2007

Dear Phyllis,

I am not quiet sure how to start this letter or if it will even be sent to you. See I have never broken my word or lied to you. When we last talked, I promised you I would not bother you again and that was truly my intent. But I cannot get over the way you talked to me, when I called as a friend nor the way you ran from me claiming you loved me so much it hurt that August night in 1978. Should I send this, due me at least one final courtesy read it before you rip it up and throw it in the trash.

Yes when I called it was done in friendship and with the hope you would tell me the truth as to why you left me standing like a piece of trash in the middle of the street. I did not deserve that. I did nothing but love you, stand by your side and support you in what you wanted to do. I never lied to you nor even bothered with any other females, you were everything to me and I thought I was to you.

I can only believe that one of two things had happened, age was not one and we both know that, I do not believe you were seeing anyone else either; I think either your parents finally gave you an ultimatum regarding me or you were pregnant and going to get an abortion. I found the second more likely, and would have stood by your side and decision and still cared and loved you, because we were together too long knowing your parents hated me and wished I would vanish into thin air. I tried to show them I would not hurt you, nor was I going to let their dislike for me push me away from you. Kids were something you did not want and if you remember correctly I told you we would marry when you decided and if we were to have children it would be your call. All I really wanted were for us to be together in life forever.

You see I feel my Lord gave me a gift the night you kissed me on the cheek and began our relationship. To that point in my life I had never felt that anyone loved or cared for me. Not even my parents, my father used to beat me till I bled and my mother always told me I should not make him so mad. My friends were non existent, I learned to cheat, lie and steal at my parent's side and how to take and not give back. Of being loved or loving I knew nothing at all. Then you were put in my life and I learned to trust another person, except their caring and their love and I learned to give back without asking or expecting anything for the first time in my life. You were a true gift from God, because of you I have been able to love, give and care for someone other than myself. You taught me that and I am forever grateful, for that gift, which will never be taken away from me.

This is my way of bringing closure to us and saying goodbye finally. You see I never morn a loss, I always have rejoiced in having known the person, and I did not do that with you. I have never allowed the kindness, love, caring and giving you showed me to overshadow the way you left my life as if there was some big dark secret. You see I cannot perceive running from someone you love so much without telling them why they cannot be a part of your life any more unless something so bad in you mind existed that you thought I would do something crazy over. I tell you this in all honesty I would never have hurt you, I would have rather died then cause you any pain, which apparently existed.

So to you my Love and friend, I bid you a found farewell. I hope the Lord continues to bless your life and bring you the happiness that you deserve. Remember we lose loved ones, but rejoicing and celebrating their lives is the greatest compliment that we can pay them. I rejoice in knowing you and am happy for the time you were part of my life.

With Gods' Love, Joe

God Bless You All and This Country of Ours!

Posted by Joseph Potocny at 12:15PM (-07:00)

How Scarry is Your Back Yard?

Tuesday, October 09, 2007

I thiink but don't remember if I have told you whoo should happen to read or check this blog at times that I have been diagnosed with Frontal Temporal Lobe Dementia, which works much faster than my old fried AD. I get lost in my own yard, I forget what I am doing how to get back intool the house and stand their wondering whatever i wonder and thus far have found my way back. I have grwon afraid to leave my own house because I am not shure that even going to the mailbox I will stop and remember to come back. I wake up generally around 6 am ad the next thing I am really aware of it is 4 or 5 in the afternoon. What scares me is not the not knowing, but when will that line come where I step over and don't come back. Of death I have no fear physical death that is, the death of me scares me for I will cease to exist and do not want to be remembered that way, if I am even remembered. Till and if I remember take care.

God Bless You and This Country of Ours!

Joe

Posted by Joseph Potocny at 09:25AM (-07:00)

Comments

—Elanor

October 14, 2007

hi joe, just wanted to say hello and I am thinking of you:)

—DirtyButter

November 13, 2007

Hi Joe,

It's ben awhoil since I stoped by. Sorry to see that you r memory has gotten so much worse. Remebered? Of course you will be!!!! {{{HUGS}}}

—DirtyButter

January 02, 2008

I am thingking about you today dear friend. God bless you and your family! May 2008 be a year of peace for you.

Farwell To All

Monday, January 07, 2008

I have attempted tho keep up this blog and it has becomme increasilngly more difficuly. I hope that I have at least showed some what My World and those like is like. Comforted some because they could not understand. Brought you some humor and education. But my AD and now Frontal Lobe Dementia my brain and atttention is not there it is on vacation I think. I sit down to post and forget and walk away and just turn off this beast. I want to THANK ALL WHO HAVE WRITTEN ME AND MADE COMMENTS. I only hope that you received in return what I had to give and you have my thanks. I am marking my calendar, this blog will be deleted on the 15th of this month. If it dosent happen you know I forgot to look at my calendar or just checked and got lost in my world.

God Bless You and this Country of Ours!

Joe

Posted by Joseph Potocny at 12:15PM (-08:00)

Comments

—DirtyButter   January 16, 2008

PLEASE DO NOT DELETE YOUR BLOG!!!!!!!!!!!! You have done something important here, Joe. It is part of history, and part of YOU!! I implore you to leave your blog on the Internet, as it will give understanding and courage to many for a long, long time.

I count it an honor to be our cyber friend, and I wish you the best as the AD takes more and more of a toll on you. I think of you often, dear friend. And God Bless YOU!!!

Before I Leave You

Monday, January 14, 2008

I have been abit taken back by those that have been reading tis blog since my last post and have beeen asked not to stop. I have tried over this time to Welcome you to My World and that of others like me. Expressing my own feelings and the loss of ones own self as it happens has not been easy, but necessary for mye. You see I have used the time to put my house in order, sort of clean my side of the street which has met with both favor and well shell we say down right not giving a damn. But that is ok. I have tried to share my humor with you, my politics, love of this country and family with you and how I feel about loosing that daily bit by bit. I have been working on this message since before eight this morning, erased it twice and it is not wha I earased at the moment that is gone. I had wanted to write my life story and started it, THROUGH THE LAUGHTER HE HEARD MY TEARS! Well I got so far and it like me are both disappearing. I do not know when I will cross that line to where what makes me whatever I am me and that new being appears, but I leave you with my love, God's Blessings and the good fortune to live in what I think is sthe greatest country on the face of this earth.

I received an email from a friend and I hope you follow the link and read the email, maybe just maybe you might wake up. Follow the link. If cliking does not work cut and paste it in your browser address bar or try the link to the right under to all that have hearts.

Subject: Fw: RED SKELTON-HOW DID HE KNOW??????

This is no joke and should be played on every news net work, and repeated by our politicians, every Day—

RED SKELTON-HOW DID HE KNOW?????? Some of you may remember him but he passed away before many of you were born. Red Skelton was a good & funny man. He also ended every show by saying, 'GOOD NIGHT AND GOD BLESS'. Listen to the end of this. It is something he said 38 years ago.

RED SKELTON-HOW DID HE KNOW??????

Very important that you listen to the very end!! Eerie! Take a moment and listen to it (from 1969). How would he have known That this is what is happening? Click on the link, and turn your sound on.

http://www.patriotfiles.org/Pledge.htm

FOR THE FEW WHO DON'T KNOW: Red Skelton was a movie star and comedian on television back in the 1950s. He created a number of characters, and his show was watched by millions. He did this on his show one evening—back when shows were live

God Bless You and Keep You and Make this Country Strong and worthy of HIm again.

Joe

Posted by Joseph Potocny at 08:49AM (-08:00)

Comments

—DirtyButter   January 16, 2008

I hope this means you have decided to keep on blogging as best you can. I know that God is blessing you each day. Peace, my dear friend!

—Anonymous   January 23, 2008

I am sorry that you are stopping your writing. I have always thought that it was a good release for you. I hope you know that you will be missed out in cyber land. I love you. Me

Having Fun

Monday, February 18, 2008

As my neurolooogist said I am tring to enjoy the time I have left in my mind as it its, that is the reaston for the new picture at the bottom. Anyway I don't look so homely. Things are getting rought, starting not to even recognize the lady next to me when staring at her in the store. No yellow brick road here, just a little broken concrete. Catch yall later, I hope.

God Bless Joe Posted by Joseph Potocny at 07:17PM (-08:00)

Comments

—DirtyButter   February 20, 2008

And God Bless YOU BOTH! Thanks for the laugh, Joe. I love the picture!! You and our family are never far from my thoughts and prayers.

Enjoy today sounds like a great way to deal with this demon!

Love, Rosemary

—JosephPotocny   February 20, 2008

DB, In you I have found a friend which I love, thank you for always showing up at teh riht time.

Joe

A Couple Of Days To Remember

Monday, February 25, 2008

Well the last coupleki days have ben interestingI have been working with some very peststy people from HBO in the process of making a documentary on folks like us with dementia. I imagine that they willl call ita show on Alszheimers, I hope the y call a documentery on dementia, since there are two many forms and they are different and people think AD is transmittable. It hwas been a strain to say the least, buth they are actually very nice folks, but we cannot let themmm no that. It is hard to tell folks what it is like, little easier to write it, because you cannot seem me or me se you. I do not know what will happen with it if anything but it has been an experiencer, they could have at least left their one crew member here. We hared some real tense moments and some very enjoyable ones. They honored our table by having a turkey dinnner with us, which makes us feel good inside. But they did not eat any of the fat raid we wnt on. Theat means goodies. WEllso mouch for now may be back soon.

God Bless You and the Country of Ours

Joe

Posted by Joseph Potocny at 06:05PM (-08:00)

As The Clouds Move In

Tuesday, March 18, 2008

"They" say whoever they maybe that thossse of us that suffer from the diffferent forms of dementia do not know that it is happening. Surprise your are full of dog dodo. I look at each day as things very slowly slip away and I see that cloud on the horizzon. I have always had a thirst for knowledge and doing things (when I was not being lazy). That once mighty river and fire that burned insside of me has slowly turned to a brook and a candle and it makes me sad. As I get lost in conversationnns and it takes me longer sometimes to recognize those I knoww, I feel the battle ground beneath my feet shake a little harder. I fought threw the cruelty of a bruttle father and naive mother, an addicted teen life and young adult drunk. I finally learned to love without strings and taking only to have it yankked from my very arms. But I had learned to finally lovve and give freely and became clean and sober in the process. Now I enjoy when I am able to my family, even with the cancers and brain injuries that occured to my children and wife the fucked up relations they had, I still was able to move forward and win the battles. Now my time has slowly come, I haaave great trouble in expressing myself anylonger, conversations and even this take a great deal of concentration and energy that I am left exhausted. I stand with open arms to welcome to my world that which is coming, for I believe that peace will be with it and this confusion, frustration and physical pain will be forgotten, at least one can only hope. Many I talk to with dementia, get angry with me when I talk of the death of me, who I am, I think it is because they know that it is true for them also. God Bless you all and one day we shall alll meet. Joe Posted by Joseph Potocny at 09:53AM (-07:00)

Humor Comes In Many Forms

Wednesday, March 26, 2008

The following is an email sent to me by a friend, who undersstandds my sense of humor and since I suffer from both thing in this, I find it funny. Enjoy or don't your chouice

In Pharmacology, all drugs have two names, a trade name and generic name. For example, the trade name of Tylenol also has a generic name of Acetaminophen. Aleve is also called Naproxen. Amoxil is also called Amoxicillin and Advil is also called Ibuprofen. The FDA has been looking for a generic name for Viagra. After careful consideration by a team of government experts, it recently announced that it has settled on the generic name of Mycoxafloppin. Also considered were Mycoxafailin, Mydixadrupin, Mydixarizin, Dixafix, and of course, Ibepokin. Pfizer Corp announced today that Viagra will soon be available in liquid form, and will be marketed by Pepsi Cola as a power beverage suitable for use as a mixer. It will now be possible for a man to literally pour himself a stiff one. Obviously we can no longer call this a soft drink, and it gives new meaning to the names of "cocktails", "highballs" and just a good old-fashioned "stiff drink". Pepsi will market the new concoction by the name of: MOUNT & DO. Thought for the day: There is more money being spent on breast implants and Viagra today than on Alzheimer's research. This means that by 2040, there should be a large elderly population with perky boobs and huge erections and absolutely no recollection of what to do with them.

Welcome to my World. God Bless Joe Posted by Joseph Potocny at 01:11PM (-07:00)

Comments

—Eric   March 31, 2008

That is some excellent stuff, Joe. Did you save that for the day your blog was featured in the Wall Street Journal, or was it providence? You made my day.

—Anonymous   April 01, 2008

Too funny Joe. I too saw the column in yesterday's WSJ and checked out your blog today. My mother has had AD for serveral years now and that's why the Living with Alzheimers' column caught my eye. I intend to check out more of your site and pass the link on to my three sisters. Keep up the good work. You made me laugh. Thank you.

A Toast to Beckey Bright

Tuesday, April 01, 2008

Ms. Bright appparently writes a coloum called Blog Watch for the Wall Street Journal. How and why she featured mine escapes me. I say thank you to Beckey. I am overwhelmed by the number of people that contacted me since yesterday. In fact it humbles me and that takes a great deaaal to do. Hopefully I made some new friends as I walk the road. There are so many out there that suffer as I do and evven worse, that I write this blog so that our side gets tolkd at least ass how it affects me and those around me. The last several weeks have been tough for me. I think my wife is getting use to me standing in the issles in the store kind of looking at her and pointing and saying I know you, then things register. My kids even ask me on the phone if I know who iam taking with. Sometimes I know right away others it takes a few minutes of talking, but I still have a ½ brain cell left so I function. To all of you that write me and tell me that you have gotten even a little comfort from

100

this blog or undersstanding, my heart goes out to you with my own tears as I sit here and write, this has taken meee most of the morning til now to get this together. Thank You.

God Bless you all.

Joe

Posted by Joseph Potocny at 01:03PM (-07:00)

Comments

—Anonymous   April 01, 2008

I am very proud of you. I knew in my heart that more people were reading what you write than what you give credit for. We are here for you. Your loving wife

—DirtyButter   April 03, 2008

I'm so glad to see that you did not quit writing, dear friend. And yes, you do a world of good just sharing yours days with us all.

Congrats on the Wall Street Journal column!! I hope I can find it online somewhere, so I can read it.

—Anonymous   April 03, 2008

Please, please, please don't delete this blog as you said you were going to do. It gives comfort to more people than you know. Leave it up forever.

—lancereyno   April 04, 2008

You are very brave Joe. As a volunteer at the Alzheimer's Services of the East Bay day care center in Berkeley I have made many wonderful friends. I will always remember the lady of few words who, one day, as we were holding hands, said "I am free now"

Lance Reynolds

—stevebogen   April 13, 2008

Joe: I just visited my mother in law at the memory care center, and came home to read your blog. I heard about it by reading the WSJ, and send your link to a few elderly clients who are beginning to want to know more about Alzheimers. I also have a blog on blogspot, which emphasizes how familes can pay for care, at www.gettingpaidinsurance.blogspot.com. My interest in Alzheimers is a lot more than having family members going through it. As a financial advisor, I see some of my clients starting down that path, and many of them have no or little family, unlike you.

Next week I am having lunch with a neurologist who I hope can provide additiona insight in noticing the early warning signs. What were some of the earliest signs for you?

Steve Bogen, Wenatchee, WA.

The Tiredness of This Week

Wednesday, April 09, 2008

When you reach your 40's you no loger have operations, you have a procedure. So my prime caregive had a procedure, yesterday. That would be my wife of 30 years, I slept little Sunday and Monday nights, Tuesday I was up I think aroun 4 AM waiting for my love to wake so we could start this day. I spent the day at the hospital, my daughter got me home areound 7pm. Needless to say I had a hard time tolleerating my grandchildren although they we just being kids. I was alone, my wife was not with me and that meant a night without her by my side. I am still up waiting to hear when she is coming home. The procd. went a ok. But that is not the issue she helps keep me balanaced and keeps me calmed down. Right now I am lost in my World wilhout her I fricken hate this crap. When I am babbling she understands me somehow, because I sure don't. These days do not help this wonder piece of a brain that I have nor my emotions or tolerancee. I almost wish I would cross the line and no longer feel this way or my Lord would just take me home. I have almost died several times in my life because I am so mentally solid, but neither he or the devil have wanted me, that makes a person feel pretty unloved and unwanted, when neitherr of them think your good enough to go live with them. I am just babbling and have lost where I am at so to all:

God Bless Joe Posted by Joseph Potocny at 08:07AM (-07:00)

Comments

—Anonymous   April 11, 2008

I'm glad the procedure went well. I have been praying for her and you as well :) Love to you both, Shannon

From a Fellow Suffer to YOU Who Care For Us

Monday, April 14, 2008

Alzheimer's Prayer

Dear Lord, Please grant my visitors tolerance for my confusion, Forgiveness for my irrationality and the strength To walk with me into the mist of memory My world has become.

Please let them take my hand and stay awhile, Even though I seem unaware of their presence. Help them to know how their strength And loving care will drift slowly Into the days to come just when I need it most.

Let them know when I don't recognize them That I will . . . I will. Keep their hearts free from sorrow for me, For my sorrow, when it comes, Only lasts a moment, when it's gone.

And finally Lord, please let them know, How very much their visits mean, How even through this relentless mystery, I can still feel their love. Amen!

—Unknown Author-

God Bless,

Joe

Posted by Joseph Potocny at 12:28PM (-07:00)

Creating Memories in The Mist

Monday, April 14, 2008

As many of you that read my blog know how I feeel about leaving my grandchildren with found memories and not those to come. Welll my eldest and her two kids have ben with us during moving, unfotunately my other two in WA have not been My grandson likes to hide behiind the couch and table and rub my hair while I try to grab his hand he is 2 and it is a game. Both him and my granddaughter help me get off the couch and want to play. This old guy doesn't last long at though, but it is form them and the joy I do get. My granddaughter is starting I feel to understand that somethiing is wrong with grandpa, but she isn't sure what it is. Even with the bad days and not remembering, I am doing my best to be happy and enjoy what time I have left. What the hell that was the Drs. prescription. I am happy most of the time and I think it is because I have accepted what awaits me and I know longer fear it or care when the line is crossed, my granddaughter is sitting with me while I write this old motor mouth. WE that suffer from various forms of dementia can live and enjoy the time we have, crap why not, we are going to forget the pain and sorrow of before so go out dancing. I weap more for those around me, because they have to watch from the otherside, see I soon forget and get lost in the conversssations and what is happening quiet often. So my sorrow is momentary. My wife shakes her head at me as we walk through the grocery store and I sing songs I make up so everone can hear, some are very colorful and I talk to everyone. Till nex time: God Bless, Joe Posted by Joseph Potocny at 06:19PM (-07:00)

103

Early Signs Differ

Tuesday, April 22, 2008

I have been asked whaat did I notice in the beginning that made me think something was wrong. On the side of my blog are places to go for the medical signs. However no two persons are alike. My Physciatrist and I talked ablut this he his opion, which to me makes sense, it takes so long to determine because it depends where you start. In other words how much grey matter do you have to statr with and have deminish. I noticed around 50, that multi tasking for me was starting to be confusing. I was able, to handle 10 projects at a time without notes and jump from one to the other and back again and never miss a beat. I was in the computer field (the beast of humanity). I started to have to pause to remember and even take notes, something I did not do, I would forget my pen, my glasses, what day it was, peoples names, stand up to do sommething and sit down again because I forgot. Eeach of these things in and of themselves is no big deal. But once I started to connect the dots, you know that old kids game where you go from one dot to another and a pickure forms, these things were happening daily and more and more often, I still functioned and got my job done, but I knew something was happening. Doctors or you are depressed, absent minded, forgetful, to much anxiety, all of a Sudden, no trauma had taken place. Things progressed slowly, but I could feel that my once active mind was slowing down and not because I was growing older. Talking to the text book guys was not helping. Finally after several years of pushing and refusing the bs answers my physcologist started to believe as I did that some form of dementia was occuring, because of my memory losses, inability to do things in minutes that now took me hours to days to do, because I forgot how. His dad had Alhziemers and he started and was the first to believe this was taking place with me. My Physc was not sure but felt that some form of dementia was occuring. My physician just plain ass was not sure, because I could still hold a conversation. Finally one day talking to him with my wife, the lights went on in his head there was something wrong because he was finally paying attention to the trouble I was having talking with him. We had done MRIs and EECs and Cat Scans, with no result, so he ordered a Pet Scan. Low and behold, his words get to a neurologist I can not help you, well none of them had been able to either. Armed with history at the PS, the new neurologist confirmed that I had Frontal Temporal Lobe Dementia along with inconsistent consistencies of Alzheimers (good one). so here I site be inconsistent and whatever else I am. All I know is that you need to look at the whole picture and stand firm and make your physicians or whatever explain why not and why something else and if their treatmenst do not work move on and kick down as many doors as needed until someone listens and starts to did. NOtes help and having someone with you that has known you for a time that can see the differences and help explaim them will help. Thankfully I have a wife that is stuborn as I am and keeps going until the truth is found. You may not like what you find but you have the right to know. I am not only having greater trouble with the grey matter but the physical affects are starting to settle in. Well you all behave and God watch over you. God Bless Joe Posted by Joseph Potocny at 12:08PM (-07:00)

Comments

—Anonymous   April 23, 2008

Hello Joe, I would like to take this opportunity to thank you for writing about your experiences and feelings about this crappy monster called Alheimers disease. My mother has dementia/Alz of some sort, and I believe that she is still in the early stages, and has been for quite some time. I am one of her part time caregivers and feel so helpless most of the time. It is like her entire path has now been predetermined by Alz/Dem. Like a train that has left the station and is on its way to it destination but we don't know how long the trip will be. I have found great comfort in reading your blogs, and I just want to thank you for giving us a peek into your world.

Gods' Circle of Life

Tuesday, April 29, 2008

As I live in this World of Mine that many others waander through with me, I come more convinced theat God has a circle of life. One dies so that another may come into being to learn of his wonders here for us. That circle got played out yesterday one passed on so that my fifth grandchild could join his family. Kobe William Abdalmelek (some name), burst upon the scene voicing his opion and ready to take on all life has to offer at 9 pounds and 19½ inches, I would say he is ready. Even in this misty world of forget fullness, God brings gladness and joy to my life. I wish to share that with you all. From the darkness comes the light.

God Bless

Joe

Posted by Joseph Potocny at 05:21PM (-07:00)

New Technology for The Eye

Friday, May 02, 2008

Do you suffer from myopia (near-sightedness), hyperopia (long-sightedness), presbyopia, astigmatism, computer vision syndrome or cataracts? Well now that is quite a question isn't it? I am using spell checker (as you know it is something

I do not do). I was approached by a site *http://www.pinhole-glasess-direct.com/* to view their site and give my opinion of the site and I would presume the product. They think I have a unique writting style, poor souls. Well what follows is my view only and not an endorsement of the product, remember that.

Pinhole-glasses are glasses that have laser (precised) cut holes in them on what appears to be a non clear plastic. Could be wrong there. You need to know that these glasses are for stationary use only. Bull riding, cow punching, climbing Mt. Everest or driving the Indy 500 are out. They are made for those folks who suffer from the question I started with, which is directly from their web site. The site makes a valiant attempt at describing the conditions and how their product works. It is pretty simple and straight forward. Even I understood most of it, of course it took me a number of hours reading it to get through it. But that was so I could write this and be fair to them. On awhole I think the product sounds good and probably, if the claims are accurate, benefit people like me who have 2000 pairs of classes because their eyes are worth not a heck of alot. See I am far, near, close and every which way sighted. Blind in one eye and cannot see out of the other. So how can I type this if I cannot see, blessed with powers beyond your belief, I look at the keys while I type.

The site is easy to manuever through and not trying to sell SNAKE OIL for 19.95 + if you order right now you get twice the amount, but wait I am not through, you order in the next 10 minutes we will add these special 10 scrubbing pads, breathing mask and Dr. Watchmacall its' famous toe remedy. I would preferr the site to be more colorfull, but you see I live in a world of color, no white walls in my house buddy (they would blend in and I would walk into them).

Check the site out let them know what you think. In fact let me know. You can leave comments right on this post (the best way) or use the email form on the side, which I never publish what is said in it. I have not bought a pair, not sure I will, and if I should, I would tell you exactly what I think of them. Good, bad or otherwise.

Well my brain hurts and I have had a few bad days so I will say goodbye for the day and when I remember I will return.

God Bless You and Our Country!

Joe

Posted by Joseph Potocny at 01:51PM (-07:00)

Crossing The Line

Friday, May 09, 2008

Some of you may have read in other entries of mine of that line that those thaat live is this World of Mine cross. Itt is that point where you cease to be who and what you are and become another entity, if you do not physicallly pass on. Yes they say this is gradual and can take many years, true but sure, it can happen in a day. Here today gone tomorrow. I have over the years since joining this ever growing community of those with dementia have seen it take place just that way. One instance my wife told me of a fellow at one of the sites she works at who has been reading my blog and hopefully gainnned some insight and comfort that he was faultless. HIs mother was fine the one day and the very next (24 hours later), knew crap, nota and required suddenly 24 hour care. So many I have communicated with that suffer have had this take place with them, because I speak (this form) with their loved ones and caregiverss and they tell me of this suddeness. What say you perverers of great wisdom and knowledge, what is that "Duh". MY own life is growing shadowier, forgetting we said grace at dinner, turning on this beast, conversations in the middle of them, physically becoming a poster child for damage of the year or how to screw up your body in one simple lesson. My time is coming when ?????? but it is on its' way. I have told my family the day will come as long as I have any ability to think as who I am, that I will kiss them all and say goodbye and be gone. I believe I have the right to passon with some of me in tact and with some dignity. I refuse to have my family see me lying with my face in my food, as I have seen from working in Assisted living homes when doing computers. Looking into the trap souls of those folks through their eyes made my decision along time ago shoulod I ever be blessed with this disease. There is no cure and most likely will not be one, until they whoever they are talk to US and really learn. For their knowledge of the brain fits in the head of a pin. Bye for now until next time be good to yourselves.

God Bless You and This Country!

Joe

Posted by Joseph Potocny at 10:27AM (-07:00)

Denial, Regret, Sorrow, Shame or just Pissed Off

Thursday, May 15, 2008

Some of you are aware that I am forard about my dealing with dementia. But many I hear from, caregivers, talk about the charges are in denial and non acceptance of what is. To this I say BS, I know you are true and giving people and really feel that way. But I have talked with over 1500 people that live in this World of MIne and they all knew from the start and still do. What follows is a typical e-mail I receive, filled with love, compassion and not knowing how to really help. I have left off the peoples names for their own privacy. After you read the email I hop to explain why i feel that DENIAL is not a real part of dementia.

"Hi Joe and Lynn.

Unfortunately I don't think that Mom is ready to BELEIVE that she has Alzheimer's. She is the daughter of a German farming family and is very stoic. She has never been known to share her emotions openly, and now the disease has exaberated the issue. Don't get me wrong, she is very sweet, we are so lucky that way. My sister and I both beleive that she sees herself quite differently than we do. She is 84 and was one of the "June Cleaver" type wives. We remember the frequency of the phrase "what will the neighbors think?" She retreats to what we call "the bubble" on a daily basis. The length of these visits to the unknown vary day depending on the good days/bad day thing. It is on these bad days that Mom will hardly speak at all. She goes far away and has a distant look in her eye. We occasionally have opportunity to gently remind Mom that she has "Alzheimer's". She says she knows. She has a very poor short term memory, and we see shades of the future now because there are times when my sister and I feel that Mom does not know who we are. We have a loose diagnosis of AD, but Mom has other stuff going on too. But, dementia is dementia. She has big-time vascular issues, and an aortic aneurysm growing in a spot that is inoperable due to its proximity to a previous stent. She has trouble breathing after just a short walk, and some vertebral fracturing too. The diagnosis of AD helps us clarify to agencies the urgency for financial aide and assistance. We just now after nearly a year have received the "Aid and Attendance" benefit from the Veteran's Administration. The money will help us to pay our hired caregivers and not have to worry as much about spending money that we don't have. We have been spending some money taken from a reverse mortgage and we're almost out after property taxes and a few other medical things, a tooth extraction, and a rebuilt crown, and then new eye glasses. She had macular degeneration and cataracts too. Mom will still do embroidery work, and she loves looking outside from her lift chair at her garden . . . and the bird feeders and bird bath . . . going full swing now.

She really enjoys going outside on the sneak, if you will to water the yard. I don't know why but it seems as soon as we leave for an errand or whatnot, Mom will have been outside watering. Bully for her I say.

Still has some spunk when it comes to her flowers . . . !

Well Joe, I think thats enough for now . . . gotta go and take core of some stuff . . .

Thank you again,"

First I say encourage here flower watering and watching. She is still in there and finds this is what she can do. Try to imagine if you can knowing that each day a little more of YOU slips away, a tiny amount of what you could due goes away.

Then the process speeds up. HOW WOULD YOU FEEL? I think pretty damned pissed off and would try to hide things, not because of denial, but your own sorrow at the lost, regretting what you did to cause this (which is most likely nothing) and there is some shame with it. You are no longer the person you were, but try to be, I see that in many I talk with. I am mentally and cognitively less then I was a year aga, I even here different words in the conversations I have. I even lose who I am talking to and come back later in the conversation. I have maybe 7 years left, believe me like those that walk with me, I plan on fighting toooth and nail till it comes time to leave. Many mistake the sense of loss that we have for Denial, it isn't we weep for ourselves, because we know better than you what is happening, I may sound quite with it, trust me it is difficult to write this without crying and focusing on what I say. The email above fills my heart with gratitude that these folks are keeping the family together and working through it, They are Heros to me, because we are a handfull. Sixtuplets don't compare to us as time goes on. We will wear you down, but we still love in our hearts and souls. Remember we still have our own brand of pride in ourselves. When I started this blog I made a promise to me to tell it as it is in me and as I see it, no matter the pain caussed me or the people I piss off.If you see our side and there are others like myself who have websites and journals maybe not as cantancerus as me and myore polite and gentle, but I find not a fricken thing gentle, fun, loving, polite in this disease at all. Thanks for your ear and being out their for me.

God Bless You and This Country of Ours!

Joe

Posted by Joseph Potocny at 07:12PM (-07:00)

A Sad Morning

Thursday, May 22, 2008

This morning has beeeen one of those moments as I call them when old things pop up that create heart ache. I was recalling when my frien Jimmie, friends since we wer 5 and lived accross the street from each other, at the age of 16 was found hung one afternoon, the loss is still with me and I cry for him and cannot wait until this fricken disease erases that memory, for he was one of two of my close friends that died that way at the same age. I talked to an old school mate this morning informing him I would not be at our class reunion from Austin High in Chicago from 1962, good thing the invitation is in front of me. We spoke briefly and asked him to say high and wish them all Gods' blessings for me. My social graces then were not very good and now I go off in a momemnt and and would be3 more of a disruption then a pleasantness to the festivities. This is my link to all of you that visit me, in My World that is occupied with outhers in the same sinking ship. I do my best to enjoy what I have, but I am noticing that I am increasingly forgetting yesterday and last year and some years before more often. I get lost in conversations, God only knows where I go because I sure the f&*k don't. Enough of the pitty potty, I am still here and able to speak to you. I truly enjoy hearing from YOU out there, so for now take care of yourselves.

God Bless You and This Country of Ours!

Joe

Posted by Joseph Potocny at 09:44AM (-07:00)

Time in a Bottle

Wednesday, May 28, 2008

Yes i took that from an old song, but that is what my life has become, just time trapped in a bottle. It has taken me several days to get to this, just keep forgetting and doing who knows what. My wife was home for 6 weeks had an operation, at our age it is called a procedure, shee had to manny kids never could say no. Had to fix stuff up. She finallly got to see ME as i really am now, not just late evenings or on weekends, but the whole day of confusssion that I go through. I accutually do get some things done, what you say? good question. I find even old memmmories are getting mixed up in their time span and order, forget the last couple of years. This life really fuckin sucks at times, but at least I still am breathing and can have solme assembalance of converstation with folks. I loose more and more of each day, I fall a lot easier, just fall get up and fall again, nothing to it.Climbing stairs is getting nearly like mountain climbing, as if I would know, never climbed mountains. MY daughter and her family came down on a surprise visit for mothhers day, I love my family to death, but tolerating them all here with the kids and the noise level is geting very difficult for me, I feel like I am on the freeway with all the cars honking, the pain in my brain, a little poetry, I still have it, becomes overwhelming and my so called social skills go out the window fast. I go hide in the bedroom or just go to sleep to escape. I can only imagine how they must feel with this behavior, I know it bothers the crap out of me. I am true royalty, as you know that we are all blue bloods, are blood is blue until it hits the air, well I have a lot of blue in my brain (dead stuff) so remember when you read this blog you are in the presence of TRUE ROYALTY

GOD BLESS YOU AND GOD BLESS OUR COUNTY! (SEE OBAMA I DON'T CARE WHO I OFFEND)

JOE

Posted by Joseph Potocny at 07:42AM (-07:00)

"I AM FREE NOW"

Monday, June 02, 2008

Those are my five pride and joys, my grandchildren. Number six is on the way. Wanted to share them with you. They are Lillian, Chase, Emma, Kobe and Malek.

Ayou know from time to time I share comments and emails I get with you. That is part of what this blog is about. My telling of my World and your response from within it or the otherside. Such is the following comment I received:

"You are very brave Joe. As a volunteer at the Alzheimer's Services of the East Bay day care center in Berkeley I have made many wonderful friends. I will always remember the lady of few words who, one day, as we were holding hands, said "I am free now"

I wonder if, I think so, this caretaker realizes the blessing God bestowed that day on the two of them. First The lady realized that the journey into darkness, frustration, aggrevation, not knowing and the fog finally for her was over and a new lite was in her life. Second he got to be there for the granting of Gods' blessing to this lady. To say I am nott jealous of them would be an outright lie. MY wife has gotten to witness things since she was off work for six weeks, with me.I think she and others of you outhere can understand how this lady finally felt and the day I look forward to. Till theen I will stumble along talk to you and respond when I remember to. Brave my friend I do not think so, scared and bewilder yes. I just feel others need to here this side of the story direct. It is different for each of us that is why it is so difficult to pin point. Thier are some things I still can do and others that baffle the crap out of me. I do not walk well, I hear different words in conversations, I don't even know when I am being talked to at times. I built a small paver patio out front, of course my hands and fingers hurt because they were to stupid to get out of the way of

111

the mallet I was using to tapp the brikcs down with into place. My darling wife has informed med that more and more of my comments in public are not in good taste and I do not use my quiet voice when saying them. Well that is just the way it is for now, exciting times to come.

God Bless You and This Country of Ours!

Joe

Posted by Joseph Potocny at 12:42PM (-07:00)

A Day of Anger
Friday, June 06, 2008

I do not know who did this sketch but it stirs my insides greatly.

This day or at least my brain and emotions ar on the rampage. Everything in pissing me off even this blog. Nobody has don anthing to me, I just am not in any type of control of myself this day.I kind of remember reding that these things would become paart of my life, and they suck. I was vacuuming the rugs downstatirs this morning and attacking them as if they were my enemies, my mind is filled with mud I think, no control. Good thing I am alone right now I think I would hit someone if the said the wrong thing, maybe this post will help who knows. All I know is I want to go home and be in green pastures with my Lords' creatures to romp and play. My mind, heart and soul are heavy this day and they should not be. I nolonger take Aricept or Namenda at doctors orders, because they did nothing for me and people I talk to with this disease seem to vary from them miraculously being sharp as ever to having such reaactions they almost died, great shit isn't it. Maybe it will or won't help and it just might kill you, great choice. I am even angry at my family, wife and all, and they have done nothing. I don't feel that they really understand the hell in my head and insides, I try to control it but of late the amountt of time I can seeems to be growing shorter maybe some so9da will help.

God Bless You and This Country of Ours!

Joe

Posted by Joseph Potocny at 12:35PM (-07:00)

What Will Your Dash Say?

Friday, June 13, 2008

I received this for a friend in Britian that suffers the pains of this disease of ours, if you read and follow the the link, you will see that we still can feel and cry for others and not just ourselves.

Subject: : remembering Suzette May 1965—July 2006

—Original Message—From:006

This is very touching, especially for those of us who have lost someone special but for all of us and how we live our lives. Hope you enjoy. You may need a tissue. It takes about 3 mins. ML

The Dash

In July 2006, shortly after Suzette left us, a 3-minute movie was launched on the Internet called The Dash. Since then, over 40 million people from around the world have watched it; and over 20, 000 a day continue to watch it as a result of people passing it along. ; The movie has been more successful than we could have ever imagined. More importantly, however, it has inspired many, many people to reflect on their lives and ask THE all important question, 'Are my priorities where they should be?'

I hope you enjoy this movie and share it with those who are close to you. as ever, Jul Click This Link to View: www.dashpoemmovie.com turn Speakers On.

God Bless You & This Country of ours!

Joe

Posted by Joseph Potocny at 12:42PM (-07:00)

A Loss In My Life Today

Monday, June 16, 2008

I am not sure if on my blog I ever mentiioned my son that I had long before I got married and he and his mother disappeared. I found them two or so years ago I think, well me and my family have tried to bring him into the other side of his world, today he made it clear that was not going to happen. So my heart is heavy and sad, but I lost him once not by my choice, now by his. I truly hope this fuckin disease takes a greater hold soon. Sounds selfish butt I want to mobve faster and get rid of the memmories and pain. Sometimes it is too much trying to live between these two worlds, I feel trapped and torn, not knowing exactly where I am or why I am. Good days and bad ones, where is the balance not with me that is for sure.I used to take Aricept and Namenda and both did nothing for me. They are hopefully supposedly to aid in slowing down the memory loss, right. Even the manufacturers do not know if they will work for sure, some good stuff. I have heard from folks who have taken these drugs and their stories range from miraculous results (i thik they were on something else) to folks that got violently ill from themm and everything in between. Me nothing just a waiste on money, so much for today, hope to meet you on the other side.

I still have demented humor, and love it.

God Bless You and This Country of Ours!

Joe

Posted by Joseph Potocny at 12:28PM (-07:00)

Comments

—Carol   June 23, 2008

Hi, I am very sorry to hear about the decision your son has made. It seems like so many people these days are so lonely and separated from people that I find it hard to understand how people can turn their backs on potential ties like they do.

One of my friends found a half sister that she had never met, and she was so excited to find her . . . but the half sister made the same decision that your son made, and it was heartbreaking for my friend. But she is glad that she made the overture anyhow, and maybe someday something will come of it anyhow . . . Hugs

My Life Passes

Friday, June 20, 2008

Lately I haave found the past getting tangled in my mind, such things as when who why and the like. My days are becoming shorter as time seems to pass and I am totally unawaree of it. I have been experiencing great difficulties in keeping old times and folks out of my relationship with my wife, needless to say this is becoming quiet a pain in the ass. I know it hurts her and it fricken is driving me nuts, to the point I am having a hard time relating to her, especially in a man and woman sense, you know husband and wife tings, the pills do not help, I think my drive and wants are getting screwed up with everything else. New or what should be new memories do not even stay with me anymore. I lock my way in sleeping at the drop of a hat, I am beginning not to care anymore, which is part of the FTD and the AD time marches on and I seeem to stand still. At times things are fine and then I have no idea of what is taking place. My tempor is growing shorter, patience is very little.

God Bless You & This Country of Ours!

Joe

Posted by Joseph Potocny at 11:33AM (-07:00)

Comments

—Anonymous   June 22, 2008

I still love you.

I think about you often, my friend. It's good to see you are still writing about your day and how you feel about this horrible disease. I would hope that you can erase some of those most painful memories, too.

God bless YOU! Rosemary

You Got To Be Kidding!

Friday, June 27, 2008

Recently I was told this about me telling you about my life with this disease. The individual even found it funny and without purpose. Wel that is ok, because I am here for me and for those who care for people like me and are like me. This is not fun and games this is real life. It iss difficult to lay out your life and how you feel. I once started sometime ago I cannot remember when posting my life story on a site, I am but one person in over 6 billion on this earth, who would care. I started getting so many emails I could not go through one days worth in a day. I was blunt and just as forthwriht in the story as I try to be here. You know when you just roll out of bed and land on the floor and are not sure why you are there I try to laugh, yes I do that. I walk into wals, sit on the floor and just fall over.I hate going past my mailbox alone, it scares me, I am leaving my security place and I actually run back, because I am afraid I will forget where it is. Sometimes you can talk like the wind with folks other times you just stare and wonder who they hell is this person and what are they doing here. The problem is you have no control over it.wrighting tihis takes all my ability to consentrate and generally I go to sleep afterwards, my brain fills like it has been crushed, I like some that live in this World of Mine do not want to be here anymore, it hurts to look at those you know, but you cannot talk to them, because the brain and mouth cannot find each other.Emotions are a real mountain, boy when they start to flow, their is no stopping them until you are tottally wiped out. The pains of the past that you thought were dealt with and now at rest, rear their ugly heads with a vengance. That is while early on in this ordearl I tried to contact old friends and put things to rest, without telling them what was happening, I got yeah I kind of remember but forget it doesn't matter, thanks but don't call again and out right anger, well that is the way it goes. If I have the time and my brain stays with me or me with it I think I shall post in segements my life story, for me. I getting lost now so good bye my friends till next time.

God Bless You and This Country of Ours!

Joe

Posted by Joseph Potocny at 01:52PM (-07:00)

Belated Freedom Wishes

Saturday, July 05, 2008

To all my friends, readers and distractors from whatever Country you live in, I send you belated greetings for the freedom that this Country has always fought for qne hope you enjoyed the day. To all of you that live in this foggy World of Mine, with AD, FTD, Picks, Lewy Bodies, Parkinsons and just plain old dementia (whatevwer that is) A special hello and thanks to you. I just was not able yesterday to put it together to write you all. As things grow tighter in my mind and ability to express them I get more and more frustrqted. But the good side is that in a short time I forget the frustration. I feel like I live in 3 Worlds, Yesterday, Something Called Today, and What is To Come (tomorrow).My temperment is slowly becoming unpleasant, I am even more straight forward then I ever was. I try to say thank you Lord for putting this asshole in my life, but I to offten find myself telling them to eat shit and bark at the moon. It is difficult to watach what I say around my grandkids, so I try to just sew my lips shut. Does it work? EEEEH It is getting harder each day to get my backside in gear to do something. The Warrior that once existed in me and fought every battle thattt came our way, has finally laid down his lance, his battle axe is rusting, but he is still moving, but I need jiff lube for the armor to stop its fricken squeaking. I do not want people to feel sorry for me because I don't, my life has been filled with battles and challenges and have risen to them all, I guess it is now my turn to rest and sort of pass the sword on to others. But I am a stuborn SOB. To all I say thank you for stopping by to visit with me. I hope your lives are filled with what the Lord wants for you.

God Bless You and This Country of Ours!

Joe

Posted by Joseph Potocny at 11:42AM (-07:00)

Comments

—DirtyButter   July 09, 2008

Joe you are just a beautiful man!! I love how true what you write sounds, and I love the fact that you spend the effort to let people see inside this horrible disease that steals a piece of you little by little.

If your grandchildren are old enough to understand why you are saying ugly things they probably would rather hear you talking than being so quiet, but the very fact that you have the determination to prevent scorching their tender ears shows there is still a warrior in there. His battles are just on a smaller scale now, that's all.

There is no way to tell you how deeply your posts affect me, Joe. Who would ever have thought that I could love someone I have never met quite the way I love you. I know your wife understands! ROTFL!!!!

{{{HUGS}}}} Always,

Rosemary

God Does Still Does Miracles
Wednesday, July 09, 2008

Some of you may recall me talking about my friend Dirty Butter, real name Rosemary. A link to her page is on the side of my blog. This daer lady was given a diagnosis of Parkinsons and some other neuro disease back 2006 or so. See they, the doctors heard houff beats and immediately saw horses and not the zebra that was in the heard. Well things progress and finally someone really takes a look at this strange looking horse and after testing and thinking and checking finds that DB does not have Parkinson's afret all but:

Essential myoclonus occurs in the absence of epilepsy or other apparent abnormalities in the brain or nerves. It can occur randomly in people with no family history, but it also can appear among members of the same family, indicating that it sometimes may be an inherited disorder. Essential myoclonus tends to be stable without increasing in severity over time. Some scientists speculate that some forms of essential myoclonus may be a type of epilepsy with no known cause. (this was cut and pasted from dictionary).

This is treatable with med, probably will not be cured but her life is becoming beter each day and will continue to. The jerks, twitches, spasms and the like are supsiding. I cannot tell you how much joy my heart is filled with for her. God loves her and so do I.

God Bless You and This Country of Ours!

Posted by Joseph Potocny at 02:39PM (-07:00)

Home Improvement Projects I Think Not

Monday, July 14, 2008

I have beeen one of those do it yourselfers, but those days are ending. Power tools and I are starting to have a new understanding. You don't pick me up, I will not hurt you. Helped the Mrs. put up new blinds in my sons room over the weekend. Those of you that live in earthquaaaake land will understand. There was a 7.2 quake going on inside me as I shook, rattled and tried to fall out the window. All this for standing up to put in a total of 10 screws. Getting to hard to handle that many even one doesnot work. I think I lost 30 pounds in sweat in the process. The time was I could paint a straight line with no guide between walls and cieling. Now we have highways with bends in them. Forget trying to mortar cracks they stick out like mountains, the crack is better.I guess this all goes with the AD and FTD. Once had pride in my handy work, now 5 year olds can do just as well.

But I can still vaccuum so there. The towels get done as long as I remember to turn them on and change from washer to dryer and take them out, now that can take as long as 12 hours. I go visiting a lot and I am not sure where it is that I go. I try to keep this light, but it is not any fun. If I get too awraped up in it I am to much to handle even for myself. But I knew that this road was to get tougher and rockier and it has not wasted much time. Well till next time.

God Bless You and This Country of Ours!

Joe

Posted by Joseph Potocny at 11:54AM (-07:00)

GOD, WHY?

Monday, July 21, 2008

You know I have asked the above question all of my life. Not just since I have gotten AD & FTD, to be sure they have not helped the situation. The question is not what you think, GOD WHY ME? No not at all. Most of my life has been screwed up, probably mostly my own fault, except my early childhood, did I have one, no I live in a house of hell part of Satans spawn. At least with the dementia some of it is leaving me now. You should see my wife as she tries to stop me from falling off the courch or the bed. It is hard to stop a rolling whale. I ask mostly, GOD WHY AM I ALIVE & WHY WAS I BORN? Looking over me and my life there is nothing special about me nor do I seem to have contributed much to this life, taken oh yes.Now my thoughts get mixed between yesterday, today and whatever comes into this brain of mush that I have. It is starting to get a bit touchier, I look at those I should know and wonder who the f&*^ is that, and it is my wife or one of the kids. I have moments that I feel perfectly "normal" (do not think I ever was that), and all of a sudden everything goes to helll in a hand basket and I have no idea what I am doing, why I am doing it or where. I spend little time doing things I used to. I start, forget and then wind up somewhere else doing something different or just sitting wondering WHY? Well enough out of me.

God Bless You & This Country of Ours!

Joe

Posted by Joseph Potocny at 02:41PM (-07:00)

A Friend Shared With Me, So I Pass It On To You!

Wednesday, July 23, 2008

THE POEM I knelt to pray but not for long, I had too much to do. I had to hurry and get to work For bills would soon be due. So I knelt and said a hurried prayer, And jumped up off my knees. My Christian duty was now done My soul could rest at ease . . . All day long I had no time To spread a word of cheer No time to speak of Christ to friends, They'd laugh at me I'd fear. No time, no time, too much to do, That was my constant cry, No time to give to souls in need But at last the time, the time to die. I went before the Lord, I came, I stood with downcast eyes. For in his hands God! held a book; It was the book of life. God looked into his book and said 'Your name I cannot find I once was going to write it down . . . But never found the time'

God Bless Your and This Country of Ours!

Joe

Posted by Joseph Potocny at 09:44AM (-07:00)

Howdy

Wednesday, August 06, 2008

It has been awhile since I posted, I sit down in fromt of this thing to do it and that is wehere it ends.I have been in sort of a place that I am not famliar with, don't ask where because I do not know. Physically I am starting to suffer more of the progress of this wonderfulo disease. It is begning to scare me more now. I stand in the house, and wonder where the hell I am. After awhile I lie down on the couch or whatever and go to sleep and the hours go away. So does the confusion and mystery fo what things are. I feel more lonely in theis World of Mine now even when people are areound me. Sometimes waking up and seeing my wife next to me scares the living (&(&^^ out of me because I am not sure who she is. Then the brain kicks in a all is well. I tire quickly and fall alot now, I guess that old Ford has caught up to me and passed me by.

I used to wonder what tomorrow would bring, now I am not sure about the rest of today. I do this for you who care for those like me so you know why we act the way we do and it has nothing to do with you, it is us.

God Bless You and this Country of Ours!

Joe

Posted by Joseph Potocny at 12:26PM (-07:00)

Comments

God Bless you Joe for giving me a peek of your world through your eyes and what is slowly becoming my mothers world, I can't thank you enough! Again may God bless you and keep you in his tender loving arms.

A WARRIOR'S LAMENT (By: j.v.potocny)

Thursday, August 07, 2008

I kneel before thee
Upon bended knee
My battle axe rusts upon a tree
The Steed that served me well
Now runs free and frail
He served us both with grace and might
Let him rest well each night
There is no deadly mace
That you can see before my face
Gone is my shield which I cannot hold
All that is before you is my sword and face
I have stood tall in all battles
With You I have won and battles song sung
Many with scars some with none
Since a child I have fought the fight
Now I wish for it to end this night
My strength is dried up and gone
No longer does exist that fierce warrior in me
I long to face only Thee
This battle I am in is lost and so am I
So before You I am on bended knee
Prostrate would I lay
But this body is to broken and brittle this day

So I lay before you all I have left
Worn, beaten, yearning, to you I give my soul
No longer in the dust of battle let me roam
I await You and Your Hand to take me in your time
I pray Thee take ME HOME
In Your Name Amen.

Joe Posted by Joseph Potocny at 12:22PM (-07:00)

Comments

—Anonymous   August 07, 2008

Where are you finding these? I really hate to cry at work. Love

—Anonymous   August 07, 2008

I did not find this, I wrote it. It is how I feel at this point on this journey that I want over. Thank you for taking time to care. Joe

—Anonymous   August 11, 2008

Hi Joe: I'm loving your website. You are doing a marvelous job with it. I wanted to thank you for helping others on this journey we're on. I know a lot of caregivers appreciate reading what their loved one is possibly going through, and can't tell them.

Hugs and enjoy each day! Mary www.simplesite.com/mothermary

Chimes & Rhymes

Wednesday, August 13, 2008

Of late my brain seems to sing In song and of different things I think and talk in rhyme Why I do not no why Is it the disease? Or am I just plain nuts? I talk the same way to So I am quiet like a shrew It drives me a bit insane But whoever said I was really sane I do not know if this is a phase Only can I hope it leaves some day I even sleep more to get away But in my dreams it follows with me I feel like part of my brain does sleep The other seems to weep Maybe this is my way to cope Before the I cross that line of no hope Even spelling seems to work this way Boy I do not know what to say I still get frustrated and loose my way Past the mailbox I do not stray There is a fear if I do alone Never will I come home If any have had this experience Please help me out of this weeeeeariness

God Bless

Joe Posted by Joseph Potocny at 10:16AM (-07:00)

My Life Today

Monday, August 25, 2008

Lately i have not told how I feel and what is happening. So, I feel like shit, the affects of this disease are catching up. I cannot be out walking and such for more than ½ hour or I feel like I am about to leave this pldace. I find converstions more and more difficult, unless I am truly angry or extremely focused on one point. Any distratction and I am lost.It is difclut I know for others to understand how hard it can be to hold a conversation, they are draining and hurt. My trembling is worse, my head spins when I turn in, hitting the ground is quiet annoying and becoming uncofortbale. Forgetting in the midle of something I am doing really ticks me off to know end, because I cannot get back to where I was, it is just plain gone. I just hope this blog helps someone.

God Bless You and This Country of Ours!

joe

Posted by Joseph Potocny at 01:00PM (-07:00)

Comments

—Anonymous   August 27, 2008

Hi Joe . . . boy do I understand! lol You know I got myself a fantastic walker/rollator . . . so no more falling down! You need to check it out . . . I call it my Hummer! It has 10" wheels . . . so I can walk safely on the beach, through the woods, and all over our campground! And a seat for when I get tired out! Hang in there Joe . . . and love your writings. Hugs Mary www.simplesite.com/mothermary

Why I Do This Blog!

Sunday, August 31, 2008

Message = Joe, First I would like to say that I am sorry for the crappy deck of carded dealt to you. It seems as if we are looking forward to working ourselves to death to enjoy our older years. And then this. It is not very fair at all.

I came across your blog while researching Dementia. My mother-in-law was diagnosed 3 years ago at the age of 51. She progressed quickly and has now lost the ability to talk and lost her ability to control her bowel movements. She is trapped in a world all alone. Do you have any advice on ways to comfort her? I would like for her to know that no matter if she knows us or not that we still love and care about her.

Thank you for your time and I hope for the best for you. (we will call her)

Pam

Subject: Your Mom

Dear Pamela,

Sorry it has taken me so long to get back to you. I keep trying and keep forgetting or start and go off and start something else. The nature of this Disease. Being that your mother and I live in the same World which is different from yours. I can just imagine your feelings as a caregiver, that is why I started my Blog, so the outside world could get at least to know how it is for one person and help some to understand those they are caring for.

The best you can do for your mom is what you are doing. Being there for her, talking to her, telling you love her, sitting with her and not speaking, hold her hand, smile at her, keep your tears to yourself, she has too many in her heart to bear yours. Trust me she know deep inside you are there and helping. This disease just stops us from responding well and takes our lives away from us. I know my family gets nuts over me, because I cannot always hold a conversation with them or follow theirs and I forget who the hell they are. I am pretty outspoken and direct if you really read my blog. I am offensive at times and I do not care, because I am discussing My World the hell of it. Be glad on this email I used spell checker, because generally do not I want folks to know how this crap really is. Any further emails I will not use it, so I hope you are good a picking something apart to understand it.

Being there for your Mom is the single best thing you can do for her. I have told my family and it is in my blog, when I get to close to crossing the line of this disease as your mom has, I will say good bye to all and be gone. I will not put myself or family or friends through the last stages. See I worked for a number of nursing homes that had those that could manage on their own and those that needed assisted living care and those who needed accute care, as I was developing this disease. I still remember going through the lunch room at one of the homes (I took care of three homes computer systems) and watched the attended lift this ladies face out of her food and clean her, never I said at that point would I allow my life to become such a burden and worthless being. My heart broke that day and I finally noticed the real death of these folks that were around me. They were gone and someone else was living in them and I cried and said never would I put anyone through that. But remember that is me and my feelings.

I may post this reply on my blog, if you do not mind. I sometimes use the email people send me and my answers back to them.

God Bless and Hold You Tight in His Arms!

Joe

Joe,

Thank you for your response. You are more than welcome to post this on your blog. Reading through your eyes has given me perspective. I hope a lot of other people, especially caregivers, can see this too. Maybe it will take some of the frustration away. Maybe it will help people be a little more compassionate and forgiving and a little less annoyed and frustrated. Thank you for your insight.

Pamela

God Bless You and God Bless This Country of Ours!

Posted by Joseph Potocny at 07:10PM (-07:00)

Comments

—Anonymous	September 03, 2008

Hi Joe and Pam!

Thanks to both of you. This is exactly what I needed to hear today regarding my own caregiving situation with my loved one. I must go there soon and she has become extremely silent and removed lately. I needed to hear that it is really best for me and her to continue to talk to her, and to just be there for her no matter what as difficult as that can be sometimes. Thank you and

God bless both of you on your journeys.

Lost in Time!

Wednesday, September 10, 2008

Wow here it is amlost the midlddle of September, where have I been. It seems like as each day passes I become less and less aware of the day, date, week, month or the time. It is all seemilgy running together. It is like today is almost a repeat of yesterday. I now have problems with some of my conversations, my tongue seems to get in the way and I get all screwed up in what I am saying, so I gust wave my hands and say latter. Which of course latter does not come because I for get what I was saying in the first place. It seems to be this whole time affect first forward then backwards, drives me nuts (that is a short drive). I find that i get more irritable as time goes on, I try to handle it but well sometimes that is just the way things happen. I did not even realise that we were this far into this mont. Halloween will be here and I will not know it, except for the candy and the tricker treators. Well I guess I will go do something, probably something of no importance, but it will be something I think.

God Bless You and This Country of Ours!

Joe

Posted by Joseph Potocny at 10:50AM (-07:00)

How things change.

Tuesday, September 16, 2008

Since I have been so blessedd with these wonderful diseasess it is strange to me how I have been changing and changing towards others. I am not to concerned with what they think or have to say. I am getting more self absorbed you could say. I am not sure if this is part of the way this thing goes, but it is how I am starting to feel, it is as if others do not exist in my World, hard to describe this feeling as my commmand of the language is going to hell in a hand basket. I more and more do not enjoy going out and having people around me. The noisse and all the hurry scurryy around me tendsl to set me off and I have to get away from it. I know because of the hlep that my famliy has given me, I have fallen in love with my wife and the rest of my family all over again. I find when I am extreemly focused on something that I can talk and wright quiet well. But that amount of concentraation is greatly tiring and causes me to become unsteady for awhile. My mind is starting to ramble to I will say good bye for now.

God Bless You and This Country of Ours!

joe

Posted by Joseph Potocny at 12:23PM (-07:00)

Those Good Old Golden Years!

Friday, September 26, 2008

Golden Years, right fillled with AD, FTD, BiPolar, Sinus Problems, cannn't see worth a damn and no left ear drum. I forget it means gold crowns not porcelian or metal, gold hip joints, gold nee joints and oh yes golden colored build up in your arteries, aren't the Golden Years fantastic. Up my patooty. I found out today that the bottom portion, the tip area of my heart does not get any blood, so I could have a heart attack, not onew that would kill me, but probably wished it would. So we go on a medical regement and change of eating habits to help correcvt it and if that does not work we become invasive and go in and look. This is why I have DDS most people call it ED, erctile dysfunction, I call it dead dick sysdrome. It stands up and salutes then dies. Well I guess soon I won't remember what it is for anyhow, I am starting to have vague memories of what it was used for. Well I am still breathing so it is ok. Just had to expound on this crap for a minute. I thank you all for listening and being out there for all of us in my World.

God Bless You and This Country of Ours!

Joe

Posted by Joseph Potocny at 01:39PM (-07:00)

Some Humor for This Month!

Tuesday, October 07, 2008

I thought that with all the humor of the elections that we, even us with this damn disease could use a laugh. The following is from a friend of mine in Britian, I hope you find the humor as I did.

Bus Ride

> > > > > A little something for you to get your mind off your troubles for a minute! > > ACTUAL AUSTRALIAN COURT DOCKET 12659—CASE OF THE PREGNANT LADY > > > > > A lady about 8 months pregnant got on a bus. She noticed the man opposite her was smiling at her. She immediately moved to another seat. This time the smile turned into a grin, so she moved again. The man seemed more amused. When on the fourth move, the man burst out laughing, she complained to the driver and he had the man arrested. > > The case came up in court. The judge asked the man (about 20 years old) what he had to say for himself. > > The man replied, 'Well your Honor, it was like this, when the lady got on the bus, I couldn't help but notice her condition. She sat down under a sign that said, 'The Double Mint Twins are coming' and I grinned. Then she moved and sat under a sign that said, 'Logan 's Liniment will reduce the swelling,' and I had to smile. Then she placed herself under a deodorant sign that said, 'William's Big Stick Did the Trick,' and I could hardly contain myself. But, Your Honor, when she moved the fourth time and sat under a sign that said, 'Goodyear Rubber could have prevented this accident' . . . I just lost it.' > > >

Got to love thos Brits.

God Bless You and This Country of Ours!

Joe

Posted by Joseph Potocny at 10:00AM (-07:00)

Comments

—JUSTAMOM   October 11, 2008

Joe, Hello nice ot meet you well I have not MET you abut plan to go back and read every post you have written. I have found the loving world of "MEMORY CARE" in my new job. I love it, I love the peopel and so SO want ot learn much more. I would like to keep coming back and seeing more post written by you as I said I will be going back and reading all you have done so far.

God Bless you and your family keep your chin up and you smile on . . .

Jaye

Where is Yesterday?

Tuesday, October 14, 2008

It is beocming harder each day to remember yesterday, let alone try today, even this monring. Here we are mid October per the calendar and I am somewere in September. I feel like I am altogether but I am totallly confused as to what to do next. This is not fun. But it is the hand I was dealt so I play the cards and see what they do and try to understand them. The new meds seem to help the pains in the chest and the sweating whrn walking or doing some work. So I gues complaining is just whimpy on my part. I wish I had the words to discribe what it is like to be in this World that I and others like me live in. It reallly sucks. First you know then you forget and then you do not remember forgetting what it was that you knew. If tha makes no sense to you ok, but it does to me. My frustration with others is growing and I go off more quickly then usual. I started this today with my thoughts all together and now they are some where in space and time. Did use postit notes but I found I did not read them or kept doing them over and over, now who knows what works. My brain sure does not know and many times I just don't give a damn, it is to hard to put the thoughts together. It is easier to just leave the old grey matter alone. Till next time.

God Bless You and This County Of Ours!

joe

Posted by Joseph Potocny at 11:50AM (-07:00)

Comments

—JUSTAMOM   October 15, 2008

That has to be frustrating for sure . . . I think I do understand as best as a person on the outside can. I have a lady in my unit who is aware of her condition, both grandmothers before her had it also so she knows what it will bring and it scars her. She talks about the unknown and not wanting to go there . . . hang in there and keep your chin up.

Only Us With AD & The Likes Would Think ofThis!

Friday, October 24, 2008

an email that was forwarded to me. my life in a nutshell.

AAADD KNOW THE SYMPTOMS . . .

PLEASE READ

Thank goodness there's a name for this disorder. Somehow I feel better even though I have it.

Recently, I was diagnosed with A.A.A.D.D. Age Activated Attention Deficit Disorder.

This is how it manifests:

I decide to water my garden. As I turn on the hose in the driveway, I l ook over at my car and decide it needs washing.

As I start toward the garage, I notice mail on the porch table that I brought up from the mail box earlier.

I decide to go through the mail before I wash the car.

I lay my car keys on the table, put the junk mail in the garbage can under the table, and notice that the can is full.

So, I decide to put the bills back on the table and take out the garbage first.

But then I think, since I'm going to be near the mailbox when I take out the garbage anyway, I may as well pay the bills first.

I take my check book off the table, and see that there is only one check left. My extra checks are in my desk in the study, so I go inside the house to my desk where I find the can of Pepsi I'd been drinking.

I'm going to look for my checks, but first I need to push the Pepsi aside so that I don't accidentally knock it over.

The Pepsi is getting warm, and I decide to put it in the refrigerator to keep it cold.

As I head toward the kitchen with the Pepsi, a vase of flowers on the counter catches my eye—they nee d water.

I put the Pepsi on the counter and discover my reading glasses that I've been searching for all morning. I decide I better put them back on my desk, but first I'm going to water the flowers.

I set the glasses back down on the counter, fill a container with water and suddenly spot the TV remote. Someone left it on the kitchen table.

I realize that tonight when we go to watch TV, I'll be looking for the remote, but I won't remember that it's on the kitchen table, so I decide to put it back in the den where it belongs, but first I'll water the flowers.

I pour some water in the flowers, but quite a bit of it spills on the floor.

So, I set the remote back on the table, get some towels and wipe up the spill.

Then, I head down the hall trying to remember what I was planning to do.

1

At the end of the day: the car isn't washed the bills aren't paid there is a warm can of Pepsi sitting on the counter the flowers don't have enough water, there is still only 1 check in my check book, I can't f ind the remote, I can't find my glasses, and I don't remember what I did with the car keys. Then, when I try to figure out why nothing got done today, I'm really baffled because I know I was busy all day, and I'm really tired.

I realize this is a serious problem, and I'll try to get some help for it, but first I'll check my e-mail . . .

Do me a favor. Forward this message to everyone you know, because I don't remember who the hell I've sent it to.

Don't laugh—if this isn't you yet, your day is coming

By the way don't forget to VOTE!

God Bless You & This Country of Ours!

joe

Posted by Joseph Potocny at 08:17AM (-07:00)

Comments

—JUSTAMOM   October 26, 2008

I LOVE IT!!!!! AND PLAN TO SHARE IT WILL MY FRIENDS . . . I hope all is well with you.

Dropped Call * Dead Zone

Monday, November 03, 2008

This is how I feel in the World of mine, like a droppped call or just the buzzing on the line. The thoughts are there but the connection to the jaw finds a dead zone. No messeages come or go out. It gets frustrating as you talk and sudddenly the line goes dead and your jaw stops and you look at the person and you choke up trying to get the words out and suddenly even the thought is gone. Emptiness in the brain cell. It happens when trying to write on this blog, I sit and have things to say and then the brain, fingers and keys on the keyboard become strangers. I go nowhere without someone with me, not good idea. Now the family worries because of the heart problems, I just look at it as one moore thing to add to the list, someday I will get through the list and have to start over, why, because i won't remember the beginning of it, so I will not know if I got to the end. This all makes perfect sense to me. But then so does waxy ear build up, whatever the hell that means. I know I do like hearing from folks who stop by and take the time to read my babble, strange humor and other things.

If you want to know about me truly, read my post, A Warriors Lament, it tells about me from beginning to where I am at now.You may not understand it, but I do and that is what matters to me. Well for now have fun and be kind to yourself.

God Bless You & This Country of Ours!

Joe

PS: VOTE TOMORROW—I HAVE ALREADY. Posted by Joseph Potocny at 11:15AM (-08:00)

Comments

—Anonymous   November 04, 2008

Hi Joe: Enjoying your website! You have such a neat sense of humor! he he So glad you have Lynn and I have Jim! Hugs and enjoy your day! Mary~Canada www.simplesite.com/mothermary

—JUSTAMOM   November 08, 2008

off to read that post.

This Belongs On My Answering Machine!

Friday, November 07, 2008

Thanks my friend Dick.

Hello and thank you for calling The State Mental Hospital. > > Please select from the following options menu: > > If you are obsessive-compulsive, press 1 repeatedly. > > If you are co-dependent, please ask someone to press 2 for > you. > > If you have multiple personalities, press 3, 4, 5 and 6. > > If you are paranoid, we know who you are and what you want, > stay on the line so we can trace your call. > > If you are delusional, press 7 and > your call will be forwarded to the Mother Ship. > > If you are schizophrenic, listen carefully > and a little voice will tell you which number to press.

> > If you are manic-depressive, hang up. > It doesn't matter which number you press, > nothing will make you happy anyway. > > If you are dyslexic, press 9-6-9-6. > > If you are bipolar, please leave a message after the beep > or before the beep or after the beep. > But Please wait for the beep. > > If you have short-term memory loss, press 9. > If you have short-term memory loss, press 9. > If you have short-term memory loss, press 9. > > If you have low self-esteem, please hang up. > Our operators are too busy to talk with you.

> > If you are menopausal, put the gun down, > hang up, turn on the fan, lie down and cry. > You won't be crazy forever. > > If you are blonde, don't press

any buttons. > You'll just mess it up. > > This coming week is > National Mental Health Careweek. > You can do your part by remembering > to contact at least > one unstable per son to show you care. > > (Well, my job is done. Your turn!!)

God Bless You and This Country of Ours!

Joe

Posted by Joseph Potocny at 08:00AM (-08:00)

Comments

—Anonymous   November 14, 2008

Hey Joe . . . I have been reading your blog for a long time now and as a fellow dementia person I want to say THANKS! for all your posts. Keep telling it like it is. Sandy

As My World Turns!

Tuesday, November 11, 2008

You know I have to get going early and do what chores I have, because about this time my world starts to slow down and crash. This won't be long, but I do apprecaite hereing from you folks, the good, the bad, the ugly, etc. It makes me feel like I am not preaching to the trees or the walls. Well my you all have a good one.

God Bless You and This Country of Ours!

Joe

Posted by Joseph Potocny at 09:49AM (-08:00)

Comments

—DomesticDiva   November 13, 2008

Hey Joe! Just stopped by to say hi and to check on you.

Hope that you are having a good day!

Pamela

—JUSTAMOM   November 15, 2008

keep writing,

—Anonymous   November 17, 2008

Hey Happy Birthday Joe . . . Hugs Mary

Happy Thanksgiving!

Tuesday, November 25, 2008

I know many in other countries and of spiritual beliefs have already celabrated their Thanksgiving Day, but I wanted to wish you one from the Good Old USA Before I forgot again, i feleet I had better get this done. May you all enjoy the day and may you always be free. From My World to yours, be good to yourself.

God Bless You and This Country of Ours!

Joe

Posted by Joseph Potocny at 10:00AM (-08:00)

Comments

—Anonymous	November 25, 2008

Happy Thanksgiving Babe

—JUSTAMOM	November 26, 2008

Enjoy your Turkey AND FAMILY!!

December Already!!!!

Tuesday, December 02, 2008

Yes it is that time of year again. For me Thanksgiving seems years ago. Time no longer has a start and finish for me. Well it will be here soon, probably sooner than I think and be gone before I know it was here. This year has been fillled with manny things for me. Or I think it was, I am no longger sure of it. But I still awake each day and breathe, I might looose most of the day but I am still there somewhere for it. Funny somedays I feel in total control and then for days I have no idea what is going on. I try to get to this each day, but at last it does not work that way. Early or not at all for the most part. Catch Ya All Later.

God Bless You & This Country of Ours!

Joe

Posted by Joseph Potocny at 09:09AM (-08:00)

Lack of Feed Back!

Thursday, December 04, 2008

I use to get many more emails and comments on my postings, with over 12, 000 visitors I brain thinks I would hear more. I guess maybe of late I have tried to show too much humor and people want the gore. Well the humor is howw I keepp my self together. Without it thiss life would be darn near unbearabel. I is no fun trust me sitting here tryiing to write to you and tell you that the wolrd really sucks.I does not get out of my head to the keyboard when I want it to. Tihngs do not get better here, they just slowly go down hill. I read all the new studiies and new stuff to try and I really laugh at this so calllled professionals. They all contradict each other, I wonder if they are not suffers as well. March to stamp out Alhzeimers, RIGHT! Asses don't even know what really causes it to start wity, great progress in over 100 years. I am not thrilled with having AD & FTD, but that is the way it is period. You should try it some day, look at people you have been with for 30+ years and not even know who they are, let alone what the hell they are talking about. Damn most of the time I am not sure what I am saying or trying to say. Well old ½ of brain cell here will say good bye for now. Be good to yourselves.

God Bless You and This Country of Ours!

Joe

Posted by Joseph Potocny at 12:43PM (-08:00)

Comments

—DomesticDiva   December 06, 2008

Hey Joe! Even though we arent commenting doesnt mean that we arent ready ;) I hope that you and yours had a great Thanksgiving! I cant imagine how hard this disease is for you. My mother-in-law was diagnosed 2 years ago and she is deteriorated pretty quickly. I am so glad that you have your family to help you through this. Have a great Christmas!

—Anonymous   December 10, 2008

Hi Joe, I too have not commented recently but still read regularly. I check about every other day for your new post. My mom has never had a 'real' diagnosis but it is so clear in my mind this is what she has, and she too is in that far away place for most of her day. We are blessed to have you giving us small glimpses into the world that you two share . . . Keep up the faith, and God bless you and your family.

—JUSTAMOM   December 15, 2008

JOE I LOVE YOUR HUMOR!!!!!!! I so firmly believe that is the only way to get through life some I come and read I some times do not comment I will from now on., KEEP it up

Have Fun While You are Here!

Saturday, December 20, 2008

Not being politically correct i wish you a happy Chanukah and a very Merry Christmas and best wishes for whatever holiday you celebrate.

I hope you enjoy the column at the right. There is a sight that shows 800 live world cams to watch. You can view the ever changing pictures of endangered animals. What you Tube also nearer the bottom there is a sport to go watch TV shows on different networks for your enjoyment. And you can also check out Big Ticket Depot: much like ebay & Craigs List where you can sell or join your choice of things to do. Also this day in History.\

So much for spel chekcer now you have me. The days messsh together and trying to get here is a real problem. The dyas all seem to run together. I hope you enjoy the smileys, just a little fun to bring into the site. I just wish this World of Mine would or colud make up its own mind as to wherre I will be during each day. Sorry but the old brain cell hass to many thoughts init right now and I am a bit mixed over what to soy so, take care for now.

God Bless You and This Country of Ours!

joe

Posted by Joseph Potocny at 11:25AM (-08:00)

Comments

—dianef   December 21, 2008

Joe—God bless you. I read your site every week or so. My mother was diagnosed about a year ago and now lives very close to me. My heart breaks for her and for you. I appreciate your insights so much. She has trouble sharing her feelings, and you give me a view into what she is feeling.

Merry Christmas—Diane from New Jersey

This Pretty Well Sums It Up!

Tuesday, December 30, 2008

The folowing is form some friends of mine, slightly more mature than I and walk in my World. Though I forget many of a friend until I get an email, it still amazesss me that you can grow to love and care about those you have never seen or shared a spoekn word with.

HOW TRUE IT IS

Another year has passed And we're all a little older. Last summer felt hotter And winter seems much colder.

I rack my brain for happy thoughts, To put down on my pad, But lots of things, That come to mind Just make me kind of sad.

There was a time not long ago When life was quite a blast. Now I fully understand About 'Living in the Past'.

We used to go to friends homes, Baseball games and lunches. Now we go to therapy, to hospitals, And after-funeral brunches.

We used to have hangovers, From parties that were gay. Now we suffer body aches And sleep the night away.

We used to go out dining, And couldn't get our fill. Now we ask for doggie bags, Come home and take a pill.

We used to travel often To places near and far. Now we get backaches From riding in the car.

We used to go out shopping For new clothing at the Mall But, now we never bother . . . All the sizes are too small.

That, my friend is how life is,

And now my tale is told. So, enjoy each day and live it up . . . Before you're too darn old!!

HAPPY NEW YEAR & thanks for making my days enjoyable by your Blog and e-mails funny or sad.

Wally & Delores

God Bless You & This Country of Ours!

joe

Posted by Joseph Potocny at 08:52AM (-08:00)

Welcome to 2009!

Thursday, January 01, 2009

Well the New Year of 2009 is well upon us. New challenges, changes and I am afraid much of the same old bullshit. I hope your year is good to you, I know that mine will only get tougher, but that is alright. Just think if I didn't have this wonderful sickness, YOU MIGHT. So I am doing you a favor. May you find comfort in you life and giving to others. My world and how I feel in it much of the time.

God Bless You & This Country of Ours!

Joe

Posted by Joseph Potocny at 10:34AM (-08:00)

Comments

—Melissa   January 12, 2009

Love your site! How courageous you are!

Best wishes,

Melissa

Lost In Time!

Monday, January 12, 2009

I have jsut relized that we are already at the 10th of January. A new president willl take office in ten days I think it is. When I first got the wonderful news of this new paradise that I am to lvie in, it did not bother me too much. I felt that as with ofther things it was just my turn, deal with it. It was not bad at first I had many good days with small moments in them and then days that just who the hell knows where I was. But they have seemed to merge together. Truly I have a proble with what day it is, even though I keep a calendar by my computer and mark the days off. I have gone back to sticky notes, but the real kick is remembering to use this stuff. I am not angry with the condition, but it really plays hell with you. I do not venture out alone, who knows where I will be. I find spending lengths of time with outrthers becoming quite uncomfortable and extremely distracting. My patients, which I never had, just does not handle it well. I am loosing my train here, so I guess I will go wait for a bus. Catch Ya later.

God Bless You & This Country of Ours!

Joe

Posted by Joseph Potocny at 09:14AM (-08:00)

Comments

—Carol   January 16, 2009

Your smileys make me smile!!! Thanks for blogging—it means a lot to my family!

—Anonymous   January 19, 2009

Hi Joe thank you so much for taking the time to jot down some words about the world you live in. I find them comforting and they help me to better understand where my mom is for much of her days. She seems so far away at times . . . anyway I appreciate you and hope that you will continue on with the great service that you are providing me and other caregivers!

—JUSTAMOM January 23, 2009

checkin on ya, hang in there and chin up

Hurray For Tuesday!!!!!!!

Wednesday, January 28, 2009

Yes normally I post how cruddy things are but Today is different. It is time to say Happy Birthday to the newest member of our family, Ms. Kiaya Lynn Patterson, born Tuesday 1/27/2009 at 2:56 PM. Towering over the Empire State Building standing 21" tall. Yes and you guys best becareful she weighted in at a solid 8lbs 14oz, more than capable of slapping you one upside the head if you get fresh. Please join these grandparents in wishing Morgan & Ross, along with Kaiya, Chase & Lilly all of God's blessing and happiness.

God Bless You & This Country of Ours!

Joe

Posted by Joseph Potocny at 08:58AM (-08:00)

Comments

—Anonymous January 28, 2009

Her birthday is on the 27th dear. I am sure it was a typo on your part. You just get so excited about the good stuff. Love

—Anonymous February 03, 2009

Congratulations to you and your wife and your entire family. I will keep all of you and especially that little cherub in my prayers.

To My Wife!!!!!!!!!

Wednesday, February 04, 2009

Happy 30 years of putting up with me. Thanks for marring me you have made it worthwhile.

Love, Joe Posted by Joseph Potocny at 12:06PM (-08:00)

Comments

—Anonymous February 05, 2009

It's been worth while. An interesting life is what you said you would give me and boy did you live up to your promise. Not always good but definetly interesting. Wish we had more years to go. Love you

To All of YOU from ME!!!

Sunday, February 15, 2009

While I know I am late, but I have not forgotten you my friends. Thanks for being out there for me.

God Bless, Joe Posted by Joseph Potocny at 11:10AM (-08:00)

Comments

—Anonymous   February 17, 2009

Hi Joe Happy Valentines day to you too! Thank you for putting yourself out there for us.

Just Another Day in Paradise!

Wednesday, February 25, 2009

No wonder it took so long to get to the truth, I went to the wrong medical practioners. I received the following from a friend.

TWO DIFFERENT DOCTORS' OFFICES

Boy, if this doesn't hit the nail on the head, I don't know what does!

Two patients limp into two different medical clinics with the same complaint. Both have trouble walking and appear to require a hip replacement.

The FIRST patient is examined within the hour, Is x-rayed the same day and has a time booked for Surgery the following week.

The SECOND sees his family doctor after waiting 3 weeks for an appointment, then waits 8 weeks to see a specialist, then gets an x-ray, which isn't reviewed for another week and finally has his surgery scheduled for a month from then. Why the different treatment for the two patients?

The FIRST is a Golden Retriever. The SECOND is a Senior Citizen.

Next time take me to a vet! (PLEASE)

God Bless You & This Country of Ours!!!!

Joe

Posted by Joseph Potocny at 11:00AM (-08:00)

Yes I am Here, I Think!

Wednesday, March 04, 2009

Beeen somewhere for ahwile but not exactlly sure where. Have been attempting to build sume businesses on-line for the family for xtra income, once I cross that line. I feel it coming closer each day. I am really getting to be a pain. I have been arguing Politics whith a friend and have not been exactly kind in what I have said. He supports the Pres. and I do not trust him as far as I can throw an Elephant.OOh well so much for that. The Joe that started this blog cple of years ago is not here anymore. Infact the one that wrote her last year is gone. This is the part of the loss of me (dying) that bohters me, who will I become and what. Death of my body does not bother me, in fact it will be a blessing. I know my family is making memmories with me for when I am not here and that makes me happy. My youngest daughter, cut my hair. She called it a caldusec look, because we buzzzes the topand just trimed the sides. The name is because we live on a caldusac. When the sides stand up, because combing is not in my world, my wife calls me Albert, because I remind her of Albert Einstein, not bad company. Well you all have fun.

God Bless You & This Country of Ours! in case you forgot BHO this is the symbol of our Country.

Joe

Posted by Joseph Potocny at 01:04PM (-08:00)

Something For You.

Sunday, March 08, 2009

If you look to the right you will see that if you have a proble reading joeneese, You can translate my blog to different languages now. Have fun. When page switches and says TRANSLATING IN BLUE click on it and it will switch back to the blog in the language you picked.

God Bless You & This Country of Ours!

Joe

Posted by Joseph Potocny at 03:52PM (-07:00)

Comments

—Anonymous   March 16, 2009

I just found you on SLE

Tomorrow is My Day.

Wednesday, March 18, 2009

Yes, yesterdaaay was the werin of the green to be sure. AAAAH but Friday is St. Joseph's Day, the werin of the red, so be carefull. Good thing I have a calendar on my desk by this beast or I would not know the day. Once I leave this point alll bets are off.

Since it is my day here is to the world:

Wish you al well.

God Bless You & This Country of Ours!

joe

Posted by Joseph Potocny at 12:35PM (-07:00)

Google Adds On My Blog!!!!

Thursday, March 26, 2009

You proobably have notice that there are adds in my postings and on the upper right side of my blog. These are additional resources for you to click and go to. I do not select them, GOOGLE does, so that they fit the blogs content. It has been difficult for me of late. I am trying to make my blog more informtavie for all. The reason for the adds. Actually they are sites for you to visit and garner what info you can from them. It is my way of saying thank you for visiting me here.

The image is about Our Country. May she ever remain strong and free. Yes I bleed red, white and blue.

For awhile I had hit sort of a holding pattern and staid stable, but noe things are getting fuzzy and I forget more easily. I guess that is hust pare of this process. Well you have a good one.

God Bless You and This Country of Ours!

Joe

Posted by Joseph Potocny at 01:51PM (-07:00)

A Change, I Am A Crook

Thursday, April 02, 2009

I OPENED WHAT IS CALLLED A GOOGLE ADSENSE ACCOUNT, SO THAT YOU WOULD HAVE MORE RESCOURES AT YOUR DISPOSAL THROUGH SIDE ADDS.

WELL GOOGLE AND OUR PRESIDENT THINK THEY CAN JUST FIRE ANYONE IN THE PRIVATE SECTOR. THE ADDS ARE GONE, SOMEONE WAS CLICKING ON THEM, GOD FORBID, WHAT THE FUCK WERE THEY THEIR FOR. ANGRY YES I AM, I DO NOT LIKE BEING CALLED A THIEF OR IT BEING IMPLIED. THAT IS EXACTLY WHAT GOOGLE HAAS DONE. SO, IN MY INFINITE WISDOM I CHOOSE TO SAY SCREW THEM AND USE YAHOO FROM NOW ON. I REALISE THAAT MEANS CLOSING THIS BLOG DOWN AND STARTING OVER. BUT I TRIED TO GIVE YOU THE STORY ON THIS SIDE OF DEMENTIA AND OTHER RESOURCES, BUT GOOGLE DOES NOT THINK YOU ARE WORTHY. SO IF THIS GOES AWAY, I WILL TRY AND LET YOU KNOW WHERE I WENT, IF I REMEMBER EITHER ONE.

GOD BLESS YOU & THIS COUNTRY OF OURS!!!

joe

PS THEY PAID ME AN UNBELIEVABLE AMOUNT FOR WHOEVER CLICKED TO GET THE INFO THEY WANTED YES I AM A REAL FUCKIN CROOK $0.81, LOCK ME UP NOW! Posted by Joseph Potocny at 10:02AM (-07:00)

Mark Your Calendars — 5/10/2009

Tuesday, April 07, 2009

On this date HBO will start the firsst in a 4 part series on Alzhiemers. As you know I prefer to call it dementia. As the council on aging testified in March to Congress, THEY DO NOT KNOW WHAT EVEN CAUSES IT. Yet they feel thaat with the right structure and funds there could be the possibility of delaying its onset. It is finnally being recognized and called a disease and not just of the aged. Maria Schiver gave a moving talk, but the gentleman from Florida much more touch me with the story of his wife diagnosed at 55, about 65 now I am guessing no longer remembers him and the pain of it. He also talked about those who are not wealthy like Maria, face challenges of care that she can afford. I am not taking things from her, the devestation of her father is real and painful for the family. But I still do not believe the caregivers truly understand the pain and frustration and anger of it in this World. You go along ok for awhile. Then you fall down a part of the stairs. You go to get back up the stairs, but no way, they are gone lost forever and so has part of yourlife and who you are disappeared. Epedemic they call it, try PANDEMIC, with more than 10 million in this country alone suffering. These people did state a real truth, when you have seen one case of AD, you have seen just one case. We all progress differently. And as they said 'YOU WILL NOT SEE ANY SURVIVORS OF AD WALKING AROUND". THERE ARE NONE!!!!!!! Welcom eo My World

I have got nasty lately on my blog and truly do not care, it is part of wo and what I amm becoming. BUT I AM PROUD TO SAY THAT I AM PART OF THE

DOCUMENTARY THAT WILL BE SHOWN ON HBO IN MAY. I thank them for having the balls to truly attack this head on. KUDOS HBO.

If science has or ever gets the courage to take live brain cels so they can truly start to find out how this plague works, I AM READY AND WILLING TO LET THEM GO AT MY BRAIN, it is becoming of smaller and smaller value to me.

God Bless You & This Country of Ours!

joe

Posted by Joseph Potocny at 08:40AM (-07:00)

Comments

—LovingGrand   May 10, 2009

Joe, thank you for inviting me along your journey. I listen very well, so please keep talking.

Spreading your words, making memories in places and through people you've never met makes your world larger than mine.

You're my hero and my favorite star of "The Alzheimer's Project"! ▢ ▢ ▢

speaking my mind????

Monday, April 20, 2009

The littttle one is my one granddaughter Lillian. You know I am finding it more and more diffficult to maintain images in my mind of those I once knew and loved and even those that I care about and love now. A feeling of urgency is starting to take hold in my life. What it means I do not know. All final arragnements have been made and paid for, so that is not a concern any longer. I do not want to be around people much anymore, it is gettinng harder to tolerate them, I am sure I am no prize either now, probably neverr was. At first I told this disease of mine, that you may win, but you will know you have been in one hell of a fricken fight. Seems I am the one with the wounds and they don't heal or go away. Well soo much for my rambling.

God Bless You & This Country of Ours!

joe

Posted by Joseph Potocny at 09:37AM (-07:00)

Comments

—LovingGrand   April 20, 2009

Joe, it's not such a small world after all as I found you and I am listening, please keep speaking your mind—all words count. I like your blog and your granddaughter is darling.

Check out mine at http://LovingGrand.blogspot.com. I'm also on Twitter, following you.

Take care and Bless You & Yours! Terrilee

WOW TO HBO, JUST WOW!

Wednesday, April 22, 2009

Last night and I need to do this while it is still fresh or atleast somewhat fresh in my brain, my Wife & I had the privilege of seeing the premier screeening in LA of the first part of the HBO series The Alzhiemers Project. What a job they did. I am humbled that I was a part of this movie. It truly shows a side that few people know about for thoose that live in this World of Mine, with me. It was done with style, grace, compassion and an understanding of what we go through.

AGAIN WOW!!!! Thank You for asking me to be a part of it.

God Bless You & This Country of Ours!

Posted by Joseph Potocny at 10:21AM (-07:00)

Comments

—userMJ   April 22, 2009

Hi Joe (and Wife)—thank you so much for sharing your story with us. I was at the premier last night, to support my friend Annie from Minnesota (who cares for her mother and was also in the film). Your wife was kind enough to keep me well supplied with tissues during the screening.

It was a honor to meet you both.

MJ from Ventura

—Kirk   April 22, 2009

My wife and I attended last night and were touched by your story. Thank you so much to you and your family for sharing your lives. We'll be sure to follow and share your blog.

—Annie   April 23, 2009

Joe and Lynn,

I just got back from the screening in LA and am back home in Minnesota. It was wonderful to meet you both. If you would like a copy of the photo with you, Nick, Shari and myself, please let me know! I'll drop by here often.

—cornbreadhell   April 23, 2009

hi joe. i'm a friend of annie's, whom you probably met in los angeles at the screening. i wish you the best and hope to see your video on hbo. in the meantime i will be checking out your blog. respectfully, rick

—rilera   April 23, 2009

Hi Joe, I'm going to add your blog to my list of favorites. Thank you for sharing your experiences with us. I was a caregiver for my Mom with AD. I'm glad that you enjoyed the HBO screening.

—flintysooner   April 24, 2009 Hi Joe,

My friend, Annie, recommended your blog so I wanted to stop by and give you my best wishes and respect.

—IRun13point1   May 06, 2009

Joe, I just returned home from a screening of the HBO documentary "The Alzheimer's Project." I work for The Alzheimer's Project, Inc. in Tallahassee, Florida, and we have all fallen in love with you, your wife, and your story. We will be following you from now until . . . well, until.

All our prayers, The staff of The Alzheimer's Project, Inc.

—Adirondackcountrygal   May 09, 2009

You are a hero Joe!

—Ruthita   May 09, 2009

Hi Joe, I'm watching it online right now, and decided to google your blog. Here you are! Thank you for being part of this important series. I am the caregiver advocate for my dear 82year-old mom, who has AD. I send you love and positive thoughts from way up here in Canada.—Ruth

—June   May 10, 2009

Dear Joe and Lynn,

Checking in from Pennsylvania. I am just watching the HBO documentary now. Thank you for your bravery in being part of this project. We love you!

We are also part of the Patriotic Resistance.

My Mom was diagnosed in 2003. http://cleaningoutalife.blogspot.com/

I have not been nearly as prolific as you, Joe, in updating her blog.

Chinese proverb, author unknown: An invisible red thread connects those who are destined to meet, regardless of time, place, or circumstance. The thread may stretch or tangle, but never break.

—Jay   May 10, 2009

thank you for sharing your life in the documentary. takes a lot of courage. the show was so well done! Keep plugging away . . . jay

—hkimaging   May 10, 2009

Congratulations! I'm watching the documentary right now and it is truly amazing!

—Dan   May 10, 2009

I watched you on the show. I moved from my home in Oceanside to Washington DC to work on an immigration program. I wish there was something I could do to help you with this. Hang in there Joe. Thank you for telling your story.

—Moonie   May 10, 2009

I watched the documentary and it was wonderful, so well done. I was just in tears. I have never seen the plight of Alzheimers presented in this way. You are very courageous to share you story. I had forgotten years ago how in Art school I did a photo essay on a nursing home that took care of women suffering from this disease. I suppose I was too young at the time to comprehend what these women were suffering with . . .

You have a wonderful sense of humor and I thank you for opening your heart and mind to complete strangers. You are mentoring in ways that cannot be put into words.

God bless you and your family!

—johnwairephoto   May 10, 2009

joe

my wife and i just watched the show. thank you for sharing your story. we shared some laughs and a few tears. i'm not sure what else i can say . . . that hasn't already been said. you've probably heard it

all by now. you're a great man! john

—Anonymous   May 10, 2009

Joe . . . I just watched the documentry . . . BRAVO! I love it, you tell it like it is. I have been following your blog for a while now . . . I also have dementia . . . Thank you, Joe. Sandy

—Danielle   May 11, 2009

Dear Joe, I am sitting at work watching the HBO Program on my laptop. I never heard the view of someone living with AD. My father's was too quick to advance. Thank You for sharing with the world your view. I blog about my father on myspace . . . if your interesting in looking. http://www.myspace.com/460578844

Thank You So Much . . . and thank you to your wife for being there . . .

—userST   May 11, 2009

You are amazing. I can only imagine how humbling this experience can be for someone that has developed and created as a pioneer in the tech industry. I love your sense of humor and that you are down to earth about all of this. I wish you and your family the best. Thanks for sharing your story and maintaining a blog even in the darker times of your life.

—Tenzin   May 15, 2009

Thank you for sharing your story with us. This journey is surely not the easiest, but I pray to God to make it as smooth as can be. Will be following your blog . . .

No Where To Go —

Thursday, April 30, 2009

The picture is of me and my elsdet granddaughter. She is 6 today, Ms. Emma Nichole.

I have ben trying to get stuf done on my computer today, but I am just lost as to what I am trying to do. Postit notes allover the place, printed emails to reed and get throug. Just is not working. I haven sitting here looking at my note that saays blog and trying to get to this. Sometimes I just feel completly lost and have no idea where to go to do things. I feel like the odl brain is really slowing down and it wants to go somewhere and not with me. I just dont want to. Whateles can I say.

God Bless You and This Country of Ours!

joe

Posted by Joseph Potocny at 02:26PM (-07:00)

Comments

—rilera   April 30, 2009

God bless you Joe!

—Cindy   May 02, 2009

Hang on, Joe. Just don't stop trying. We're here.

Thank God For Friends — They Make Me Laugh!

Sunday, May 03, 2009

This came from a frien, who rote it I do not know, but you will find me in this.

I was gonna write something here _ _ _ _ _ _ _ _ _ _ _ _ _

Forgetter Be Forgotten
My forgetter's getting better,
But my rememberer is broke
To you that may seem funny
But, to me, that is no joke

For when I'm 'here' I'm wondering
If I really should be 'there'
And, when I try to think it through,
I haven't got a prayer!

Oft times I walk into a room,
Say 'what am I here for?'
I wrack my brain, but all in vain!
A zero, is my score.

At times I put something away
Where it is safe, but, Gee!
The person it is safest from
Is, generally, me!

When shopping I may see someone,
Say 'Hi' and have a chat,
Then, when the person walks away
I ask myself, 'who the heck was that?'

Yes, my forgetter's getting better
While my rememberer is broke,
And it's driving me plumb crazy
And that isn't any joke.

CAN YOU RELATE???
I DON'T REMEMBER WHO I SENT THIS TO ! LIVE, LOVE & LAUGH A LOT
God Bless You & This Country of Ours!!!!!!
joe
Posted by Joseph Potocny at 12:40PM (-07:00)

Comments

—Annie   May 04, 2009

I don't like to admit how many things I know I have in safe places!

—Adirondackcountrygal   May 09, 2009

Hi Joe, saw you profiled in our newspaper for the HBO program that is coming on about Alzhiemers. I want you to know that I care about you! I am a CNA caregiver for Alhiemers patients and understand what you are going through. Hang in there! Linda

—fidelcatro   May 10, 2009

hi joe,

i had never heard of your blog before i read the article in the NYT about the HBO stuff coming up.

i want to say that i've had the pleasure of spending a lot of time with guys who are diagnosed with early onset AD/Frontal Temporal Lobe. i wish you could have been part of our group!

i hope you do know that many people who have not commented have seen your blog and it has helped them . . . find support, humor, identification, understanding, inspiration.

thank you. rebecca

—tksinclair   May 10, 2009

Hi Joe, I live in Oceanside and I'm watching you on the HBO special. Thank you so much for allowing us into your heart and mind. Both my grandmothers had Alzheimers and as a caregiver I wish I'd found your blog a long time ago.

Just wanted to say "hi" and encourage you to keep moving forward. I live nearby and if you ever need anything I'd be happy to give you a hand. I know what you mean about living in the moment. I'm 55 and just can't seem to stop worrying about yesterday and tomorrow. It's a waste of time really, isn't it? I look forward to following what you're up to and again, thank you so much for allowing us to share your life.

Terri Sinclair Oceanside, CA tksinclair@cox.net

—BrianChristopher   May 10, 2009

Saw the special today. Thanks for your contribution to understanding this disease and good luck.

—Anonymous   May 10, 2009

Dear Joe,

I just started watching the HBO program and found your blog i wanted to share with you that my father also has Alzeimer he was diagnosed 8yrs ago . . . bless you and your family for sharing your story.

Thank you, Valentin

—newlyweds   May 10, 2009

Hi Joe,

I just watched the Alzhiemers special this evening and wanted to say that your story has really touched my heart. God bless you and your family.

—taysmommy   May 10, 2009

Just saw the documentary and I had to become a follwer. Bless you

—Lorie May   11, 2009

Hi Joe,

Saw you on HBO last night. I wanted to say thanks for sharing the good, the bad, the funny and the uglies of this disease. You rocked! Lorie

—Jules   May 11, 2009

Hi Joe, I saw the Alzheimer's Project last night and immediately grabbed my laptop to see your blog. AD affects so many friends, family, and loved ones . . . yet it's hard to truly understand

what a person with AD is feeling and thinking. Thank you so much for this much needed insight into your courageous and inspirational world. Stay strong . . . thank you so much for all you do! Julie

—Gayla   May 11, 2009

(((Joe))) I've been watching "The Alzheimer's Project" and saw you featured. You have an awesome, infectious sense of humor. The 'DDS'-dead d—k syndrome-is a classic! I'm truly not making fun of you or the situation, but it did make me laugh and others I'm sure. I admire you personally and I've just seen you on TV and now I'm reading your blog. I'm a Hospice/Palliative volunteer, and a strong advocate for rights of all. :) Keep blogging Joe as long as you can—your fantastic! Hugs from Las Vegas, Gayla

—ToddandStephanieRice   May 11, 2009

Hi Joe!! I saw The Alzheimer's Project last night as well . . . I have to say that you are truely inspiring. I'm an occupational therapy assistant student and we just finished a semester on Aging and Alzheimer's was a big portion of it. I know that is the population I want to work with when I graduate. Please keep writing as long as you can . . . this is such a wonderful insight to a horrible disease. May God Bless you and your family and know there are people out here who care!! Stephanie Peoria, Illinois

—Anonymous   May 11, 2009

Dear Joe, I saw you on TV and I fell in love with you (don't tell your wife, ok?). You made me laugh! You made me cry. You are a wonderful glowing spirit. I don't believe that even though you may disappear from those around you that you beautiful spirit will ever disappear. Love from Ruth in Washington, D.C.

—Anonymous   May 11, 2009

Hi Joe! I love this poem! It says it all. I copied it and printed it out to read to my mom. She is an extremely intelligent lady who just happens to have Alzheimer's. She will for sure relate to what you wrote!

Keep up the good work.

#1 daughter

—JimandAmyRennie   May 12, 2009

Hi Joe. I saw the HBO doc, and I wish I'd known about this blog a long time ago! I am now a follower. My grandmother suffered for many years until she passed away, but she never understood that she had an illness and could never talk about it with me. This helps me to understand a piece of her better. Thank you for being so brave and sharing your journey.

—Anonymous   ay 12, 2009

My grandmother is in the latter stages. I tuned in to the HBO special and am shocked and amazed at how similar all the stories are to the one I live.

Thank you, sir for being part of it. It brought me to this fine blog. I look forward to reading your thoughts as you fight forward!

Thank You All

Tuesday, May 12, 2009

I hav been deeply moved an honored by the number of people that have wirttin me and sent me emails over the last few days. The words used pay me an honor that I do not deserve. I am but one of many on the journey, I jus am able still to let you know hte rotten side of it here. In watching the HBO special, the real heros were the kids, I cried over their pain and frustration and the absolute resolve they had to love their grandparents and want ing to understand. See you have the tuff part, we just keep forgetting and reach a point that nothing matters as it once did. Someday, they may really know what causes this and may even find a way to stop it, reverse it I do not think so. But wha the hell we are talking about me thinking. I have one brain cell and more than one thought causes a traffic jam and I get totally messed up and confused. It is harder for me to talk these days, words come out kind of liek my typeing. If I get to it today or the nxet couple of days I will be adding some links to other blogs for you to read.

Till next we meet.

God Bless You and This Country of Ours!

joe

Posted by Joseph Potocny at 11:28AM (-07:00)

Comments

—johnwairephoto   May 12, 2009

true . . . you are 1 of many . . . but each 1 is important. the kids were heart-breaking. keep blogging joe and keep fighting!!!

—foodhoe   May 12, 2009

Thank you so much for writing about your journey, I have so much respect for you and your family in dealing with this so openly! My mother was diagnosed last year with Alzheimers and we are still just coming to grips with what this all means . . .

—rilera   May 12, 2009

Joe, I'm a friend of Annie who with her Mom is in the HBO special. I admire you for allowing your story to be included in the special. I wish the best for you and your family. I agree with you, the tough part was watching the kids who care for their grandparents.

They are indeed heroes, and so are you! Robyn

—Anonymous   May 12, 2009

Take care of your self and be blessed! I got the chance to see the HBO special and I identified the same characteristics in my grandfather. Is like looking back to someone that I loved a lot and remembered like time hasn't passed.

God Bless you.

—CynCity   May 12, 2009

Thank you for sharing your story Joe. I am an only child caring for my father who suffers from AD. I am 24 and he is 76. He is not my grandfather he is my FATHER. I look forward to following your blog. Keep your light shining bright.

—Liz   May 12, 2009

Hi, Joe. I didn't see the television show; I just want to thank you for writing and telling us how you feel. Most people don't write enough these days, so I enjoyed reading what sounds like a personal letter, and your spelling is still better than a lot of other peoples' attempts! Thanks again, Joe-I hope you have a good day today, and a good meal, too. Signed, Liz in New Jersey

—JonathanJAaronson   May 12, 2009

Dear Joe, You are a very intelligent man Joe. From the context of the HBO special which I have had the opportunity to watch . . . And trust me as it was a opportunity for me to see you and your family come to grips with a hard reality only because it reached desperately into my soul as one human being to another. I have no idea if you will remember this comment but what does not kill us makes us stronger. You will be remembered even if you don't remember me and I shall light a resounding pray for you and those that love you because you have such lovely things to live for even if you may not remember them in the future. God Bless you and yours, Sincerely, Jon Aaronson Tampa, FL

—Tasha   May 13, 2009

I'm watching your HBO special now and I am touched by your story. You are a strong person and your family loves you. I don't think you should feel badly about your children suffering, they love you so much and want to be there for you. I know this is hard, but it's okay. We are here with you and I will continue to follow your blog, pray for you, and your family. Can't wait for the next post. God Bless.

—JoelthePastor   May 13, 2009

Joe,

I'm grateful to you for allowing us to see into your life through the show. My hope is that people would have compassion on those affected by dementia/Alzheimer's Disease and that it might lead to research that might slow the progress of the disease, lessen the symptoms, and maybe even lead to a cure.

My thoughts and prayers are with you and your family.

—Anonymous   May 13, 2009

dear joe—i just finished watching 2 of the specials. a friend taped them for me. thank u for letting HBO use your kindness and your empathy toward all suffering with this disease. My father-in-law is in the middle stage right now and watching the special gave me not only head knowledge . . . but heart knowledge. Take care.

Joan Mobile, Alabama

—Mary   May 13, 2009

Joe, You are my hero. I was amazed at your attitude towards AD. My mom has AD and we are all affected as a family. I have been watching the HBO special. I can only hope-that if i am ever diagnosed with this disease that I have the strength and courage to handle it as you do!!

—Colleen   May 13, 2009

Thank you for sharing your story. My father in law is 82 and has been diagnosed for about 2 years. God bless you and your family.

155

—Danielle   May 14, 2009

I cried through all of them but the Momentum of Science . . . the Caregiver one really hit me. As a daughter of early onset alzheimers . . . I really appreciate you sharing your journey. Makes me realize how hard it really is for my father. Feel free to share my blog www.myspace.com/460578844

Thank you!! Danielle

—userAL   May 14, 2009

Hi Joe, I am American Muslim, Pro-palestinian woman in NH. I wish you the best and hope sincerely that you remain strong.

salaam cali

—Anonymous   May 14, 2009

Thank You for sharing your story Joe. I knew that AD was difficult on the person who has it but I never knew that it was not only scarey but painful. I pray that you will continue to "fight" this horrible disease with the courage I know you have inside of you. God Bless you dear man, I shall keep you and your family in my thoughts and prayers.

—ClaytonDavis   May 14, 2009

I'm watching you right now. You are an awesome man. I pray to be half as cool as you are when I'm your age.

Be well!

—LidnaBurke   May 14, 2009

Thank you, Joe, for chronicling your situation. I care for my great Aunt, who is 82 and has been stricken with Alzheimer's for 15 years. God Bless You.

—ArtistVictoriaONeill   May 14, 2009

I'm watching you on HBO and it's a real pleasure getting to know you. xox

—TishiraBrown   May 14, 2009

God bless you! You are so courageous and I'm so glad I found your blog. You keep up the good fight and know you and your family are being prayed for in my little tiny corner of Texas.

God bless, Tishira

—Sherri   May 15, 2009

I looke forward to getting to know you. You are touching many lives by sharing your journey with us so honestly. Thankyou!!!

—Gargeyi   May 15, 2009

Hi Joe,

I watched you on the HBO special series on AD and cried through the entire show. All the stories screened got me so emotional and I just wanted to let you know you are such a trooper. March on! We love you and we will always pray for your good health. I look forward to reading more of your posts.

God bless, Gargeyi

—Anonymous   May 16, 2009

Hi Joe! You are a remarkable person!. I walk every year the memory walk to raise money for people like you. I like someday to have no more AD!. My name is Kathy Wood. I live in Oakland, Ca.

—Christine   May 16, 2009

Hey Joe! You don't know me but I watched the HBO special and I decided to find your website! I really like all of the pictures, your blog entries, and the webcams. You seem like a very special person. I will be sure to keep checking your blog!

—Lizzy   May 16, 2009

Hi Joe. I'm watching the HBO Special right now and am so touched and moved by it, especially when I learned of your blog and then found it!

My mother also has Alzheimer's Disease, although the rest of my family (except for my brother), including my father, is having a very hard time accepting it and dealing with it. The most tragic part is the pain and loss she is experiencing as she realizes she is

slowly sliding into dementia. Thanks for sharing your story; thanks to HBO for making it happen. Lizzy Woodfield

—Sherry   May 17, 2009

Hi Joe,

I really appreciate your appearance on the HBO special, your candid openness about your dementia, and your sense of humor about it. My Dad also has Alzheimer's. Unfortunately our family is spread out geographically, and I live 3000 miles away, coincidentally just a few miles from you in fact. It is times like these when so far away from our families, that we feel so helpless to assist in the caregiving, the support, or just be present in our family's lives. The passage of time between visits also makes the reality more difficult because we see the changes in more drastic chunks, rather than gradually bit by bit.

Of all the victims in the HBO special, I think my father would relate to you the most. His name is Joe too, and like you, he is very intelligent and struggling intellectually as well as emotionally. He is still "together", but "not", and like you, he is at the point of being aware of the things he does wrong or can't do, "crossing over" and coming back. I think that my Dad would identify with your comments made at the psychologist on the show, if you remember them, and that hit home with me.

I am glad that you are blogging. Most of our family can only "see" my father's decline through my mother's e-mail descriptions, which help us all, including her. I really wanted my father to record his thoughts, feelings, experiences, struggles, and fears in some written manner as you have done, but he not only doesn't have an inclination to do so, but has given up trying to write since even a simple gift card is difficult for him to compose, and he gets frustrated. I would have really liked to have something in writing from him, an interview, or even a video . . . something to document what he is going through, something to allow him to express his inner struggles, something to help us understand them, something to give us memories of him to hang onto before he is gone. However, it is more difficult for him to face it and talk about it. His "bloopers" are embarrassing for him, and he struggles with desperately trying to preserve his dignity. Your family is very lucky that you are more willing to share yourself and your struggles openly. And I thank you for it too; since my own father can't be as open or write about it, seeing and reading it from others such as yourself really helps me to understand it better, and understand him better, and what he may be experiencing. Thank you so much for giving us that gift.

God bless you and your family. You seem very brave, and your wife, Lynn, is very brave too. It's amazing that you both let the world in on such a touching and emotional personal part of your lives. Thank you so much for sharing it with us. I will continue to follow your blog, and for those of us sharing the journey in some way, I hope that Lynn or another member of your family will share some updates with us after you are unable to.

Many blessings, prayers, and Peace

—Sherry					May 17, 2009

Dear Joe, P.S. I forgot to mention that in a few weeks I will be going to see my father for the first time in about two years, and will experience his "new behavior" for the first time, the descriptions of which my mother has been writing to me. Watching the HBO specials has helped me to prepare for this visit and experience. Thank you again so much for being a part of that and helping people like me to better understand the disease, our family victims, as well as prepare ourselves emotionally to meet them. You've been a blessing to us.

Stay strong. Sherry

—Anonymous   May 19, 2009

Dad no matter what you say you will always be my hero. Love you always your daughter Morgan

—dragyonfly   May 29, 2009

Joe, I love your sense of humor . . . thanks for your bravery and insight. I enjoyed your part in the show, you are one fine human.

Who Am I?

Sunday, May 17, 2009

For some reason many of you have called me hero, courgeous, generous spirt, wonderful person and all type of kind things. Truly I am none of these, just another one among millions with this fricken disease. No cure, no real meds, no real scientific finds, just one end. At firstm many thought I was bitter orver it, I never have been. Pissed at a medical profession that would not get its head out of its ass and listen yes. You see it is just my turn, I was called and well I answered, oh well. Often wanted to write my life story, maybe that is teh real reason behind this blog, I do not know. Now I have difficulty putting it into a time frame since time does not exist for me the same as it does for you. I was going to callthe booke THROUGH THE LAUGHTER, HE HEARD MY TEARS! So much for that.

If you want to know who and what I really am, there is a post 08/0/2008 called A Warrior's Lament, an attempt at a poem by me saying where I have been and am and a post 09/29/2007 Farwell To My Old Friend Pain, to post is self explaining I thing.

Well Lakes to HBO this blog has been buzing. They are the Heroes for doing the series that needed to be done. Five hours cannot cover it all, but they did a one heck of a knock up job. Shit the brought back long lost friends to me because of it, I sure benefited by it. Well tooo much rambling.

God Bless You & This Country of Ours!

joe

Posted by Joseph Potocny at 11:24AM (-07:00)

Comments

—Adirondackcountrygal May 18, 2009

You are a hero Joe, because instead of burying your head in the sand, you are fighting this and informing others so that they may be better prepared to help a loved one, or themselves.

—Anonymous   May 18, 2009

I don't think you are a hero, nor do I think you are especially courageous, but what I do think you are is IMPORTANT. Your work with this blog and with the HBO documentary is helping to put a human face on this disease and to give insight to those with loved ones afflicted by AD/dementia who may never experience it from the inside looking out. Thank you.

—tksinclair   May 18, 2009

Anonymous really said it. Yes, you are important whether you want to believe it or not. You've not only touched every one who has written you but you've also made so many, like myself, stop and take inventory of "what the hell am I doing?!" AND, you've made a call to action that there is work to be done. For every person you touch there might be an additional donation, a contribution of any kind, that will bring us a step closer to ending this disease. If you can keep us thinking for one more day, one person at a time, it's a contribution you can't deny this world Joe. You've sure made me take stock in some of my crap and there's not a day that's gone by since I saw the documentary where I haven't thought of you, your family, how I can make my time here matter more . . .

I know I for one am glad I got to know a little about you, your life and your family. My life will not be the same and I learned more about Alzheimer's since I've "known" you than I did before and both my grandmothers died with dementia, one with Alzhiemers. Thanks. A Warrior's Lament . . . really liked that.

—TishiraBrown   May 19, 2009

You are courageous and a hero to me. You are putting yourself out there and bringing much needed attention to a disease that not only affects the person with it but their families as well. My Momma was a victim of this terrible disease and I know she would think you were a hero too. God bless you for all you do. Tishira

—newlyweds   May 19, 2009

Joe you are a hero for fighting this disease with all your heart. That documentary was so special and helped more people than you will ever now. Take Care!

—Anonymous   May 29, 2009

I just finished watching the memory loss tapes. The program was first class and very educational. You are an inspiration to me.

I Do Not Go Away — Google.

Monday, May 18, 2009

I sure many thougt I would not follow up on my distain with Google, but I have a very angry side to me, especially when being called a thief. Years ago maybe, now no way. So here is to google, using spell & grammar checker so they could understand. Also, no answer from them yet. No balls I guess.

April 28, 2009

Mr. Eric Schmidt Chairman of the Board & Chief Executive Officer Google 1600 Amphitheatre Pkwy. Mountain View, CA 94043

Dear Mr. Schmidt:

I am sure that you maybe wondering why there is a check for $0.81 attached to this letter.

Well there is a good reason for that, I do not appreciate being basically called a thief and a purveyor of illegal intent of taking funds from anyone. This blood money is repayment for what I was paid by Google Ad sense, because someone unknown to me was clicking on the ads on my blog. I presume from the insulting email I received from your outfit, they were not justified. I appealed, since I did not even know that I was to get paid, and basically as far as I am concerned was called a liar and complicter by your staff.

You see I suffer from Alzheimer's and Frontal Temporal Lobe Dementia. I have a blog located at *http://living-with-alzheimers.blogspot.com/*. On this site I tell of how the disease affects me and how I cope with it. I started it to help caregivers, physicians and those whose loved ones suffer from the disease, what it is like in Our World. Maybe in a small way giving them some comfort as to how it is not their fault and that they could do very little.

I thought Adsense would be good, because it listed sites and places for people to go on my blog as well as in the posting. The ads were pertinent to the blog and entries. This was my whole thrust. But YOUR PEOPLE, I guess felt I was just trying to steal from you. So hence I return the $0.81 to you, I would not want your firm to suffer any financial hardship over this, or your dog not be able to eat because of it.

As a point of interest, The Wall Street Journal thought enough of me and my integrity to feature my blog in the paper. HBO Media also has honored me by including me in their The Alzheimer's Project, which airs in May 2009. By the way you can find the information on Google.

I remain, Joseph Potocny Posted by Joseph Potocny at 12:52PM (-07:00)

Comments

—Wendy   May 18, 2009

Love your letter. I hope they respond.

—Anonymous	May 19, 2009

you go dad . . . tell them like it is. Morgan

—TishiraBrown	May 19, 2009

OOOOH! That makes me soooo mad! Awesome job on the letter. Some people don't have the sense God gave a goose! As my momma would say. Way to go Joe! God Bless, Tishira

—CynCity	May 20, 2009

Excellent letter! You inspire me so much, that I started a blog too http:// caringfromtheheart.blogspot.com/

Stick it to them Joe, don't let them get away with that BS. Let us know if/when they respond.

—Anonymous	May 20, 2009

this was amazing. i loved every little part of it . . . but i think my FAVORITE was the last line that says they could find the information on google. nice job, well put.

—Danielle May 23, 2009

Good Job!!!

The Grewsome Foursome!
Wednesday, May 20, 2009

Well I thought you should seem some of the folks respoonsilge for the HBO Special.

Starting on the right: Sherry the Nick they along with Elisa (not in the picture) produced Memory The Lost Tapes. Give them a bid hand for a job very well done. Next is Annie daughter of Josephine that were in the special. Picture was taken in LA at a priemer showing. The old fart, well he is not going to beat out robert Redford. He is the mystery person.

God Bless You & This Country of Ours!!

joe

Posted by Joseph Potocny at 02:40PM (-07:00)

Comments

—rilera   May 20, 2009

Thanks for posting this picture you and Annie and the others. You look great Joe!

—AimeeCarlen   May 22, 2009

Joe,

I'm watching you on HBO right now, which is kind of strange to watch you on TV while at the same time reading your words on the Net. Such is the world in which we find ourselves. Your humor is very much appreciated, as I am a genius in my own mind, and you are actually a genius. I am a registered nurse who has seen entirely too much of AD, and watched my father-in-law deal with the disease. What you are doing by putting your words out there is invaluable, and we all very much appreciate you and your indomitable spirit. God bless you and your beautiful family.

No Wonder My BackYard is a Challenge.

Friday, May 22, 2009

I was sittting here reading my last entry, I knew something was wrong with it, but I had to study my own hands to figrue it out. It should have read starting on the left. See I do not know my right from my left anymore. Might be one reason I don't drive anymore and I turn into the wall when walking. I think I have it right now, if not you figure it out I am done.

You know this thing is gettting the better of me, we knew it would happen. I am having greater difficulty in remebering what day it is and am getting lost in conversations more often now. I am trying to follow the note that hangs on my computer desk that just says BLOG. I feel that I will soon not be doing this, having too much trouble with my thoughts, fingers and the friken keybaord. So much for my crab, you all have a great ad wonderful life.

God Bless You & This Country of Ours!

Joe

Posted by Joseph Potocny at 10:00AM (-07:00)

Comments

—Anonymous   May 22, 2009

I am with yiou in your heart Joe. I wish more than anything that I could make everything good for you. No matter what you may think of yourself at this time-Many people still love you and ALLWAYS will.

—TishiraBrown   May 22, 2009

Joe, you are an amazing person and no matter what you always will be. I too am with you in heart and spirit. You and your family will always be in my prayers. You have touched so many people's lives, mine included. I've decided to go ahead and get my degree in nursing so I can work with Alzheimer's patients. I want you to know that you had a part in that decision. I admire you so much for your courage. God bless you! ~Big Hugs to you and your family~ Tishira in Texas

—maria   May 22, 2009

hey Joe i read you blog every day and you have inspire me so much please dont stop bloging even if it dont make sence any more at lest it will give me some thing to look farward to (and i dont mean it in a bad way) since that HBO specail ive been readin your blog every day and keeping you in my preays if one day you cant type any more you can always find stuff online that will type it for you while you talk it out Maria riverside ca

—Anonymous   May 25, 2009

Hi Joe,

My sons and I just watched you on the HBO documentary. Everyone wanted to say hi to you and that you are truly such a wonderful person. This came through in the documentary in shinning colors. My sons said please be sure to take lots of vitamins and minerals. We all hope that you get stronger and that one day we can all meet you.

Sincerely, Joseph, Charley, and Jonathan

—Anonymous   May 25, 2009

I am watching you now on HBO as well. I wish you all th best. Shawa from the Bronx, NY :-)

—JoAnnFyfe   May 26, 2009

Hi . . . my mom has alzheimers, and I see it literally getting worse by the day. I wanted to thank you, first, for opening up your story on the HBO special. It's not until you deal with this horrible disease that you realize how devestating it is. I truly wish you the best of days. You have a wonderful family to support you, and that is a true blessing. God bless you all . . .

—Anonymous   May 26, 2009

Hi Joe, You are providing such a priceless gift to those of us who have a loved one that is afflicted with the crappy (sp?) disease! Words cannot express my gratitude to you for giving me a glimpse into what my mom's world is and will become . . . thank you!

—joyceseckendorfyahoocom   May 27, 2009

Joe, I just read your comment from May 22, 2009 and was in tears. I am grateful to you for your blog—it is a great inspiration to me to live every day of my life to the fullest! I pray for you and your family and hope you don't mind that I do. I saw you on the HBO special. I watched it because my 88 year-old mom has started exhibiting signs of this disease. God bless you and yours, Joyce Seckendorf-Falstrom Park Forest, Illinois

—CynCity   June 02, 2009

Hang in there Joe. Your blogger family is with you. My dad often doesn't know what day it is or what time of day it is for that matter. I think he takes comfort in the fact that I will always be there to remind him. Just as we are here in spirit with you.

God Bless!

We Will Always Remember!!!!!!!!
Monday, May 25, 2009

Lest we forget why we are FREE!!!!! To OUR TROOPS and FALLEN COMRADES, I Salute You.

God Bless You All & God Bless Our Country!!!

Joe

Posted by Joseph Potocny at 01:34PM (-07:00)

Comments

—TerryGold   May 25, 2009

Hi Joe,

I just discovered your blog today and wanted to say hi, and that I hope you had a good day today. I'm a techie myself, and a blogger too. Thank you for putting your thoughts out there—I just wanted you to know there is a guy in Boulder, Colorado who appreciaties your writing and wishes you the best.

Take care,

Terry

—Misty   May 27, 2009

i saw you on the HBO special and knew that I had to check out your blog! your story was so touching and you made me laugh and cry. i have enjoyed reading through your blog. thank you so much for sharing your story!

misty in Colorado

—AleceK   May 27, 2009

Dear Joe,

My name is Alece and I am an occupational therapy student in Seattle. I just watched The Memory Loss Tapes online—thank you for sharing your story. I am now enjoying your blog and will continue to check back for updates.

~Alece

—Laur   June 01, 2009

Hello my name is Laur, from Ohio

I watched your story on HBO and I had to find you because something about you made me think of how this terrible disease can take away even the most intelligent people and I am talking about you Joe Potocny and his beautiful wife and family. My heart goes out to you for ever . . . and i plan to keep checking to see what happens to you and I am sometimes so angry on if they can send a man to the moon why can't they fix these terrible diseases like this one especially? This must be a very scary time in your life . . . but please do not give up. If i were you I would fight to the end and ask questions and why so many people have this and what is the cause? and for research to get off their butts and do something fast!!! This could happen to anyone . . . including me . . . and I've looked at your blog and it just blows my mind to hear that you have this disease. I will check back . . . and i will pray to god for you Joe and your family. You have a great sense of humor . . . You showed it on your documentary on HBO . . . that's what made me try to find your blog and write to say . . . you have some friends over here on the other side of the map and you need to keep exercising your mind to keep blogging!!!!! Don't give up!! have at least 5 cups of strong coffee!! every day . . . We love you Joe!!! email me if you want. I'd love to hear from what has been happening. laur98@yahoo.com

My View On The World Today.

Monday, June 01, 2009

Nothing Else Be Said! Posted by Joseph Potocny at 11:49AM (-07:00)

Comments

—laur   June 01, 2009

well let's put it this way Joe . . . Do monkeys have this? . . . at least you have a great personality that keeps not even me laughing . . . but others I'm sure that reads your blog page here . . . Did you have that cup of coffee yet?

—colleenmc   June 10, 2009

if it's any help, you made me chuckle, and I thank you for that, hope your day turns around

—LovingGrand   June 19, 2009

You're right—nothing else be said.

♥ ♥ ♥

Through The Fog Comes Anger.

Thursday, June 04, 2009

I have beeen reaing some of the blogs I follow this morning, which I can do from inside my blog. I get disturbed easily, especially by those in the "Medical Practice" and what they try to push. These are the very people (not necessarily the ones I read) that have told somany that live with me in theis World of Mine, that we were ok, just anxious, depressed and absent minded. See we did not fit in their fuckin little box, we did not adhere to pages 89-101 so we could not have any form of dementia. Now some of them have joined us in this world of ours and are bitching that people say they cann't have it because, THE BOX, is square not distorted. Mean this may sound but, you diserve to

hear that crap your profession spit out at me and thousands like me. I make no appologies for letting you know how I feel, you see my life is worth just as muchas yours and I am loosing it more and more each day. It is harder for me to talk, walk and maintain train of thought in a conversation. I even forget who the people are around me more now. Probably by this time next year, if I am still around, my body will be here, but I will not. Alhziemers is doing its job on me and having a good time at it. I saw a youtube asking fatso Oprah to help. This woman is only interested in her money and famous friends that may have this disease or know someone that does, than she does a show on it. It just discusts me to beg such people. It is us who do these blogs and what HBO did for us that is going to make the difference. Yeah the baby boomers are getting worried, WHY?, because a whole hell of alot of them are starting and will joine us here in the World of Forgetfullness. Where we these people when we cried out for help, toooo busy to hear us. Wait till you look at your wife or children and have no idea why these people are in your house and what the hell do they want. Then the old mind comes back and you know you left, you want terror there it is. Come walk with me in my World and see how brown the grass is.

God Bless You & This Country of Ours!!!

joe

Posted by Joseph Potocny at 10:55AM (-07:00)

Comments

—CynCity   June 05, 2009

You are a quite eliquent writer Joe. Know that anger is passion and passion is the driving life force in us all.

God Bless

—Anonymous   June 05, 2009

Sometimes the truth is not pretty and neither is this disease and what it is doing to you and my mom. Thank you SO much for sharing all of your thoughts about it and your walk. May God's peace and blessings surround you and your family.

—ColourBeauty   June 09, 2009

Thank you for sharing your experience with Alzheimer's on your blog and the HBO series. My mother, a former journalist, has AD but she no longer sends me emails or writes me letters. She has no insight into her disease.

God bless.

—tksinclair   June 17, 2009

Reminds me of the first self help book I can remember seeing . . . "I'm Okay, You're Okay" Well, you know what? We're not all "okay" you medical SOB's. Medical "Practice" is just as it sounds . . . practice.

BTW, I hope you never make apologies for telling we minions here how you feel. That's why I come here. To get the "real" answers from your experience not some gobblely gook a professional is spouting from a journal they read. This is the real deal and I hope that never changes. It may not be pleasant to read or hear all the time but it's real and from what I've learned about you in the short time I've been reading here Joe is you'll tell it like it is, the good, the bad and the very very ugly.

God Bless you right back Joe,

Terri, from Oceanside

I Am Back, Ready or Not.

Thursday, June 18, 2009

You know, no you don't, but this damn disease is a real bitch at times. I find myself having to seperate and kind of hide to keep from lashing out. We have had our one daughter and grand kids and son in law with us almost 3 weeks I think, am not handlin this well. I love them, but.

My wife and I are starting to lock horns more, she thought my last post was rather mean and spiteful, I think that is how she put it. My reply was, well you guessed it eat shit and bark at the moon. I write what I feel and how I see it. It may be clouded it maybe one sided, but it is all I know. I make no excuses for what and how I put it. Those that live in this World with me, they know, they understand and hopefully I say what they cannot at least for now, while I am able to. Yes I am angry as I write this today, better to put it here than where else I might.

Ino We that live with AD, really find ourselves fucked up alot of the time, understanding the real confusion and loss we feel is difficult I know for those on the outside looking in. See we can not get back to the outside to look in, we are stuck here and sinking deeper. Try to imagine the darkness starting to encase you slowly and you cannot stop it and you want out and NO not for you. What is that old saying when Casey at The Bat struck out, there is no joy in mudville.

Well enough from me. You all have a great day and wonderful life. God know the idiots in Washington won't fix it, but only screw us more. joe

God Bless You & This Country of Ours!

Posted by Joseph Potocny at 07:37AM (-07:00)

Comments

—colleenmc   June 18, 2009

God bless you too, Joe.

—kenju   June 18, 2009

You are entitled to be mean, Joe. I think I would be too. You need a place to put that anger, and where better than a blog?

—CynCity   June 19, 2009

I'm sorry you and your wife are locking horns. This cannot be easy for her either and I'm sure she has her own anger and pain to deal with. On some level I think she understands where you are coming from and there is lttle she can do.

That being said . . . please do not censor yourself or water down your thoughts (not that you would). We followers appreciate the REAL JOE so much. It may not always be easy to hear, but your blog is so necissary and important to a lot of us.

God bless you and your family.

—LovingGrand   June 19, 2009

Went to write a comment and Cyn Cyn already wrote my thoughts. Once again someone else beat me to it.

Oh well—I ditto her comments and ask that you not censor anything, the good, the bad, and the really ugly.

♥ ♥ ♥

—Dezi
June 19, 2009

Joe, I have to be honest I fell in love with your disposition towards AD, and I appreciate so much that you made a blog devoted to dealing with it. I originally heard your story from The Alzheimer's Project on HBO, and as soon as you mentioned your blog I got on my laptop to find it. My grandfather was diagnosed with the disease about 5 years ago, I love him dearly but it kills me to see what he goes through. Just know there are people out there to support you Joe. All the best!—Dezi

—tksinclair
June 21, 2009

I can't imagine being in your or your wife's position. And let's face it, I hope I never have to. I have been a part-time caretaker of my grandmother who had AD but that's not even close to what you are both dealing with. I can't bear to imagine the darkness encasing me. It's both terrifying and horrifying. Sometimes anger is the only choice a person has when the darkness closes in. At least with anger you feel like you have some control.

BTW, we've been supporting nine people for over a year now due to unemployment and while I deal with it better than my husband it's a challenge at best. I can only guess that with AD the extra confusion, noise—brought on by a house full of people, just being people—in your house is at times incredibly difficult to handle from everyones position. I would also guess that the frustation of AD doesn't allow for any extra patience it may take to deal with the "normal" absurdities of life and a house filled with people.

There's no sense keeping a blog if you're not going to be, at least at times, brutally honest. I find I write when I know what I have to say (yell or scream) would most likely knock the other person out of their shoes!

—Anonymous
June 23, 2009

There is nothing easy or helpful I or anyone can say from the outside world, Joe. I am moved to tears, and sometimes a smile sharing your journey with you via this blog. Do what you have to do to do, Joe. If your blogs bother your wife (which may be understandable) perhaps she needs to take a break from reading them. Or you can warn her you are having a bad day and she may not like to read it. Just a thought . . . I am sure it will all work out. For my own selfish interests, I hope you continue to be honest in your blogs. Wishing you Peace and clarity HOLLEY

—Anonymous
June 25, 2009

Joe,

I work in Geriatric Neuropsychology and have been involved in dementia research for several years now. However, seeing the HBO series and your story in particular has given me a new understanding of the personal experience of the disease. I am truly grateful that you were willing to share your story of stuggle and resilience as you battle this condition. I look forward to hearing more from you in the future.

Pat Sleeth B.S.

—Anonymous   July 01, 2009

hey dad, don't worry (and i know you're not) but we were ready to leave too . . . it was a bit overwhelmong for us to be there as well, but thanks for having us. i love you dad.

morgan

From The Clouds Comes The Darkness.

Sunday, June 28, 2009

Some or many of you know I quit drivnig a long time ago, by my choice because of the danger I was, then my drs. told me not too, they were a litttle behind the curve. Well now the check book has a problem, ME. so the wife has to take that ove now. See they call this MCI (mild cognetive impairment), up my ass. Come live in my brain and tell me how mild this bull is. See how you like it when you stand up turn around and do not know where the hell you are or the wall hits your face or your world spins. Get lost in the talk you are havngi. Set and stare at the computer and not know why you are looking at it. MCI explains it all. The Dr. who first coined this phrase had brain cell farts in my book and sure didn't know mild from a hole in the ground. But of course he knows it to be so, he is smart, right.

Well let me go I need to practice for Moderat Cognitive Impairment, so I don't know what the fuck or what the hell I am doing. That should be fun.

All you caregivers remember MCI and see how you think of it. Your thoughts much welcomed. By the way you Drs. and Holistic nits that send me your causes and cures go away, I have checked out studies and they do not work. Some provide a year or so of added time, then the person is right where they should have been, big service you do. Yes, I was told how herpes causes AD and then had an advertisement at the end of the email for vits and herbs to help cure and slow down. I guess I must really come across as a moron and totaly stupid. But this posts are getting harder and I am getting more, well less friendly and tired.

God Bless,

Joe

Posted by Joseph Potocny at 08:42AM (-07:00)

Comments

—colleenmc   June 28, 2009

Dear Joe, You are a very compelling writer. It bums me out that you have to deal with this and all of the frustration. I am really bummed that people would be assaulting you with their causes and 'cures', although they may mean well, I guess. God Bless you, I look forward to reading your next blog. You are a better writer than I am. Colleen

—kenju   June 28, 2009

Joe, I hope you can find some peace.

—Anonymous   July 01, 2009

Joe just wanted to thank you for keeping up the great fight on your blog . . . I look forward to reading your posts even if you are pissed off . . . it's part of your reality and that emotion needs to be shared too! Keep up the faith and the good fight!

—dragyonfly   July 01, 2009

Joe . . . you got a right to be less friendly and tired. You keep holding on. We know you are strong and determined. I'm a nurse and I know what you are talking about with all the conditions reduced to initials. It makes it so impersonal. I also get mad when someone refers to a patient as "room 3".

People think I'm kinda crazy, too because I speak out.

—Danielle   July 20, 2009

My father THE DEMENTIA GUY decided on his own to stop driving. It was good because when I was getting the car ready for sale . . . I saw that he put motor oil in the transmission and coolant . . . I have no idea how that car survived but it did. At the same time I saw a little bit of my father's spirit die because it was one more thing he couldnt do. So we took lots of road trips that I made him decide where we were going and what he wanted to do. I think that helped him feel better for the moment and more like my dad and not my kid in the passenger seat.

Something Different From Me

Wednesday, July 01, 2009

Yes a big HELLO to you all. I wish to thnak all of you who write to me. And those of you whose blogs I have listed although I may not leave comments I do read them in the back office of my blog, where I constantly recieve your updates. This morning is calm for me, feels strange. But it is like the weather wait a minute things will change, so I though I would get this off now. Your sharing of your troubles with your loved ones brings a sense of calmness to me at times. See it is nice to know (unfortunately), that I am not alone out here. I want to say thank you for being there for me, it truly helps. You know you can comment however you chose, good, bad, rotten, ugly, beautiful, your choisce but remember I do not edit comments and they get posted as written. That is how I post and you deserve the same.

God Bless You & This Country of Ours!

Joe

Posted by Joseph Potocny at 09:24AM (-07:00)

Comments

—colleenmc   July 01, 2009

love the picture on the webcamera and loved your message today, we are with you too

—lindsaylovesyou   July 01, 2009

Joe, I found your blog after seeing your special on HBO while writing a report on AD. I was worried after seeing you on the screen, because I liked your spirit and sense of humor. My grandmother is suffering from Alzheimer's and its very hard to see her slip away. Luckily, she still remembers my name—something I'm very thankful for. I'm glad you're still around :) Lindsay

—Adirondackcountrygal   July 01, 2009

I hope you continue to have good days. Linda

p.s my word verification is lessabl but I think you are very able!

—dragyonfly   July 01, 2009

Joe, I love your posts, they are so real. You are an amazing human. Never forget that.

—James   July 02, 2009

Joe—I've been following your blog since seeing the HBO series, and have learned a lot from the twists and turns that you've faced. I'm glad to hear of good days and can only imagine how so many of your days are not good. You are in my prayers and thank you for sharing your journey!

—johnwairephoto   July 02, 2009

hope you have a great holiday weekend joe! . . . and that more days are like this one for you :)

—Anonymous   July 02, 2009

Joe,

Whether you are pissed off or calm, please come to your keyboard as frequently as you are inclined to express yourself. My mom has PPA, FTD and a little AD mixed in. I can only wish she could continue to express herself the way you do. Keep fighting the fight! God Bless and Happy 4th!

Bz

—Anonymous   July 04, 2009

Hi Joe Happy 4th of July! I hope you are surrounded by loved ones today . . . even though they may be pissing you off . . . LOL! I am with my mom today and I'm happy I can be here to try to make her 4th a special day . . . even though she won't remember it tomorrow, it's all about the here and now for her and for me. I hope that you keep up the great blogging I look forward to reading them.

—Annie   July 07, 2009

Joe, I have learned a lot reading your posts. I never realized that there was a physical aspect to AD, as you describe feeling fuzzy and dizzy. Thank you for your insights. I think it helps me be a better caregiver for my Mom.

To All True American's — Happy July 4th.
Saturday, July 04, 2009

TO ALL WHO HAVE FOUGHT AND DIED FOR OUR FREEDOM. THIS IS OUR TRIBUTE TO YOU! THEY WILL CARRY ON FOR YOU AND CONTINUE THE FIGHT REGARDLESS OF THOSE IN WASHINGTON THAT WANT TO SELL US TO ILLEGALS AND CHINA.

Our Country is based on the Christian and Judeo principals, no matter what the "I'm Just A Boy From Kenya" has to say. I am not normally this political on my site, but this man and the present congress are not worthy of the support of REAL AMERICANS.

So let me have it back. Just remember I will forget it and go on with what is left of my life and brain, you will be living in yours. Little AD sarcasim.

I hope YOU ALL have a geart 4th of July and remember why we have our freedoms that others even here what to take away from us.

God Bless You and This Country of Ours!

Joe

Posted by Joseph Potocny at 05:50PM (-07:00)

Comments

—Danielle   July 20, 2009

My father THE DEMENTIA GUY was a Vietnam Vet. I cant wait to get replacement medals and his flag that I ordered from the VA. I just wish I had a photo of him in his uniform. Even though he was bitter about it all I am still proud to say I am the daughter of a Army Vetran who served his country in the Vietnam War

Who & What Am I Becoming?

Thursday, July 09, 2009

There once was a tmie I could answer that but not anylonger. I have for the last several months porued myself into trying to start some things for the family to help make their financial future better. However, I remember the comment I made in the HBO thing, Once I was a genius, now I'm not. How true, it seems that once what I touched I mad work and well, now it goes to hell in a hand basket. My thoughts seem to be of the same charge and push each other out of the way, leaving avoid for confusion. That is the disease at work and having a good time of it. I find myself much more pissy and angry now, but I try to keeep the old trap shut and carry it alone. I am beginning to understand why we in this World of Ours, just sit alot and say nothing or just wander. We no longer have a grasp on things, what is real is it, I don't know any longer. I do not want to say things to family and friends because I don't want the constant hovering or them walikng on eggs. Frankly i do not know what I want, who I really am, where I have been or am going. Things from the past seem to be from yesterday and yesetrday seems to be the past. I feel truly helpless for the first time in my life. Where do we go from here? Down the tunnel.

God Bless, Joe Posted by Joseph Potocny at 09:34AM (-07:00)

Comments

—Lynn   July 09, 2009

Not yet you don't. Love

—rilera   July 09, 2009

Joe, you are allowed to be pissy. This disease sucks. As a family member who watched this happen to my Mom, I can truly say that it was by far the hardest thing that I ever had to do. It hurt so much to watch someone I love suffer. I know that your family and friends feel the same. Hang in there Joe. I'm rooting for you.

—kenju   July 09, 2009

No one blames you for being pissy. You're allowed. But remember that your family members love you and try not to be pissy with them.

—lindsayelyse   July 09, 2009

like Dory from Finding Nemo so famously quoted . . . "just keep swimming . . ."

You're life is giving me hope. AD runs in my family and I'm slowly watching my grandmother leave. I wouldn't want to miss a second of it.

Be good, and take care.

Lindsay

—colleenmc   July 09, 2009

I'm listening and I hope you know that you still write a heck of a lot better than most that I know. I wish I could say something meaningful to you except, God Bless you back Joe.

—Annie   July 10, 2009

Be pissy, but please understand if once in a while your family is pissy back. Cut them some slack too. As hard as we try, us caregivers aren't all happy and light either. It's admirable that you're doing what you can to take care of your family. You're a good man, Joe! Give that lovely wife of yours a hug from me!

—joyceseckendorfyahoocom   July 10, 2009

I am a caregiver also and get pissy—I'm glad you wrote pissy in there; Your blog reads of so many of the things I am experiencing, and, because of your blog, I get to read all the comments we folks post. Joe, you are serving a purpose for me and many others, know that. God bless you, Joyce Seckendorf Park Forest, IL

Yes, it's a bad situation. I hate this disease for you and for every one that has it. I am terrified of getting it. I imagine you daily try to create some order in a situation where there virtually is none. I think you have to, yes, sorry for the dang cliche, "take one day at a time" . . . keep up as many daily routines as possible. Regardless of how small. There's sometimes comfort in those things Joe. Maybe it's a false sense of order but it's something. Unfortunately as you well know entire families suffer from Alzheimers. Try to have as much meaning, compassion and mindfulness as you can (yeah I know, easy for me to say—you'll note I'm saying this from a distance way over here hiding behind a tree where you can't slap me silly).

Joe, many of the things you are and were are still there. Okay, maybe not all of it, I get that. But there are still some challenges you can meet and a warmth of relationships you can enjoy. Are there any daily tasks that are enjoyable? Achievable? Rewarding? I know it's Herculean.

Actually, the truth is, I don't know crap Joe. I have no advice or magic wand. Just a sympathetic heart. I guess you'll have to change your standards—what else can you do?

Melville said, "Life's a voyage that's homeward bound" and you're heading home—as we all are. Sadly your path is taking you down a tunnel. A long dark tunnel. Have you given up on Organizations? Have your family and caretakers exasperated books and agencies to support caregivers? I don't know about these things. Maybe they are useless.

I wish, like I'm sure others who come here do, that I could give you hope or meaning as you live with AD. I've read and heard that many with this disease can still learn things and appreciate things. Again, what do I know? Nothing. It's just what I've heard. Your brain is damaged but it's still there, right? It seems like you're suffering from loneliness, helplessness and boredom . . . these things alone can kill a person and you don't have to have AD to suffer from them.

I don't know crap . . . all I can do is encourage you to live in the moment, something we all should do, and understand that especially through your blog you are a value to society. I think if I were you I'd stick close to plants, animals and children. Or maybe right now you're in a situation where nothing happens spontaneously therefore, BOREDOM. Maybe it's all routine. Meaningless activity will kill you too I guess. If so then you have to figure out something meaningful to do not so easy while living with AD right?

Anway, for someone who doesn't know anything I sure have a lot to say huh? Sorry bout that.

I guess I'm just "typing" out loud . . . sorry . . .

—Anonymous   July 11, 2009

keep hope alive. you are stronger than the disease. WE WILL WIN THE BATTLE

—June   July 12, 2009

Dear Joe, As Glenn Beck says, "You are not alone"! And, fellow Patriot, your brain is working superbly, since you know that the emperor/czar obamination isn't wearing any clothes! Hang in there, Joe! June http://cleaningoutalife.blogspot.com)

—Danielle   July 20, 2009

I am reading this book called "Still Alice" by Lisa Genova. I cant seem to put it down. The character Alice was a top notch Harvard Professor and I see the same comments you make in this character. As my father's caregiver I see inside a little when I read this book and read your blog. Makes me feel that much closer to him even though he is gone now.

THE DEMENTIA GUY's Daughter

OK Let's See If You Use This.

Tuesday, July 14, 2009

After slaving for 1000's of hours and bangnig my head on the wall to clear my ½ brain cell, and much swet, tears and blood and of course countlsse 10000000's of dollars, sound like I am going to make you rich scheme? WRONG!!!!!!!! This is more torturing than that. There is a small blue statement with a red under line on the upper right hand side of the blog it says live chat. Yes click on it and if my beast of humanity is on it will ring and we can chat to one another if you want. If not fine. I will take my milk and oreo's ago elsewhere.

God Bless,

Joe

Posted by Joseph Potocny at 06:14PM (-07:00)

Comments

—johnwairephoto   July 15, 2009

box opened. i typed my name, my number and a message and hit enter. box closed. nothing :)

—Lynn   July 15, 2009

Give him a chance to wake up. He decides to crawl out of bed about 8 and has to feed his bird and fish. talks to them alot. Also this is pacific time. If he is on the computer he will answer your call.

Still Buggy Operator

Wednesday, July 15, 2009

I know you were there john, the operator was just signing on and signed himself right off. Give us a break, not much, just a little. Program works, I just have to get the fingers working right. it showed you at 5:29am where ever that is. it is 8PST am here. God Bless, Joe Posted by Joseph Potocny at 07:57AM (-07:00)

Comments

—johnwairephoto   July 15, 2009

i'll give you a break this 1 time :) i'm on the east coast . . . in baltimore, md.

Friends You Got To Love Them.

Friday, July 17, 2009

This came from a friend of mine, who knows there is not much upstairs anymore and that I love old jokes and humor.

A distraught senior citizen phoned her doctor's office. 'Is it true,' she wanted to know, 'that the medication you prescribed has to be taken for the rest of my life? "Yes, I'm afraid so,' the doctor told her There was a moment of silence before the senior lady replied, 'I'm wondering, then, just how serious is my condition because this prescription is marked 'NO REFILLS'.' *** An older gentleman was on the operating table awaiting surgery and he insisted that his son, a renowned surgeon, perform the operation. As he was about to get the anesthesia, he asked to speak to his son. 'Yes, Dad, what is it?' 'Don't be nervous, son; do your best and just remember, if it doesn't go well, if something happens to me, your mother is going to come and live with you and your wife.'

~~~~~~~~~~~~~~~~~~~

Aging: Eventually you will reach a point when you stop lying about your age and start bragging about it.—The older we get, the fewer things seem worth waiting in line for.—

Some people try to turn back their odometers. Not me!

I want people to know 'why' I look this way. I've traveled a long way and some of the roads weren't paved. ***

When you are dissatisfied and would like to go back to youth, think of Algebra.

~~~~~~~~~~~~~~~~~~~

You know you are getting old when everything either dries up or leaks.—

One of the many things no one tells you about aging is that it is such a nice change from being young.

<><><><><><><><><>

Ah, being young is beautiful, but being old is comfortable.

<><><><><><><><><>

First you forget names, then you forget faces. Then you forget to pull up your zipper. It's worse when you forget to pull it down.—Long ago when men cursed and beat the ground with sticks, it was called witchcraft . . . Today, it's called golf.

~~~~~~~~~~~~~~~~~~~~

Two old guys are pushing their carts around Wal-Mart when they collide. The first old guy says to the second guy, 'Sorry about that. I'm looking for my wife, and I guess I wasn't paying attention to where I was going.' The second old guy says, 'That's OK, it's a coincidence. I'm looking for my wife, too. I can't find her and I'm getting a little desperate.' The first old guy says, 'Well, maybe I can help you find her. What does she look like?' The second old guy says, 'Well, she is 27 yrs old, tall, with red hair, blue eyes, long legs, and is wearing short shorts. What does your wife look like?' To which the first old guy says, 'Doesn't matter, let's look for yours.'

*   *   *

Lord, Keep Your arm around my shoulder, and Your hand over my mouth! Posted by Joseph Potocny at 08:21AM (-07:00)

Comments

—WLataneBarton   July 19, 2009

glad to have found your blog. It, it am sure, will give me a new prospective on the male side of Alzheimers. My husband has had this awful disease for 9 years.

—Anonymous   July 20, 2009

These are great. The first one made me laugh out loud!

How Chat Works

Tuesday, July 21, 2009

When you come to site you can click on the blue Live Chat and we can talk. Aslo if you do not the system notifies me that someone is on my blog and I can invite you. What happens is this beautiful young lady in a box (my alter ego) comes across the screen says her name is Jane and Hello and asks if you need help. Actually that is me inviting you to talk. Just click start chat or no thanks. Sorry if the hi tech scares you, but I am having fun with it, of course the folks in Israel you created this program meant it for companies and they have spent hours explaining things to me. This am I am ok, will see what the rest of the day holds. Be Good. You never know when you may here my voice when you come to the site.

God Bless You & This Country of Ours!

Joe

Posted by Joseph Potocny at 10:07AM (-07:00)

Good Morning

Thursday, July 23, 2009

Wanted to say thanks to those of you taht have used the chat link, it has been fun for me. I think when i request it and the icon goes acros the screeen it scares people out, because they leave. I must admit it has woren me out. I am talking with some folks I hope to put a full time live chat room on. My hope is that it will give those who come to might site a chance to exchange ideas of this disease. Mabee it will help some of you caregivers to have others to talk to and help release some of your frustrations. Hell I know we with the disease are a handful. I find as it is progressing that I am less talkative to others, cut them off or just go to my own world and leave them out.

Physically it is getting more demanding as well, was not prepared for this part and it pisses the hell out of me. I get to ill easily, to faint and way to exhausted. Shopping is not something I tolerate well at all anymore. But there are those that are worse off than I, but I am sure I will goin them soon, the way things are progressing. Even these entries tire me out, takes to much concentration that is getting harder to hold onto.

Well enough pitty potty. You all have a great and wonderful day.

God Bless You & This Country of Ours (we need it now)!

Joe

Posted by Joseph Potocny at 08:40AM (-07:00)

Comments

—Anonymous   July 23, 2009

Good morning Joe, hope you have a great day too! Thanks for keeping up the hard work . . . you are a blessing in my life!

—tksinclair   July 26, 2009

Hi Joe,

Just checking in to see what you're up to. I'm heading to Boston tomorrow for a week I'm not too happy about it but I'm visiting a friend. Hopefully when I return I'll try to figure out this chat thing sometime.

Do your best to continue the fight. I'm reading "Measure of the Heart" A Father's Alzheimer's, A Daughter's Return by Mary Ellen Geist. It's insightful, powerful but painful to read. Still I recommend it to those caregivers. My "patient" has passed but I wish I'd read this prior to her illness getting Herculean.

Another book although a novel, not a memoir, is Still Alice by Lisa Genova. It won the 2008 Bronte Prize and I think is a pretty decent portrayal of one woman's Alzheimer's journey.

Maybe it will be helpful to some other caregivers. It was recommended by Charley Schneider who wrote "Don't Bury me, It Ain't Over Yet" . . . which for some reason the title reminds me of you.

So for today that's my message to you Joe . . . I know you get tired. I know it's hard to fight but remember, at least for today, it ain't over yet! Check in next week. God bless you Joe.

—CynCity   July 27, 2009

I know its getting harder for you Joe. I just wanted to say how much I appreciate your effort and everything you are doing for the cause. We caregivers look up to you a lot! Keep fighting the good fight!

—Annie   July 27, 2009

In case you don't realize, the book mentioned above Measure of the Heart, is Woody's

story, who was also in the documentary.

GOOD MORNING WORLD!

Tuesday, July 28, 2009

hope you are all fine. Chat seems to be working out ok. Have gotten to talk with some nice people. One in particular a 21 yr old woman in Boston, who at her age has taken on the daunting task of working in an Assisted Living Facility and going to host an Alhziemer's Proget meeting. I know what it takes to work in such a facility, you see that is where my mind was made up at an early age, while I handle the computer systems for 3 facilities, never would I live the way I saw. My heart broke working there.

I have gotten a few that well shall we say have not been really forward, challenge them and they disappear, oh well.

I have been told to write a bok about this journey and I hae tried but you know I thought about it and said yes good ideaa. But then I started to think, something ya thnik. I am writing a book here, completely unedited. Certainly not proof read and things but neatly. But this is a living book ever changing, always wanted to write one andnow my brain realizes after how many years at this, that I am.

A little slower on the uptake these days. Well now, I lost my train and my thoughts, fuck I hate this shit. Catch Ya Latter.

God Bless You & This Country of Ours!

Joe

Posted by Joseph Potocny at 09:49AM (-07:00)

New Chat Room

Friday, July 31, 2009

Hopefully you will note the new chatroom feature. You click wait for the chat request to appear, you put in your name or alias short discription and click chat. The room has room for more that one person. So I may or not may enter the chat. Please feel free to be open about why you are there. GIVE PEOPLE A CHANCE TO ANSWER. Try hard as it may or will be not to talk oevr one anotehr. I can it is my chat room. The LIVE CHAT will probably leave as this only alllowed one to talk to me at a time. I hope caregivers that are on at the same time as us looney tunes will enter and share. I am trying to make this site yours as well as mine, hopefullly we can all learn from each other.

God Bless You & This Country of Ours!

joe

Posted by Joseph Potocny at 01:31PM (-07:00)

Comments

—DavidSchantz   August 01, 2009

Joe,

I need to check out what the Java plugin would do to this old computer before I can enter your chat room. When I was looking to see if anyone had set up a blog site on Alzheimer's yours was the first I found. It looks interesting, so I will return. Four months ago we found out my Wife has Alzheimer's. This will be the second time I lived in the home with an Alzheimer's victim. I've set up a new site to tell about the effects the disease is having on us, Alzheimer's In The House. I hope you'll stop by to visit us.

God Bless America, God Save The Republic.

As The Weeks Go By

Sunday, August 02, 2009

The last few weeks I have beeen working with others to bring more excitement to my blog things I havve added, I once could have done in minutes by myself, they have taken days with help. Things are not well in my head nor do they seeem to be inside either. My shrink has suggested I go back to my physco. guy and my physician for some help. But I am a stubborn bastard and well you can guess the rest.

If I can remember why i have the note on my computer that says "BLOG" maybe I will post more often, even when I have nothing to say, which is gettting to be most of the time now.

God Bless You and This Country of Ours!

Joe

PS No brains, if David S. would send me the linke to his blog, use the email form near botton I would be glad to read & comment and tie to my blog.

Posted by Joseph Potocny at 05:01PM (-07:00)

Comments

—Anonymous   August 04, 2009

Good morning Joe! I'm left sometimes with no words after reading you blog . . . just all sorts of feelings and I think that it is a miracle that in this day of where everyone is trying to numb our feelings or avoid them . . . that you "in the face" blog can make me feel . . . I feel for you and your family and I also feel for me and my mom who has some sort of memory affliction . . . it sucks! It's plain and simple english for me too . . . she's been robbed and so have I so has her other kids and grand kids!!!! Hang in there and I look forward to reading every word you are brave enough to write down . . . bring it on! BTW . . . just a bit angry today in my tone . . . sorry for that. Signed, one worn out caregiver

—Anonymous   August 04, 2009

Hello Joe, even though you have no idea who i am I'd like to thank you for helping me to deal better with my grandma's disease. She is pretty well for someone who's been living with it for almost 10 years and who is almost 80 years old!! I've just watched the HBO project and that's where I found out about your blog. I guess i just felt like i had to really thank you for opening my eyes and I´m pretty sure your posts will always have sth to say!! PS: just so you know you just helped sb who doesn´t even live in your country so thank you so much!!

—Danielle   August 08, 2009

Hey Joe, Thanks for the times you do remember to blog . . . I like checking in and seeing how you are doing.

For You Caregivers

Sunday, August 09, 2009

How I got this is beyond me but it may help some of you. You wil nk I did not write thsi spellings is to good. Hope it helps.

Welcome to the Combination Care for Alzheimer's program

As a caregiver for someone who is living with Alzheimer's disease, your role is to make sure your loved one is getting the most effective treatment possible. This means using a combination of approaches—medication combined with other activities can help expand what you're already doing. By enrolling in this program you'll have access to information and resources that can help you learn more about the disease and treatments you may not have considered, such as combination therapy. (Combination therapy is when two Alzheimer's disease medications are used together to increase the benefits of treatment).

Based on what you told us when you enrolled, we have created a personalized Doctor Discussion Guide just for you. This guide offers important tips that can help you work with the doctor and talk openly about your loved one's condition and treatment plan. It also offers a series of questions that may help you have an informed conversation about how you can continue to enhance your loved one's care. As time with the doctor can be limited, the personalized Doctor Discussion Guide can help you maximize your office visits.

Please PRINT this Doctor Discussion Guide now, review it, and make note of any topics you'd like to discuss at your next doctor's appointment. Beyond this, you will also receive a series of personalized emails over the next two months, providing you with educational and supportive information on how you can enhance your loved one's care. They will also help you learn about ways you can look after yourself as you continue managing your loved one's disease.

Doctor Discussion Guide:

Your Role as a Caregiver Is Essential. As you continue to care for someone living with Alzheimer's disease, it's important that you work as a partner with the doctor. Your doctor relies on you to communicate openly about how your loved one is doing and how treatment is working. The more information you can provide the more you'll be able to help your loved one get treatment that will make life more manageable for both of you.

One treatment option that you and your doctor may want to consider is combination therapy. In the treatment of moderate to severe Alzheimer's disease, doctors may prescribe a combination of medications, Namenda® (memantine HCl)* and Aricept® (donepezil)**, when they believe it will be more effective than a single Alzheimer's medicine alone. Use the following tips and questions to have an informed discussion about whether combination therapy may be the right option for the person you care about.

Questions to Ask the Doctor: When it comes to treatment:

1. What additional treatment options are available for Alzheimer's disease?
2. Based on the treatments we've tried before, is there anything more we can be doing?
3. I understand there is an option called "combination therapy." Can you tell me about it?
4. What are the benefits of combination therapy?

When it comes to daily living:

1. In addition to medication, are there any lifestyle changes that you would recommend?
2. What type of mental activities will help my loved one?
3. What type of physical activities will help my loved one?
4. Can you tell me what types of support services in my area are available to us, such as in-home assistance, adult day care, assisted living facilities, etc.?
5. Can you recommend a support group in my area for caregivers like me? Tips for Partnering with Your Doctor

Keep track of changes in your loved one's behavior—It may seem obvious and you may have been doing it for a while, but it's very useful for you to track and tell your doctor about any changes in your loved one's behavior and symptoms such as increased difficulty in performing everyday tasks, agitation, or even increased deficits in intellect and reasoning. Ask family members or friends if they notice any changes that you may miss. And, if you aren't already, consider keeping a journal or diary to note any changes in behavior, so you can share this information with the doctor. You can also write notes on this Doctor Discussion Guide and take it with you to your next appointment.

Prepare for doctor visits ahead of time—Taking the time to write down any questions or concerns you have can help make your office visits more productive. You may also want to bring articles or online resources that you have found with you to the appointments. This way the doctor is aware of what you're learning and where you are finding additional information.

Listen carefully to the doctor and take notes—To be sure that you clearly understand everything the doctor tells you and that you remember it once you leave the appointment, it's helpful to take notes. You can take notes on this Doctor Discussion Guide. You may alsowant to consider using a tape recorder or bringing a friend or family member with you.

Think about yourself too—It may be difficult to consider yourself when so much of your energy is spent caring for someone else, but by staying healthy you're better able to provide the care your loved one needs. Don't hesitate to ask your doctor what you can be doing to take care of yourself so you stay strong too.

Notes: *Namenda is indicated for the treatment of moderate to severe Alzheimer's disease. Namenda® (memantine HCl) is a registered trademark of Forest Laboratories, Inc. **Aricept® (donepezil HCl tablets) is a registered trademark of Eisai Co., Ltd. and Pfizer Inc. © 2008 Forest Laboratories, Inc. Welcome to the Combination Care for Alzheimer's program

God Bless You & This Country of Ours!

Joe

Posted by Joseph Potocny at 08:54AM (-07:00)

Comments

—Anonymous   August 09, 2009

Dear Joe, Your postings are read with much interest and appreciated greatly. Thank you for sharing your thoughts and feelings. Despite your struggles, your sense of humour comes through in your writing. Please know that your efforts are very much admired and that you are thought about each day by many people. Thank you!

—OscarScheepstra   August 11, 2009

Hey Joe!

I just saw you on tv on HBO. It was quite nice to meet you—even if it lasted for a few minutes. I must be thankful for you—as I am always surrounded by technology. So I think I must say thank you :). I like the way you see your condition and your sense of humor. Keep on being that nice person you are, mate. Hope one day we can meet.

Kindest (technological) regards,

Oscar Scheepstra

—AngelaScheepstra   August 11, 2009

Hi, Joe, I am Angela from Brazil, 55, married with a Dutch man. I have just watched the documentary on HBO about Alzheimer. I was really tauched by it. My mother-in-law, 96, —Alzheimer's patient—live with us, hier in Brazil for 10 years and the documentary was very familiar to me. I whish you and yorur wife the best. I loved your sense of humor. Like we say here in BrazilUm grande abraço

A Special Request.

Friday, August 14, 2009

I would like to add a slide show to the side of my blog. I want to make this a memorial to those who have passed from this disease. So I am asking you to email me a picture of a friend or loved one with their name and birth and deceased years so I can make the slide show. I would like to honor those that have gone before me and paid the final price of this disease. Maybe their faces will prompt those who visit this blog to take some type of action or get involved some way to get those needed to help out (government????). I hope this is not offensive to anyone, if it is well then.

Thank you in advance. jolynn1@cox.net is the email to send to.

God Bless You & This Country of Ours!

Joe

Posted by Joseph Potocny at 01:16PM (-07:00)

Comments

—lucianokf333   August 14, 2009

Joe,

You are amazing !!!that's what I can about you. To the ones that felt themselves offended . . . go visit the Disney World's website !!! Wake up Alices!!!You are not in wonderland!!! Life is not easy, it sucks sometimes and we have face the truth . . . We are proud of you and love you Joe.

—dragyonfly   August 18, 2009

Joe, I love that picture of you with the tigerface . . . as for your idea for the slideshow, I say go for it.

—Danielle-daughteroftheDe   August 24, 2009

Great idea. I sent mine. Hope you got them. Hope all is well. Happy Monday

Time Marches On

Thursday, August 20, 2009

My wife and I were discusing what cognaitve and occupational skills meant. Because they confuse me. Of course cognaitve is thinking, record keeping, more complex problem solving, well forget hat one. Occupational are those things such as typing, cooking, walking and general doing things. Well we looose on that score to. At least I still can brush my teeeth without putting the brush up my nose. That is it for today, whatelse is there.

God Bless You and This Country of Ours!

Joe

Posted by Joseph Potocny at 06:57PM (-07:00)

Comments

—colleenmc   August 21, 2009

I love the talking host with instructions on chat etc . . . this is great, I hope you're well and God Bless you and yours too!

—Mary   August 25, 2009

hi, i saw u on HBO's program . . . i like what to do on internet with the blog . . . great idea . . .!!! i'm to Guatemala City, America Central, God Bless you.

Marisol

—keek   August 25, 2009

Hi Joe, I just saw "The Alzheimers Project" this evening. You are still an insightful and brilliant gentleman. Thank you for sharing your life and experience with all of us. Don't give up the blogging, your blog is one of the few worth reading.

—HugoEscudero   August 26, 2009

Good Morning Joe,

Hope you had a good night. I also saw you on TV. My father started its Alzheimer at the age of 54, aprox. 1984. I very much appreciated your comments on TV and in this web. Best wishes to you and your family. Hugo

Hi! I'm from Brazil, I saw you in a documentary of Alzheimer on HBO. My grandma has Alzheimer, and I really wanna help her. I'm only sixteen yet, but I'm studying Alzheimer for a couple years . . . She's forgeting a lot of things now, sometimes she even doesn't know who I am . . . It's difficult, but I understand. Well, I thought your great idea about your blog . . . It's good to help other people that live the same life as you live . . . I'm sending you a big hug!

Pushy Friends!

Tuesday, September 01, 2009

I am glad I have some, they help remind me of what my postit notes seem to fail to do. I have not written in while. I have been elsewhere lately, not ecxalty sure where, but I have been there. Getting more tests, health is well not what is used to be. Age this disease, rotten lyfestyle when I was youndger who knows, I do not. What is starting to show more offten then not, is I have no idea what day it is and yesterday seems not to have happened. Hard to explain. But there is no longer any time frame in my brain to connnect things to, so they all seem recent and mixed up. True moments of knowing exactly what I am thinking or doing are growing fewer by the day. This is not a lot of fun and am starting to looose my humor about it. But I am getting to meet someone new each day in the mirror, so I guess that is ok.

God Bless You and This Country of Ours!

Joe

Posted by Joseph Potocny at 10:37AM (-07:00)

Comments

Hi Joe, I always look forward to your posts. I wish you the best day possible, as always. God bless you!

Hi joe, I watched the hbo special you were on today in my nursing school class. And I just wanted to say thank you for sharing your story to us. It truly taught us to understand Alzheimers, and how it effects everyone around you. thanks again.

Lisa m.

—newlyweds September 03, 2009

Hi Joe, so glad you posted, still see that witty humor! Your so right everyone needs some pushy friends. Keep in the light!

—Brangane September 04, 2009

Hi Joe. I am so glad you posted. Thanks for continuing your blog.

God bless.

—alzheimersandmomblog September 08, 2009

great post. You make my day. Good luck and God Bless.

—Anonymous September 15, 2009

Hi Joe thank you so much for continuing to post, I will continue to read them as long as you put them out there. My mom was finally taken to her heavenly home, and so my duties as caregiver have ended, for now. Who know's who might need me next!

What is a Friend?

Tuesday, September 08, 2009

I have become very confused oevr this. It seems that what I think (have to be easy there) and others is different. Maybe because it is more difficult to talkto me and keep things on track and the fact that I get angry easier has changed things betweeen me and others. I always thought and still do that you are honest totally with a friend and not afraid to be calllled on your BS and not afraid to call them on it. That seems to be a problem in theis world today. It is costing me friends. Even trying to explain things to them doe snot work. I guess this is going to be a new part of my life that I am going to have as this keeps getting harder.

I am still waiting for pics and info to start the memorial post for those that have proceeded me and are now at rest. I think they are the faces of this disease. Their fight was bvaliant and brave, they fought and tried against a foe that is not beatable at this time. They are my heroes for hanging in ass long as they could. They helpeed to pave the road I have to travel and I thank them for making it a little easier for me. The millions that suffer now and to come are my family now.

This is my story on this blog, but I want it to be a home for you as well. That is why things haveeeve ben changing and will continue to do so. Those of you that take care of us extreemely unpredictable persons, need an outlet and I am going to try and succeed with you help making this blog one outlet for you. It maybe moving to more of a website and changing the address, so that it can be more interactive for you who take the time to read my ramblings and need to converse with otherers in your position.

I have to stop now, my brain is not holding thoughts rifht now.

God Bless You and This Country of Ours!

Joe

Posted by Joseph Potocny at 02:14PM (-07:00)

Comments

—Anonymous	September 08, 2009

Dear Joe, you are not alone in sometimes receiving a negative reaction from friends when you try to be honest. It can help if you first tell them you care about them and don't intend to hurt their feelings—and that sometimes it is just hard to find the right words to say. Friendships are special and it sounds like you understand that and value your friends. Hang in there with those friends!

—dragyonfly	September 08, 2009

Hi joe, I love that photo of you painted up like a tiger . . . As for the friend thing, I would imagine people don't want to engage you because you have nothing to lose by stating the obvious. You are more aware of your mortality, and are light years away from those who are not as aware. It puts you in a special category, I believe.

That, at least, is my philosophy. You may call it bullshit if you like . . . LOL . . . I mentioned you in my blog, by the way, because I really like what you say and represent. You are very brave. Peace . . . Deb

—alzheimersandmomblog	September 09, 2009

I like your post and I bet your friends will forget what they got mad at you for saying. Keep it up it makes things interesting.

—lucianokf333	September 13, 2009

Hi Joe, the ones that are really friends will always understand what you've been thru.Just like us, lots of people that have read your blog had never met you before and I am sure that for most of us you are a hero in so many ways, not just because of that stupid Alzheimer thing but how brave you are, I know there are so many people that got inspired by reading your blog, people like me. Although we are miles away from you, know that we will never leave you. God bless you and all your family, you are special.

Your friends from Brazil, Luciano and Lumy

—June   September 14, 2009

Dear Joe, "Be Who You Are and Say What You Feel Because Those Who Mind Don't Matter and Those Who Matter Don't Mind." (quoting Dr.Seuss0.

An Email Identity Secret

Wednesday, September 16, 2009

Message = Hello I work at a local Alzheimer Society . . . My co-workers and I have been watching the HBO series over our lunch hour. I wanted to stop by and visit your blog.

Thank you for having the courage to share your story so publically. You have made such a huge difference for other people with ADRD because you have put a face behind this disease. Your story is particularly important because it shows that anyone can get Alzheimer's disease . . . even someone as accomplished as you.

Not everyone is interested in being the "poster child" for Alzheimer's disease (for lack of a better phrase). It is such a personal journey. Thank you for the courage and commitment to do this.

Our chapter is marking it's . . . Anniversary this year. In fact we are having a . . . on . . . with over 150 people attending it (i.e., to honour the occasion). There are so many people who have touched the chapter . . . be it person's with Dementia, their family, volunteers and staff.

There are so many people who are working towards improving the quality of life all of those affected by Alzheimer's disease. I know that each of them would send you and your family their well-wishes.

I have worked at the chapter for about half that time. During that time, there have been incredible strides in research and public awareness about Alzheimer's disease. It is encouraging to see this but we all know that there is so much more that needs to be done. Your story will bring much needed awareness to this disease and will help to move things one step further in search of a cure.

Anyway, I just wanted to say hello and THANK YOU!

Sending you and your family warm thoughts . . .

I have removeed info that would id this person to keep them anoynomous. I am using this email because I have received countless numebers that call me the face of alhzeimers and the voice. I am neither. Just a person with this fricken disease who wants to share our side of the story with you.

I have asked all of you for pics and dates of you loved ones that passted from this disease, as all of us with it do. I received one. So I will be posting it. You see those before me are the face and voice of this disease and should be remmembered and I want this blog to pay tribute to their fight for life. I get tired of hearing about all the big people who have survived this and that, big fuckin deal. We all die period. I am tired of all the crap about cures and how to stop this disease, well prove it to me with a survivor of it. No matter the advancements the real cause and any real treatment exscapes the med prof., maybe someday, I wonder.

I hope Bill's daughter does not take offense at the pic that I have because hers did not come through so I took one from his site. To me it shows the real heart of the man and how he felt about this disease and inate love of life.

God Bless You & This Country of Ours!!!!!!!

Joe

PS: I received a very sad email of the passing of one in my World, but it is sad for the daughter, for mom she is free now. The whole left of years of caregiving will be difficult I believe at best to deal with. To you my love and prayers. Posted by Joseph Potocny at 08:31AM (-07:00)

Comments

—karen   September 16, 2009

You are one of the many faces of this nasty disease.And may I say a very nice face. Keep happy thoughts. And I am sorry for the passing of one the other faces of alz. God bless her daughter has she rebuilds her life. http://alzheimersandmomblog.blogspot.com/

—Danielle   September 26, 2009

I opened up your site today . . . I see my father sticking his tounge out. It was one of the ones I sent. I have such a difficutly with hotmail. Sorry I didnt get you the pictures. I was going to let you choose anyhow . . . PERFECT CHOICE.

This was in the elevator at his Dr's office and he was being playful. I have a couple of him with his tounge out. It was our thing.

I put on a BIG party last weekend for the Nor Cal Alz Assoc and it was a success. I thought of you because I did it for my father and for all the other Dad's. I hope to work with the next generation (under 30 year olds)and get them to open their eyes . . . and hearts. My Memory Walk is next week and as the Team Captain of Team Bird House . . . we walk in your honor as well.

Thanks Joe!!!!

Danielle

Daughter of Alz

195

Alhzeimer's & Marriage

Tuesday, September 22, 2009

I received a comment from a gentleman whose wife has early stage AD. It seems this has affected his marriage quite a bit. Trust me that is an understatement, it has litterally screwed mine up. I have asked my wife to post her side on the blog, but she is reluctant for whatever reasons.

I know that she has one heck of a time with me, I am extremely moody at times, I get lost in conversations and I go off elsewhere in my mind on a dime. The other day we were talking and as usually Mr. Brilliant here got lost and could not even get a word out, the wife answered for me and was right. Her words to me were "Aren't you glad I know you?" my reply was yes someone has to because I do not know me anymore. This is starting to get scarey now. I have been going to post for the last couple of days, just does not happen. It certainly has messed up our sex life, I cannot even keep things going, because my mind suddenly goes off to War, or the Circus or some such fuckin thing and I am no longer involved in the situation or I just plain fall asleep.

I cannot even imagine how my commentor or my wife feel. I am not even sure how I feel at any given moment. At times I am on my game and then there is no game I have lost my processes and cannot get back. Yes I can write because I can stop and come back and start over, but in my real world it just does not work that way.

To my friend I am truly sorry for your situation, I will not say Hey it is ok it will be fine, because the truth is it will not get better only worse. I do hope the Lord continures to give you the strength you need for each day, we are a hand full.

God Bless You & This Country of Ours!

Joe

Posted by Joseph Potocny at 01:50PM (-07:00)

Comments

—karen   September 23, 2009

I am so sorry. Your wife must be a wonderful to put up with you.LOL! I know it is no laughing matter. God Bless you both.

http://alzheimersandmomblog.blogspot.com/

—QuLocura   September 23, 2009

Hey, I'm just 16 years old and I'm from Colombia. Two nights ago, I watched HBO Documentary: "The Alzheimer's Project" and I didn't know how hard is live with this disease, and I want you to know that maybe I don't know you and you don't know me, but here in my country, in Colombia, someone know that you're trying to fight against alzheimer's. Next year i'll go to college and I'm gonna be a doctor, I promise that i will do anything to help people with alzheimer's. Cuz I watched you talking about your life, a great life, you made great things . . . maybe in future you will forget all you did, but people wont do it.

My name is Jessie and now, you have a friend on colombia. I'll think of you and I'll think of your family.

Live, Love, Laugh.

—JUSTAMOM   September 23, 2009

good to see ya hangin,

—Annie   September 25, 2009

As hard as it is dealing with AD in a parent, I cannot imagine the difficulty of doing it with a spouse. Hugs to you and Lynn.

—colleenmc   September 26, 2009

Hi Joe, Yours is one of the first blogspots I check daily and I'm always happy to read a new post. The picture of you and your wife speaks volumes. And, especially, I want to thank you for having the God Bless in your signature, so thoughtful. Take care of yourself and pass that on to your spouse. Regards, Colleen

—Anonymous   September 26, 2009

Dear Joe, thanks for sharing the personal struggles you and your wife are going through; it helps other people in the same situation to know that they are not alone in how they feel. Please keep on posting your thoughts and feelings; you are providing very useful information about this difficult disease. Hang in there—you are in my thoughts.

—CynCity   October 07, 2009

I really enjoy reading your posts Joe and I am a big supporter so I hope you don't take this the wrong way . . .

My dad has been really moody since being diagnosed with AD and various other health problems that required surgery and physical therapy.

It was very hard to deal with but his doctor perscribed him an anti-depressant that has been helping a lot. It doesn't really help him remember things, but it makes him less pissed that he can't remember which has improved our relationship a lot.

I know the dynamics of father and daughter are a lot different then husband and wife but I just thought that I would give my two cents. I wrote a post about it over on my blog if you're interested.

Keep fighting the good fight Joe. God bless.

Good Morning From Nutsville!

Tuesday, September 29, 2009

Yes it is your on the scene reporter coming to you from his favorite City. I have not the faintist idea what is going to come of this post. I had it thought out and as usual as I type it flutters away.

My wife, Lynn the crazy one that married me, and I were talking one day, when who knows. I told her that my feelings and emotions have real problems with themselves, half the time I do not even care or love my family, other times the opposite is just as strong. I guess this wonderful companion of mine the big Dementia, is doing its job on me as it should be. Time means nothing anymore, a good deal of the past is leaving along with the supposed friends. But I think maybe it is reallly me that is leaving and not them. As Sherlock Holmes once said, I think it was him, Come On Watson The Game is A Foot. That is how i feel.

The cursor is flashing at me, like I should know what the hell it wants. I am not even sure what I want. My head hurts, my thoughts wander and the damned things do not even take me with them, that's the shits.

Well till I remember to come back.

God Bless You & This Country of Ours!!!!!

Joe

Posted by Joseph Potocny at 08:25AM (-07:00)

Comments

—karen   September 29, 2009

I wish you would write everyday. But I know it is hard. I love reading your stuff. http://alzheimersandmomblog.blogspot.com/

—Anonymous   October 02, 2009

Joe . . . see you when you remember to come back. Yeah, the nerve of those wandering thoughts not taking us with them . . . how rude! Take care Joe . . . Sandy

—Anonymous   October 05, 2009

Dear Joe,

I check your writings every week and always find them very interesting. Thanks for sharing your thoughts about the meaning of time to you. Also, your comment about sometimes caring and sometimes not caring about family and friends is helpful to those of us who love someone suffering from this disease. There are a lot of people out here who care about how you and your wife are doing. Thanks again.

With Sadness & Great Joy!

Wednesday, October 07, 2009

I will be posting another who has left this hell in which I live, that I call My World. Friend Arlene has pasted. I read it said of her that she lost the war but won the battle. I greatly disagree, she lost the battle but WON THE WAR. This disease takes our minds and bodies while it works, but you know the stupid bastard that it is, it winds up setting us FREE of its grip. So I ask in the final analysis, Who Wins?

I am sad that Arlenes' family has lost her vibrant character, but what joy they must also feel that she is now at peace and I believe with our Lord. I am jealous, her hell is over, mine is still going on and getting worse. Yes I can write, but I no longer can do the things I once did, my normal conversations leave some empty spaces. As I have said I have no concept of time. See I am writing now, I just got up and this is when I am at my best, few hours maybe less, well hello mindless.

I will post Arlenes picture later after I finish transfering it to my computer and stumble through the process of the posting.

Till Then.

God Bless You & This Country of Ours!

Joe

Posted by Joseph Potocny at 08:20AM (-07:00)

Comments

—Florencia   October 08, 2009

Dear Joe, I thought i'd never find your blog, but I actually did. I was just seeing you in The Alzheimer's project, and I was quite impressed and curious of your blog. I'm from Chile, a small country very far from yours, but I'm closer to you than you think. You see, my grandmother used to had Alzheimer, she passed away in April 2009, and believe me Joe, you are better than you think. How I wished my grandmother could have been as well as you are. She was diagnosed in 2003, so she wasn't very far from you. I know that probbably (and I don't have a doubt about it) it's much easier to say this from my teenager point of view but: keep the faith. :) I don't know if you care about what I'm going to tell you, but maybe you do, I'm making a lot of research about the disease for my school, I'm focusing a project we're doing on AD. Tomorrow it's my due date for one of the assignments, I hope it goes well haha. nothing much to say, but take care :)

greetings from chile !

Florencia

—karen	October 08, 2009

God Bless

—Anonymous	October 11, 2009

Hi Joe,

Thank you for posting my mom Arlene's picture on your site, I miss her very much, but I know that she is finally happy. Now she can once again watch over me instead of me watching over her like it had been while my sister and I cared for her. By the way I love that you share the anger you have in your latest blog. It speaks the harsh reality of this crappy disease that so many suffer from. I will continue to read what you have to say.

Anger Sits With Me This Day.

Saturday, October 10, 2009

Since HBO has ran and is running the documentery on AD, I have had a slew of emails from this country, Chilie, Brazil, Canada, Australia, Israel, just all over. What has gotten to me is the YOUNG PEOPLE, who have suffered the loss or are suffering a parent and a grandparent and because of this special they want to do something to help. Wow I say, and the adults in this country and around the World have sat on their asses all this time, yes even the tauted medical profession. I hear we have come along way since 1906 or 1908 whenever AD was coined. How far have we come is it in real knowledge, help, knowing the CAUSE, curing or is it just plain ass TIME? I read the studies and that contradict each other, the so called quak cures and how to stop and cure it. But yet I have not read on single word mentioning a persons name that has been cured . . . Oh let us march for a cure, bull shit. Let us first march to find the cause, no cause no cure, that is how it works. Yes these folks will do good in raising funds and maybe some awareness to help in the research on the disease. But since it does not affect your boobs, balls, prostate, colon or lungs, I guess it just does not warrant the NFL or other major playes to do anything. You know I have seen the cancer marches, heart disease, etc. and people where T-Shirts, "I AM

A SURVIOR OF CANCER". Watch the walks for AD and find me a picture of just one person that has a shirt that says, 'I AM A SURVIVOR OF ALHZIEMERS OR DEMENTIA"! find it, it will not exist, we all die period. I know Iwill get hate mail and the such, but bring it on, truth stands on my side. Ask the literally 10's of millions around this World that have been affected by it having or knowing one. I do not take the other killers, cancer, heart disease, diabetes, obesity, aids, etc. lightly but boy are there a lot of people (baby boomers) in for the ride of their life, with no real help.

Straight talk from one who suffers and is declining, I hope that I enrage you enough to do something and get rid of socialized medicine it is a failure and by God, do not just take your Drs. word for what is wrong, make hin/her explain why and in detail. It is your LIFE and your BODY that is at stake.

God Bless You & Keep You & This Country of Ours!

Joe

Posted by Joseph Potocny at 08:31AM (-07:00)

Comments

—Anonymous   October 10, 2009

Hi Joe . . . all I can say is . . . "BRAVO!" I feel every word you say is true . . . there are no survivors of Alzheimers or Dementia. Keep on talking straight talk. Also, thank you for the photos of Bill and Arlene who are no longer suffering.

Hugs to you, Sandy

—karen   October 10, 2009

Good Job. I feel very strong about all the other causes you mentioned too. But your right about Alz. Being left behind.

—Annie   October 12, 2009

You know what enrages me? The commercials for the drug that makes your eyelashes grow darker. WTF? There are people dying of AD and other hideous diseases, but we need a f'ing drug that makes eyelashes grow darker. Again, WTF?

—Anonymous   October 13, 2009

Dear Joe, I commend you on your straight talk. As a caregiver, I too am angered by the lack of knowledge and research of this diabolical killer. My mother was diagnosed with AD 3yrs ago. In looking for an AD Housing Facility, I was told by an ombudsman that I was not to mention the word "Alzheimer's". Even though these facilities claim to specialize in caring for residents with AD, I was told that the minute the "A" word was spoken that upwords of $1000 would be added to my bill. In this day and age there is still such a stigma attached to AD. Unfortunately, I believe that if my mother had any one of those other diseases that you mentioned it would be a blessing. I truly hope that I will see the day when the cause of this horrible disease is discovered. Thanks so much for your blog, you help shed some insight into a world my mother can no longer describe to me. God Bless, HS

—karen   October 13, 2009

Anonymous thanks for the advice about not mentioning the A word. Every place I visit is around $4000 a month. I will try not saying the A word next time.

http://alzheimersandmomblog.blogspot.com/

—Anonymous   October 14, 2009

I am outraged that this takes place in homes that are supposed to be "caring" for our loved ones who have been so "unlucky" to get this crappy disease. That is simply unacceptable, I would be doing anything I could to keep my loved one away from a place like that. I am so happy that we were able to keep my mom in her own home until the very end . . . good Lord what is this world coming too? Mom is the lucky one, she doesn't have to watch or hear about all of this insanity anymore. Keep up the good work you're doing Joe, and may God bless you and your family!

—rilera   October 14, 2009

A year ago we thought we were being proactive. We had chosen 3 places for mom when the time came that I could no longer care for her. Once place called and said they had a room. We said we would take it. I phoned to follow-up a few weeks later and they had 'given the room to someone from assisted living'. Back to square 1. Next place called and had a room. They did the eval and said they wouldn't take Mom, she had behavioral issues. Put Mom in the Geri psych ward at their urging where they put her on anti psychotics. We finally placed her somewhere for over $7000 per month. She lasted there for a little over 3 months before she passed away. Lesson learned: memory care facilities that are private pay can be very, very picky and usually only want the cream of the crop.

God Bless you Joe.

—Anonymous   October 22, 2009

My Grandmother has AD and there isn't one day that goes by that I don't think about her. I wouldn't be the person I am today if it wasn't for her. Recently my mother, aunt, two friends and I formed a team to raise money for the Alzheimer's Association and we walked with hundreds of others to help end AD. I know that walking isn't going to end it, but I do know that it is a way of me helping and showing support for my Grandma. It is also a way for me to cope with the fact that we are going to lose her eventually. My heart is breaking, she is the most important person to me and just thinking about not having her is heart-wrenching. Thank you for having this blog and sharing your story with us. Take care.

—Anonymous   October 26, 2009

Not a day goes by that I don't look at my children and pray they will not suffer the pain and anguish in trying to cope as I do with my father's AD. The fact that my g-mom suffered as well and my father described it as hell then only adds to the pain. My fate has been sealed I fear—no cause no cure on the horizon—so I only hope I dodge the inheritance and save them the suffering.

—DanielleBillsDaughter   October 26, 2009

Right on Joe . . . I did the Alz Assoc walk here in Sacramento and was interviewed on a local news station. I talked about the same thing . . . We need to act up and do something . . . the more I talk to people the more that phrase "Alz is the second most feared disease, second to Cancer" the more I convince people that it is the number one thing to fear. I am out there marching and yelling for our fathers . . . mine and fathers like you. I talk to people my age (30) and younger. I will continue and I hope it is catching on.

Fight the good fight Joe. I am right there behind you!!

What is Important in this World?

Tuesday, October 13, 2009

Last post has drawn some hard comments, which is great. But the one I am going to post here comes from a friend whose mom is suffering a great deal from this disease.

You know what enrages me? The commercials for the drug that makes your eyelashes grow darker. WTF? There are people dying of AD and other hideous diseases, but we need a f'ing drug that makes eyelashes grow darker. Again, WTF?

2:21 PM

My point exactly.

I was informed that they found the protien believed to be the culprit. AMALOIDs probably speeled wrong. But guess what Dr. A. in 1906 or 1908 made that discovery, boy we are moving fast. By the way this same protien can settle anywhere in the body, and that means any organ and cause failure. It is produced by the body. As I understand it, and we have to remember my brain here, they are formed by an auto imune sysdrome that attacks the white corpusles in the blood and breaks them down into these things and they do not know how to stop it exactly. Got a lesson these on Discovery Health, where a lady was in almost complete kidney shut down from these wonders and I forget what they did to help her, but they did say things could happen again as they did not know how to really stop it. Let's grow those eyelashes, boobs and fix up our stomaches and loves handles guys and gals.

The word AIDS was a stigma but it is ok now, not having it but talking about it. But Alhziemer's get away you with the plaque.

God Bless & Keep You and This Country of Ours!

joe

Posted by Joseph Potocny at 04:08PM (-07:00)

Comments

—karen   October 13, 2009

I hate the comm. about the eyelash's. It is the most stupid thing I have ever seen. Almost.

—JosephJSivakMD   October 15, 2009

Hey Joe,

I just found your blog, and it is great. Your comment about the previous stigma of AID's is so correct. I am so tired of the stigma of Alzheimer's. My mother died from AD 22 years ago, I was still pretty young, but so humiliated when I tried to explain what she had to other people. Sadly a lot has not changed. I look forward to following your blog. God Bless. Joe http://alzheimmers.blogspot.com

Freedom Rings Once More!

Sunday, October 18, 2009

Thursday this disease took another from My World. You know it takes owr minds, it takes our emotions, it takes our feelings, it takes our abilities, then it takes our last breathe. But what it does not know iss that it returns it all to us and sets us FREE from its crips. Yes from the grips we snatch Victory. To you my friend Josephine, I can hear you sing your song of Freedom, see you running through the tall grasses under the blue skies. I was blessed, I got to share the big screen with you, but for a moment. Now I know you are free and it brings me hope. Annie God Loves You and so do Lynn and I.

God Bless & Keep You and This Country of Ours!!

joe

Posted by Joseph Potocny at 08:32AM (-07:00)

Comments

Dear Joe, I am an avid fan of yours and read your blog with interest as often as possible. I am sorry about Josephine and yet I love the way your picture her running through the grasses and being free from the grips.

I am curious if you believe that if you get angry about something, if anger allows you to remember things a little bit better or longer.

I hope you don't mind me asking. I wish there was a cure and i wish I could help some how. My best friend's mother is suffering from a.d. and it is not easy, as you know. i agree with you how sickening it is that our society spends time on things such as making lashes darker, putting fake plastic bags in women's bodies . . . overeating and then sucking fat out . . . i agree that our country is distorted in its priorites, but i also feel that most people don't know where to begin and what to do.

i am going to try to look up josephine on the internet now because i watched the hbo series but i don't remember which person was josephine.

lots of love and wishes for your well being as much as possible. ruth

Thank you Joe. Deep down I am glad she is free too, but I'm missing her too much right now. The thought of her running through tall grasses brings peace.

You have a wonderful heart sir and I support your anger at this disease and the lack of treatments available so far. God bless you and your wife and thank you for continuing to share.

Free at last. I felt the same way when my father past. I curled up in bed with him and listened to his heart beat and then when it was gone I knew he was free of the chains and the prison of Alz. I cried for 10 mins and then I shouted to the night sky . . . Youre free Daddy . . . youre free!!!! Though I miss him terribly . . . I know he is better and I couldnt have a better person to watch over me.

Thank You Joe for being so open and honest with the world.

To You Who Care For US!

Wednesday, October 28, 2009

This is my Thank You to all of you that give care for those in this World I live in.

Strange this may sound, but when we are set free from this disease, something really wonderful happens, YOU TO ARE SET FREE. The great burden you shoulder with us on a daily basis, which can be unbearable at times, is lifted from you. You once more are blessed to live your life. Maybe caring for another, or just getting a very well deserved rest for your heart, soul, mind and body.

From thos stil in my world and those that have been set free: THANK YOU11

God Bless You & This Country of Ours!

Joe

Posted by Joseph Potocny at 12:43PM (-07:00)

Comments

—jncsundbergcomcastnet   October 29, 2009

Hi Joe, and Lynn,

The burdens are born of LOVE. They are at times heavy, and overwhelming, but truly, the memories we take from this Labor of Love help to mend the wounds of grief. I miss my Mom (Arlene) so much. I don't think we can prepare for a loss such as this. The freedom you speak of is bittersweet, as it's cost is the loss of a loved one. Yes, the burdens have been lifted, but we cannot go back to the life we had, as it has been forever changed. There is now a strangly empty space in my heart that has become a part of me (caregiving). There are times now when I am overwhelmed by the feeling of having forgotten some detail of Mom's care, as if she is still here with us. I hope that this feeling will pass with time.

Lots of love to you both, Cheryl

—JUSTAMOM   October 30, 2009

I find my JOY in caring for those like you, again and again over and over as they come into our care and as they leave us . . . I LOVE MY JOB. THANK YOU

When Will They Get IT Right?

Saturday, November 07, 2009

The so caled pros that know everyghing, you know the PHDs, the ones with the Paper Hanging Degrees, they still know Jack Squat about this disease. Ant those of you out there withit, that write your wonderful books and taught your abilities to do so, you sure are a big help. Dr. Joe (not me) runs a blog that makes my fires burn, because he knows his mom died from it and still hears all the bs of 20 years ago today, with new hair brained ideas. You want the answers here we are standing ready to show you the way, but you alas are to stupid to realize that just maybe we hold the key and the lock.

Yes I am a tadd upset, because each day we help keep them boobs healthy and 15000 less a year die (which is good), more of us are let to go by the wayside. You see my world is getting worse each day, the one in my head, the one outside of me has been really fucked for just over a year now and going to get worse. Maybe it isn't so bad that I suffer from this Disease, soon I won't give a shit about any of you, because I will not know who the hell you are.

Well it is Turkey Month, this year I give it to the Medical Profession and The Do Nothing Politicians. Uncooked, ungutted, feathers and all, you won't be able to tell the difference any how.

To those I still love and care about.

God Bless You & This Country of Ours.

Joe

Posted by Joseph Potocny at 01:34PM (-08:00)

Comments

—karen   November 07, 2009

I hear you. It is Alz's Awareness Month and I still have not heard hardly anything about it on tv. It sucks. Hang in there.

—Lynn   November 11, 2009

To all of you reading Joes blog thankyou. When he says that his world is getting worse he is correct. It is getting harder for him to remember things such as what day it is and what he is doing. Before I leave for work we talk and he will ask what day it is and I tell him. It is hard to know that while I am at work he is losing more of himself. Mornings are a good time but come the night he is distant and moody. But not all the time. I know when he says things in his blog you may want to have an explanation on what he is talking about. I have been reluctant to get involved because this is his, but as things go forward I will help him get out what he wants to say.

Lynn

A Request

Sunday, November 08, 2009

Many of you may not know, because the media does not care this is NATIONAL ALZHEIMER'S AWARENESS MONTH. Let your local papers know, let us see if they have the balls to say anything.

Again I ask for pictures, birth year and year of passing of loved ones that died from this damnable disease. Two of you have heard. They need to be remembered for they are the faces of Alzheimer's.

(Yes I used spell checker, so I cheated)!

If you like this blog I ask you to click on the Wellsphere voting Icon on the right and vote for it. I know that many on Wellsphere do not necessarily like it, I am not a caregiver or dr. I just suffer from the disease and try to tell how my life is deteriorating and getting worse as we move to my physical death. Yes the 7th leading cause of death. Probably if death certificates showed the real agent that caused death I am sure that it would be higher. Most to feared diagnosis so it is said, is you have Cancer and You Have Alzheimer's. Help me spread the word Please.

Till next time thanks for your thoughts and help.

God Bless You & This Country of Ours!

Joe

Posted by Joseph Potocny at 08:42AM (-08:00)

Comments

—karen   November 08, 2009

I voted and great Idea on telling the local news. I will.

—ScottJudyandJackie   November 11, 2009

Joe . . .

I do not how to contact you any other way, but I wanted to say "Thank you" for allowing HBO to include you, your family, and your horrific journey through Alzheimer's. I am an instructor at a Tech center in Oklahoma that teaches certified nursing assistants. Oklahoma State Department of Health has stated that every nursing home in the state has to provide proof that every certified nursing assistant that works in the facility has attended a 10 hour in-service on Alzheimer's. I have included the Alzheimer's Project in both my teachings. Every student has commented about you and your straight forwardness concerning your every day life. I want to let you know that I personally appreciate you and your family very much. My prayers are that you and your family can spend as much time as possible together for as long as you all can. Again, thank you for being such an inspiration to me, my students, and every single person going through this dreaded disease.

Judy Pearce, LPN judy_pearce@hughes.net

—Anonymous   November 12, 2009

I just saw the documetary that you're participated in today, and It really touched me. I hope you're doing well, and that I can follow your blogg for a long time. :)

From Linda 31 years, from Norway.

AS ONE READER SEE'S IT!

Thursday, November 12, 2009

userid = jpotocny FirstLastName = Email = Message = why yu gotta be such a curmudgeon? i got on ur sight for some insight into the disease, my mom has it too. but i dont want to listen to yur ranting and bitterness . . . not that i blame yu but i wont be bak. life is hard enuf for us without listening to someone elses negativity. i thank god my mom aint bitter and angry like yu. she so sad at times but othertimes she is happy too and like my own child. sorry for yu

Thank you for using Bravenet Email Form Processing!

(YES I AM CHEATING AGAIN USING SPELL CHECKER ON MY PART even used grammar checker)

As many of you know I invite all comments and emails. I publish them as received. So that you all know, I get many like the above. Of course I hide their identity on emails, but did not have to with this one, them, him, her or it, did not have what it takes to give a first name. This comes from the email block I have on the right side of the blog, so you can email instead of leaving a comment, if you do not want it published.

But I have not edited it, spells like me, because I do not change comments and the like. I have said in the past and still do, bring it on as you feel.

I am sorry that your mom has joined this ever expanding World of Alzheimer's or Dementia. It is not a fun way to live. Try reading my blog from the beginning and then judge me. You got insight, but could not hear it, your ears and eyes are closed. You think with your heart, which is wonderful, but this disease gives a damn about your heart. It wants and is taking your mom away, like it or not. I am not bitter at the disease or people in general. But I am offended, slighted and angry with those who claim to know how we feel and are making progress. Progress in what? Same info we have now existed over 100 years ago so where is the progress, I keep asking and hear nothing but silence.

I do not enjoy this disease, it will KILL me period. Not only physically, but it is the loss of me that is taking place that just rips at my very fiber. I say to you who will not return, yes you will, as you see what takes place with you mom. Here you will hear and have heard the truth from one who suffers and is declining. From others you can find the soft gentleness that you seem to want to hear, but not the harsh reality of it all.

If you have the chance to see the HBO documentary, The Alzheimer's Project, pay close attention to the time of diagnosis and the immanent decline of the people and how quickly it can come and see what is ahead. You see Josephine just pasted away a couple of weeks ago. Of course Cousin Cliff passes in the documentary (for real). I do not know about the rest how they are but sure would like to know.

Well I have said what I needed to, I did walk away from the computer before doing this because I wanted to really strike out, but I still have some control over my emotions. Not very often but, once in awhile I manage. So before I go off in another direction Good Bye for today.

God Bless You & This Country of Ours!

Joe

Posted by Joseph Potocny at 09:50AM (-08:00)

Comments

—karen   November 12, 2009

Good response to bad email.

—Anonymous   November 12, 2009

You are so right Joe . . . they will be back. People need to educate themselves. And personally, I believe your website is an education for me as a caregiver. If only . . . Alzheimer's was a "memory loss" disease as many people think. God Bless, HS

—kenju   November 12, 2009

Joe, you are right, of course. That person should have read your posts from the beginning. He apparently does not understand much about the progression of the disease. I know very little about it, except what I read here and on the site of a wife whose husband has it. I would NEVER presume to chastise you for being angry or bitter-you have every right to be.

—rilera   November 12, 2009

Joe, thank you for refusing to 'candy coat' your journey through alzheimer's. The disease just plain sucks. We need to get to the point where those afflicted can be survivors of this disease. it's time for the researchers to get going on a cure.

Robyn

P.s. I lost my Mom to ALZ in January. I miss her so much.

—colleenmc   November 13, 2009

What a wonderful photo you have put on your blog, I love it. I feel for the pain the emailer expressed, we all know how hard it is . . . my mom is much older and was diagnosed some years ago. But she is angry at the disease and her loss of independence, clear memory. Your blog expresses so much of reality. God Bless you and our country.

—Anonymous   November 13, 2009

I find your blog has helped me understand where my dad went. I am also so glad to see someone angry about the disease. Have spent so much time with my family making this a "positive" experience, "being brave" and not "wasting tears". I come home from visits(live 500 miles away) and scream "THIS SUCKS" to my husband over and over until it doesn't hurt some much. You have exposed this disease for what it is . . . a demon, a monster. Thank you

—Lynn   November 14, 2009

To one reader, I am so sorry that you have not had an easy time. I am glad the your mother is not angry yet, and that she is happy and has good times. Joe is a happy man and he has good times. He can be a curmudgen at times too just like anyone else. I live with him. He has not been bitter about the disease. He is angry that he is losing who he is. Not that he is actually going to die. Our grandchildren will not know the man that he once was. The see a papa who falls, sleeps, gets lost, and snaps at them when they to be too much. He tries real hard not to do that but somtetimes it just happens. When they are over here and getting to be too much he goes upstairs and lays down. Papa disappears. So for now enjoy the fact that your mom is sad at times and that she is not bitter. But be prepared that that can and will change at any moment. Joe has tried to convey what it is like to have the disease. He is not the cargiver. This is all on his side of the fence, to give those of us on the caring side an insight as to what those you are taking care of feel and think like. It is not easy.

—Amy   November 15, 2009

Joe, I thank you for writing this blog. My grandmother has Alzheimer's and Dementia. Papa never said a word. We all saw little things from time to time, but thought . . . she was "just getting old". She's in her 80's. It wasn't until my aunt, her youngest daughter, was ill and in the hospital a few years ago that the rest of us saw more clearly what was happening. Papa didn't want to admit that anything was wrong and he still has a very hard time with it. He wants things to be back to "normal" I can't blame him, I'd be angry and confused and sad, too, If I were losing my husband—especially after 70 years. I wish that one of them would have reached out and said something earlier or that we would've been less preoccupied with our own lives so that we could've spent more time with her, could've written memories down—SOMETHING—ANYTHING. But, I suppose there will always be wishes and things we'd do differently. The Granny we know now is not the Granny I grew up with. I wish my son would've been able to know the amazing person she really is. Again, I thank you, for writing this blog and giving the rest of us insight into what it's like and what our own family members must be going through. I applaud you for being so open and honest about it all.

—Annie   November 18, 2009

Joe, just keep doing what you're doing. I thank you for it.

—Anonymous   November 28, 2009

Joe, to me you are genius and you are the winner. Look what you are doing expressing your feeling. That's healthy whether it is negative or positive feelings, it is the true feeling that you are feeling and sharing it with us. There are many people out there living without AD and they do not appreciate what life is and they do not know how to express their feelings so To me again you are the Genius.

Another Day in Dream Land!

Wednesday, November 18, 2009

where i get my titles is unknown to me. But it seems that my dreams and my reality are starting to be one in the same. I wake up hear voices, it is my dream entering my what ever you call it, I guess my here and now. It takes awhile for things to clear up. I am normally fine until this time of the day, after this 11:30 or so, the day just plain disappears on me. I no longer can do math by hand and mind, need a calculaor, pisses me off to no end. I had to leave twitter, sokule & facebook, could not keeep up with them. Hells bells I have enough problems with this thing. Had numerous on line business and affiliate accounts have closed them as well. Although things were witen down and all in a book organized, I got to confused and angry and just could not handle things. As of today the Joe that I once kew no longer exists. I am becoming someone else and I am not happy over that. Yesterday I turned 65 an age I never ever expected to reach or frankly wanted to, especially in my drunkin druggie days of my 20's. In my 20's did not know what the hell I was doing, somethings never change back in the saddle, no drugs or alcohol, don't need it now, brain is fucked as it is. Strange family was over last night but yet I was alone and am most of the time. Feelings towards others seem to keeep getting farther and farther from me. They are not leaving, I AM. I do not hear words right anymore, no car, problems with the bills and the check book, my wife Lynn can go to give me a kiss an it will scare the crap out of me. I forget who she is. So much for my babeling soon it will be Turkey Day, yes I will over eat and be in gastric distress big time. I even got some of the big words right this time, no red lines under them, look out. Bye for now.

God Bless You & This Country of Ours!

Joe

Posted by Joseph Potocny at 11:34AM (-08:00)

Comments

—karen   November 18, 2009

Happy Birthday and I love your new picture. I am glad you are still doing this blog. I am a caregiver and now I know what my mom was dealing with in her early stages. It makes me better care for her now. She was in Hell and we did not know it. I hope she forgives us.

—rilera   November 19, 2009

Thank you Joe for your insightful posts. It helps me to understand my mom in her early stages. She must have been so fearful. Hang in there Joe. God Bless You.

—Malin   November 23, 2009

Hi Joe! I just finished watching "The Alzheimer's Project". My grandmother was diagnosed a couple of years ago, and God knows how many years the disease had been growing inside of her before anyone really understood that it was more than just her age playing tricks on her. She turned 90 today actually. The reason I think we didn't notice the amount of her dementia earlier was because of my grandfather, and the way he covered up for her. As long as he was around, we didn't notice anything wrong. But then he passed away and my grandmother was alone. Years went by, she got worse and finally we managed to get her into a nice home for people with Alzheimer's. She doesn't remember us anymore. Sometimes she yells at us to go away. Sometimes she cries. Sometimes I'm convinced she knows who we are, or at least that we care about her and love her unconditionally. Why am I writing all this? I don't know. I hate this disease. It's a thief of souls and hearts and memories. But you have to fight back as hard as you can. Watching you on the TV made me smile. You're a fighter, Joe. Hang in there and take care of yourself!

—shellyk   November 24, 2009

I voted for you on Wellsphere and am making my way through the archive. You are an amazing man and I appreciate your willingness to share your thoughts. I just found your blog when I googled your name—I am a nurse in a nursing home and my company used the Memory Loss Tapes from HBO for "sensitivity training". More important—my husband's mother died in January 09 after suffering with AD for 16+ years. Your frank comments remind me of her—she used to tell me "my mind is a sheet—it's a blank sheet". I try to keep that image in my mind—a plain sheet on a clothesline, swaying with the wind—nothing on it—blank—where her memories were. I will be reading regularly. Keep your comments going to remind the medical "professionals" how much we DON'T know. WE have NO idea what you're experiencing and I hope we all are smart enough to admit it!

Happy Turkey Day!!!!!!!

Wednesday, November 25, 2009

I wish to you all a very Happy Thanksgiving. Eat well and stay safe.

I was thinking of this now and felt I better post it before I drift away again this day. My thanks are for all of your support and comments.

God Bless You & This Country of Ours!

Joe

Posted by Joseph Potocny at 01:54PM (-08:00)

Comments

—colleenmc   November 28, 2009

I hope you had a wonderful Thanksgiving. Love what you posted, wish I did things like that. Take care, Colleen

—Anonymous   November 29, 2009

Didn't know how else to get this to you. Don't have much info(picture birth date etc) but felt it should be posted somewhere. Jack, my dad's roommate, died of Alzhiemer's last week. He was 89 years old and my father's main transporter(as he was mobile and my dad wheelchair bound). In the short time we knew him he was a wonderful man who saw to it that my dad was up and going everyday. At the end of every visit I would always thank him for taking care of my dad and he would always say the pleasure was his, that he so enjoyed talking with my dad and having someone to hang out with. I can only imagine the adventures those two took around the grounds of the VA. So glad he is now at peace but so sorry to have my father feel such a loss.

—SeanS   December 03, 2009

Joe,

My aunt is in her early 60's with Alz, grandfather passed from it also 5 years ago. I am a 39 yo male, was injured at work and can no longer work, major back problems. I can relate to your frustration of watching myself deteriorate over the years, although my body is going and not my mind yet, I dreed to find out if I have the gene.

At the moment I can still take care of my home, dog and myself but get anxious at the thought of having to be cared for by strangers and sharing a room in an institution.

I have read that THC fights off the Alz, but further checking on your end may be needed to start that type of medication. I'm watching the HBO canada Special and I trully hope things work out for you. Take care Joe, and thanks for sharing your story with the world. I am certain it will help people in many ways. Thank you Joe.

Sean S.

—DollySheriff   December 06, 2009

Just saw The Alzheimer Projct on TV. Your Blog is inspirational!. Well done and keep going Joe. Love Dolly

CESTMOI

Monday, December 07, 2009

Yes, it is Tis I. Camelot humor. It seems to me that I just posted, by my wife reminneded me that it had been over a week. Time is becoming of little meaning to me and I no longer seem to have a grasp on it. Today is raining and windy, here in Sunny So. CA, love the rain. At one time it use to charge me up when it would get stormy, now nothing. I feel things moving faster now. I sit here and have to close my eyes to concentrate on what I want to say, and damned if I can figure it out.

Yes it is the Christmas time again. I hope you have a Jolly and Peaceful one. Maybe this time you and I can find away to keep this feeling always not just now.

This year let us not forget for they give us the freedom to live free and enjoy our lives. They sacrifice their lives for us and should be honored.

I know I am not staying very well on ssubject, byt my thoughts are getting in a bind you could say. I wish the old me was here, he could at least most of the time stay on topic.

I doubt that by next year this time, I will be writing here. Hopefully my wife will take over and let you know, where mindless has gone to.

A VERY MERRY CHRISTMAS TO YOU ALL!!!!!!!

God Bless You & This Country of Ours!

Joe

Posted by Joseph Potocny at 03:24PM (-08:00)

Comments

—kenju   December 07, 2009

Merry Christmas, Joe, to you and your family. I wish you well.

—Anonymous   December 08, 2009

I really enjoy your posts, thanks for sharing your experience with us.

—Lene-Therese   December 08, 2009

Merry Christmas to you to! :)

—JosephJSivakMD   December 08, 2009

Hi Joe,

I love the picture at the top of your blog. I think you captured all the meaning of Christmas with it. Keep up the inspiring work. I wish you the best and blessed Christmas ever. Joe

—karen   December 10, 2009

Merry Christmas to you and your family. You are the best. I look forward to all your post. Merry Christmas !!!!!

New Studies — These People Are Idiots!

Monday, December 14, 2009

Yes that is my take on this. They do not have a clue to what they are doing.

NEW STUDY: Gist of the study is that those who have 5 cups or more of coffee each day can slow the onset and progression of Alhzeimer's. Now is what few cells I have left are working, I believe studies in not to distant past showed that this type of coffee consumption put you at a higher risk of Bladder Cancer. Well I guess drink the coffee, get the cancer, stop drinking the coffee and forget the cancer. Maybe I am wrong but seems to me, that spirits were part of this one.

Next & I Love This One: proves a point made in one of my listing.

Salk Institute scientists in La Jolla, CA: major incredible fantanstic break through. Of course we used GENETICALLY MODIFIED MICE:so normal humans won't work in this one. The GM mice "not only lived longer, but the onset of mental decline was also delayed". Reports Andrew Dillion of the university as reported in the North County Times by Bradley J. Fikes. This gets more interesting, I love amoloyids, they do not know what they are to do. According to Dillin (A Professor at Salk), their research shows that th plaques of these toxin protiens in those of us with AD and the like: ready for this: ARE NOT THE CAUSE OF THE DISEASE. Guess allyou PHDs outhere need a brain transplant. Instead and this is a quote from the article: "Instead, the clumps of beta amyloid proteins are how cells stow away the toxic proteins where they can't do damage, Dillin said." Well now, rest of study is to be published in the 12/11 issue of Cell. Have not gotten to it yet.

I hate to rain on a parade but these folks are all over the place. This is why I am so harsh on them. They can not get their heads unstuck from their a***.

Cannot repair brain cells from what I know. So I see no cure, and all meds may slow down the progression no solid proof they do in at least 85% of AD patients, that I have found, more like maybe 20% if at all.

This is just interesting to me. You may or may not know that many NFL players over time have donated their brains for study, after they are dead to see the affects of all the concusions and blows to the heads they take do. In the group thus far checked of those in their 30's to 50's that have passed, it was noticed that, all though no signs at least know showed, but these guys had brains that looked like they had some form of Dementia for YEARS. just something interesting. So you folks know that I do try to keep up as much as possible on my disease and the tinker toy ways they are working on it.

Blast me, but these folks still do not get it.

God Bless You & This Country of Ours!

Joe

Posted by Joseph Potocny at 10:18AM (-08:00)

Comments

—karen   December 14, 2009

you are right they don't get it. God bless you and our country. And Merry Christmas!!!

—rilera   December 14, 2009

Joe, I get angry over the studies that say exercise can prevent alzheimer's. They don't get it, but at least they are trying. God Bless.

Caregivers — They Need Love Too!!!!!

Friday, December 18, 2009

Yes those caregivers need a lot of love and tender care. You all know what us with AD & FTD can be like to care for. Talking to us or at least trying to can be very trying and nerve racking. My ability to hold meanningful concersations is starting to waine quite a bit. I get lost in them not to mention the poor person who talks to me. What follows is a picture of my beloved wife and I holding such a conversation. Do not lauugh to loud it is serious.

217

God Bless You & This Country of Ours! Merry Christmas!!!!!

Joe

Posted by Joseph Potocny at 02:09PM (-08:00)

Comments

—kenju   December 18, 2009

God Bless YOU, Joe, and your lovely wife. Merry Christmas.

—userdd   December 18, 2009

Merry Christmas to you and your family! God bless you all!!

—JUSTAMOM   December 19, 2009

YOU are those who cary what you do are the REASON I for one am a caregiver. I LOVE my job, it is SO much harder for the wife who has you in her view 24/7. God Bless her for keeping you in your home! THAT IS WHERE YOU ALL BELONG AT "HOME"

HAVE A GREAT HOLIDAY

—AlzheimersDiseaseSupport   December 25, 2009

Merry Christmas to you and your family.

To All The Best.

Tuesday, December 29, 2009

I hope you all had a great Christmas. We spent the time at the US Coast Guard Training Center in Petaluma with my daughter, son-in-law and 3 grand children. Now I am sick, kids were sick so gramps got it also now. Today we will be having Christmas with the rest of the family and grandkids.

I hope that next year is peaceful and blessed for you all.

I see my friend Mary in Canada has been going to town with her new site which will be updated on my links today, I hope. Need to remember to do it.

We have been putting in our third pond, moved my koi to the bigger one and lost my big guy. He was about 14 inches and around 3 pound, had him since little. Hopefully we can save the others, moved them back to old pond and started treating them, will see. So far we have lost about six. I do not know if I am sad, mad, pissed or who cares. This disease has really messed with my emotions and state of mind. As you can tell I am ok at this moment. Later who knows. So before I babble on like a brook, you all have a great day.

God Bless You & This Country of Ours!

Joe

Posted by Joseph Potocny at 10:28AM (-08:00)

Comments

—colleenmc   December 29, 2009

Great to hear about your trip to see family, sorry about the koi, hoping for the best for them. Take care and God bless you, your wife and all of your family and friends.

Better Late Than Never.

Saturday, January 02, 2010

I know I am a day late and a dollar short but; HAPPY NEW YEARS TO YOU ALL. I want to thank all of you that have followed my blog, sent me coments, emails, good and thos not so. Even the ones I had to have interpreted for me or replying with, WHAT? See you need to keep it simple and clear for me, my one time brain cell hsa shrunk to about ¼ of its size this past year.

My family and I hope and wish all the best for you and yours in the coming New Year and years to come.

For me 2006 was not as good as 2005, 2007 got a little worse, 2008 things got on the move, and last year 2009 this disease reallly started to make itself known. So things being what they are I would imagine 2010 is going to be interesting as I trudge this happy road of Alhzeimer's and FTD.

For now take care catch you on the other side.

God Bless You & This Country of Ours!

Joe

Posted by Joseph Potocny at 08:30AM (-08:00)

Comments

—kenju   January 02, 2010

I hope that 2010 will be a better year for you, Joe. What a nice photo of your family!!

—karen   January 03, 2010

This is my fav. picture you have ever posted. I love it. You all look wonderful. Happy New Year!!!

—Anonymous   January 03, 2010

Happy New Year to you Joe and your family. I will also be trying to hang in during 2010 so looking forward to reading all about your continuing journey.

Hugs, Sandy

—Moonchild   January 05, 2010

Happy New Year Joe!

—Anonymous   January 06, 2010

Happy new year and thank you for helping us see the good, the bad and the ugly—no matter how hard it is.

—useraj   January 11, 2010

Hello Joe,

I am very sorry to here of your situation, however, your positive attitude and approach are an inspiration to all.

I am a nursing student in Canada currently working on an Alzheimers project. I would appreciate the opportunity to include some of your comments as a way to provide others with some insight to this terrible disease and its effects on individuals.

I wish you and your family a Happy New Year and thank-you for sharing.

Amanda

Days Lost.

Tuesday, January 12, 2010

First to AJ if you read this you have my permission to use any part of my blog you wish, with the exception of the In Memory of Photos. I do not have permission to allow that. My stuff have at it pictures, posts, etc.

I am starting to loose more and more days and time. I am feeling a sense of loss in my life now more than I did when I started this journey. It confuses me, for a period I am normal and can do anything I know where I am and then someone comes along and turns the lights out. I guess this is the way it goes and will continue until. I hear from folks how well I am handling this, and how great the HBO special was, etc. I am not that person anymore, he disappeared almost 2 years ago when the filming was done, at least I think it was that long ago. It is more difficult to concetrate on writtting these posts now, probabbly why I am not doing so much anymore.

Well the best5 to all of you.

God Bless You & This Country of Ours!

joe

Posted by Joseph Potocny at 11:27AM (-08:00)

Comments

—colleenmc   January 13, 2010

Joe, I am still reading your posts. They come from your heart. I am glad you still write them. Take care of yourself sir; best to your family also.

—useraj   January 13, 2010

Firstly thank-you for permission to use excerpts from your blog excluding the In Memory of Photos.

I do understand what you and your family are going through. My great grandmother suffered with Altzheimer's while I was a teenager. Now I am helping my partner while he sees his father becoming lost to the same disease.

I realize that it must be very hard for you to keep up with writing the posts, but please continue for as long as you can. It helps keep the mind active and also helps others understand better what you and your family are going through.

I wish you all the best and will keep in touch. I will also let you know how my project is going. I have also been very fortunate to be in touch with Mary (through your blog). Thank-you for that.

Keep the faith and thinking of you and your family.

Amanda (AJ)

—Anonymous   January 13, 2010

Dear Joe, thanks for continuing to share your thoughts and feelings. Thanks also for sharing the photo of your beautiful family—those are sure happy faces on those grandchildren. Wishing you a peaceful 2010.

—namie							January 14, 2010

愛情是盲目的，但婚姻恢復了它的視力。...

—Anonymous						January 15, 2010

Hi Joe . . . sorry to hear you feel a sense of loss more so now than when you started your journey. I know your feelings well . . . especially about you not being able to concentrate on writing your posts. You are in my thoughts and please keep blogging as long as you can . . . even if it is not as often because I do understand your feelings totally and know I am not alone with mine. Hugs . . . Sandy

—rilera							January 16, 2010

Joe, thank you for the insight into this awful disease. God bless you.

—Anonymous						January 19, 2010

Joe As hard as it may be I am happy that you continue to try. You have helped me understand where my dad went and how it must have been for him . . . and continues to be. Wishing thoughts, prayers and words of encouragement were the cure . . . but sending them your way all the same. Will continue to check in on you so continue to post.

Couple of Things.

Wednesday, January 20, 2010

Well I am back here at the monster again.

I am still asking for those of you who would like their loved ones, friends, etc. who have passed from AD to send me their picture, first name, birth year and year of being set free. As you see so far only 3 people have felt that their loved one's should be honored, what about the rest of you? Yes I can get snotty.

The chatroom will disappear soon, I only paid for it for a year and I do not know if anyone has used it, so goes life.

Also NOTICE if you have skype on your computer, headphones, microphone and speakers you can call me free just click on CALL ME button. If i am on we will talk.

Things in this world of mine are getting a bit out of touch with me. I feel like I am beginning to seperate into two different folks, the one who knows (as if I ever did) what they are doing and one who hasn't a clue.

We finally finished our second KOI pond, Sept to now, not bad. Waiting for the season to warm up to bring in new fish, lost ½ of my others. Home projects I still like but they are becoming very hazardous to me. I built a square box around the pond for cemment so that the pavers vor the patio could be laid straight and shot my self in the finger with the nail gun. Then while laying the bricks one by one and setting them I smashed the same finger with the mallet, of course I really warmed up for that brick setting. Finally has feeling coming back in it. Golden years, kiss my butt.

Wife is now home with me for not sure how long, I guess until she cannot take me anymore or I send her back to work. Wants to do toooooo many things. What a pest, but I love her, so sorry guys I am keeping her, in it for the money now.

I am still amazed at my friend Mary in Canada, how she posts almost daily, I just cannot get it together to do that.

If you have a blog or website, that is not in my lisk of links and want it there email me jolynn1@cox.net with the name and I will enter it. I do follow alll the links I have, in the back part of blogger you can list those you want to follow and you get continual updates as people post, really neat. I just need to comment more, get to involved then forget what I am doing and walk away in disgust,

Well before I babble a brook you all have a great day. I am going to hide from the rain.

God Bless You & This Country of Ours!

Joe

Posted by Joseph Potocny at 01:36PM (-08:00)

Comments

—karen   January 20, 2010

My mom has not passed yet. But she is in her own world not ours anymore. Sometimes she talks to me. But she just sits or lays where ever I put her. No moving. I do wish you would read my blog. Come visit me. Tell me what you think. I know you will tell me the truth.:) http://alzheimersandmomblog. blogspot.com/

—Mary   January 22, 2010

Hi Joe . . . I'd love to come see your KOI pond! I'm visualizing it, as I gaze out over our snow covered lawns. Oh well . . . summer must be just around the corner! Hugs Mary~Canada

—JosephJSivakMD   January 23, 2010

Hey Joe, Thinking of you. Thanks for picture of my mom, Madeline. You should be getting some mail from me next week. Can't wait to get your opinion and reviews. Keep the faith. Joe

—Anonymous   January 24, 2010

Hi Joe . . . I agree with Mary. I would love to see your KOI pond. The three of us could sit around and talk . . . talk . . . talk. Take care, Joe, hugs to you.

Sandy

—JUSTAMOM   January 25, 2010

Hey Joe stoppin in to check on ya . . . your doing great . . . be back again. keep warm

Grandparents Again!

Tuesday, January 26, 2010

Yes at 10:26AM our 7th grandchild was born. His name is Lucas, by emergency C section. 2 months early. We are leaving for Petaluma, early tomorrow to help or do what it is grandparents do do.

Fish pond disaster after our storms, but what the heck we are fixing, repairs now on hold. My brain hurts and is not handling this well. Till next time. God Bless You & This Country of Ours!

joe

Posted by Joseph Potocny at 10:25AM (-08:00)

Comments

—Anonymous   January 26, 2010

Congratulations Joe. Safe journey.

—Anonymous   January 27, 2010

Joe, Both of you have a pleasant trip. Congratulations! Hugs, Sandy

—JosephJSivakMD   January 28, 2010

Hey Joe,

Don't worry about the fish pond, congrats on the grandbaby, hopefully he will make your brain hurt a little less. I wish for everything to go well for he and you. Keep the faith in the cycle of life. Joe

Hello From Petaluma!

Friday, January 29, 2010

We are here in Petaluma. That is between San Fran and Santa Rosa. Wheather has been ok.

Our Daughter Morgan is doing fine and grandson Lucas is progressing well. He is breathing totally on his own and is now eating. So tense times are lessening. We will be here another week or so. I really wish I was home, that is safe haven for me. Plus I have some idea wherre I am there.

Other three grandkids driving me a little batty, have hard time dealing with them and their energy, trying to keeep things straight is not easy, oh well.

Will keep you updated as I reemember.

God Bless You & This Country of Ours!

joe

Posted by Joseph Potocny at 12:30PM (-08:00)

Comments

—karen   January 29, 2010

so glad your grandson is better. I know not being home is hard on you but you being there is great for your daughter. So nice of you to go. Best wishes to all.

—jncsundberg   anuary 30, 2010

Hey Joe and Lynn . . .

Im so happy that it looks like a happy outcome for all of you with this new grandbaby. Congratulations!

Have you ever been to Petaluma before? We live just a stones throw west in the little town of Guerneville. Mom(Arlene) lived in Santa Rosa. Hope you all get to see some of the area, so many neat things to see. We think it's pretty special anyway . . . its been called "God's Country" by many folks.

Best and warmest regards to all of you, Cheryl

—Annie   February 03, 2010

Congratulations on your new grandson!

—June   February 03, 2010

Hi Joe and Lynn, Long time reader of your blog. Glad that Lucas is doing so well! Congrats on being grandparents again.

I started a blog about my Mom, havent updated it very recently. Not sure I like the title of it, but don't feel like re-doing the whole thing.

http://cleaningoutalife.blogspot.com/

Add it to your blog list if you want! I like your blog and your political views.

225

June in PA (we are about to get another major snowstorm, so you got mega rain, here it's being called a paralyzing storm).

—Mary February 04, 2010

Hi Joe . . . good news about your new grandson for sure. I totally understand about wanting to be back in your 'safe haven'. You need to do what I do . . . find a quiet room, and just stay there! (hopefully with a computer!) Hugs and best wishes to the new family! Mary~Canada

—Felipe February 04, 2010

Hi Joe. My name is Felipe, I'm a 17 years old boy from Chile, a country from South America. Last night I watched the documentary "The Alzheimer's Project" and it really touched me. I didn't know how mucho ago it was filmed or anything, so I started to research a little and I found your blog. I really like how you write and let all those thoughts free, and I think I'll be reading your entries now and then. Hope you're having a great time there at Petaluma.

—JUSTAMOM February 06, 2010

new babies are fun!!!!! hope your trip is a safe one back home.

—useraj February 06, 2010

Hi Joe,

Congratulations on your new grandson. Glad to here that your daughter is doing well and Lucus is getting on track—a sign of strength on his part.

I know that the kids can be tiring sometimes even when we are in the best of health.

Take one thing at a time and follow Mary's suggestion of giving yourself a brain break when you need it.

Take care and God bless to you and your family.

Amanda

Hello My Friends, Hello!

Monday, February 08, 2010

We are back from Petaluma. Daughter and new grandson doing well. She is home, Lucas still in hospital hopefully home this Saturday.

We finally got a room on base in guest quarters. Gramps here could not handle staying with the kids, even though we had our oun room. I needed a hide out period. Had to increase meds while there just to try and cope. Am Losing control of my emotions and ability to keep calm and mouth shut.

Came home sick again. But we have figured out the problem, their is mold and mildew all over tha t base and I am highly alergic to mold. So from now on will have to build up with antihistamines before we go.

Now to start back on the pond. God this disease just makes me not want to do things, forget what the hell I am doing and really now mly emotions and starting to not care about others, they are starting not to exist for me. I have a very hard time writing on this thing now. Mind wanders toooo much. But still can get out something. Body is starting to rule itself and not tell me. Eating I forget to eat or tha t I ate real pain.

Until we meet again.

God Bless You & This Country of Ours!

joe

Posted by Joseph Potocny at 12:39PM (-08:00)

Comments

—karen   February 08, 2010

Glad all is well. Sorry you got sick. And I hope you get your pond done soon. It is snowing here so no outside work for any of us.

—useraj   February 10, 2010

Hey Joe,

Glad to hear all is well with your daughter and grandson. Handling kids for some can be a challenge even without your issues. In the end you were still their for your family when they needed it—hats off to you. Now you are home and can work on your koi pond . . . fish are pretty quite, so, as Mary puts it, you can have a brain break.

Have finished my project . . . I am presenting it to the class tomorrow—hope I can do it without crying (that's O.K. have a box of kleenex with me). Thank-you for allowing me and others into your world—it is a great educational lesson that is never ending. I only hope that those listening to it tomorrow learn some of what I have learned and also keep learning, listening and advocating for patient's and their families.

I will continue to read your blog and stay intouch . . .

Keep smiling . . . my thoughs and prayers are with you and your family

Amanda (AJ)

—jncsundberg   February 11, 2010

Howdy Joe, Welcome home. Im so glad everything looks good for the new and wonderful Lucas. Sorry you got sick, and hope that you feel better soon. The Koi pond sounds like a fun project. Good luck, and I hope you make quick progress. It'll be a nice place for a comfy chair to just sit and try to have a little peace.

Think about you often. Love, Cheryl (Arlene's daughter)

—Marion   February 13, 2010

Hi, Joe,

It's been awhile since I've commented . . . I lost your blog! So glad I've found you again. I've been wondering how you are doing. And here I discover you are a new grandparent! I will be catching up on what you've been up to, now that I've found you again.

—Anonymous   February 16, 2010

Hi Joe Love the pictures and the blog. We will write soon. Randy and Deborah

Hello All!

Tuesday, February 23, 2010

My ggrandson Lucas is now home from hospital and out of the NICU and mom is fine, so they do not have that stress anylonger.

We built a cover over the pond and have started to plant the area, should be done soon, then will post pictures. We have a new femaile Koi that is pregnant. She is black with a white belly and white nose so we call her Orca. Have to get a male for her, since I lost mine.

I have been trying to read a book from a friend who has been published and it comes out in June, so I cannot tell you the name yet. I am having problems with it, very slow reader I am. But what I see in it that for you care givers it probably will be good. I cannot relate to the person's feelings from this side of the fence, except to let them know that many of their feelings we have on this side. Of course we don't have the family BS of what to do with us to tend with, we just keep going on and forgetting. But I can see how it could get tacky, since we are still locked away and forgotten about. Not alot has changed over the decades.

I am starting to become disconnectd from life in general and my past and who I once was. Things seem to be of little importance anymore. Ask me this afternoon what I did this morning and I will have problems telling you and so goes the day and my life. Trying to keep a sense of humor is becoming hard, I do not like this world of mine but I cannot change it, it is what it is, shit.

Posting is getting harder. The note on my computer to do so does not help much, I just start and forget and walk away. telling of the misery of this does not even fill worhwihile anymore. There is a lonelyness that is setting in a feeling of being apart from everything, and trying to hang on I feel like I am drowning in a vast void in my mind.

So much babbling.

God Bless You & This Country of Ours!

joe

Posted by Joseph Potocny at 10:37AM (-08:00)

Comments

—karen   February 23, 2010

So glad the baby and mommie is doing well. And Can't wait to see photos of the pond.I bet it very pretty. You are very brave writing this post and sharing what you are going throw. I am a caregiver so I don't know what it is like on your side of the fence. I can only say God Bless and Good Luck.

—kenju   February 23, 2010

I'm sorry, Joe.

Your "telling of the misery" can help others understand what to expect and help us understand others who may be going down the same path.

—Anonymous   February 23, 2010

Glad to hear Lucas is home and that you are back on track with our pond. I know posting must be getting harder and harder but you really are helping some many. Continue on for as long as you can.

—Moonchild   February 24, 2010

All I can say is I really feel for you.I can't imagine what you are going through. The fact that you have kept your sense of humor for as long as you have is amazing. What struck me about your piece on the HBO special was your biting sense of humor and honesty. We are rooting for you and your family.

—user   March 01, 2010

原來這世上能跟你共同領略一個笑話的人竟如此難得 . . .

—JUSTAMOM   March 01, 2010

I am AMAZED at your writing I LOVE COMING AND READING YOUR WORDS!!!! PLEASE KEEP WRITING!!!!

—Mary   March 02, 2010

Hi Joe . . . glad to hear the good news about Lucas. I'm so sorry that you are struggling these days. Please write whenever you feel up to it! They keep telling us that brain exercise will keep us going longer . . . I do hope they are right! Hugs Mary~Canada

A Favor to Ask.

Tuesday, March 02, 2010

My friend Mary, who's site is listed in my linkes, is having some real troubles health wise. Also her doctor is being a pain about meds for her hubby who has AD also. Please say a prayer for the two of them so that they get the right help. I would appreciate it. I am starting to loose to many friends to this disease.

They live in Canada and their whether is nowhere as nice as my haunts.

If I remember I will post pictures of THE POND, yes it is 95% done, need to get an electrician to run the out door cables for me. Me and electricity, not a good match, never was and even less so now.

Until later:

God Bless You & This Country of Ours!

Joe

Posted by Joseph Potocny at 03:50PM (-08:00)

Comments

—JUSTAMOM   March 03, 2010

PRAYERS!!!!! can't wait to see the pond!

—Anonymous   March 03, 2010

Joe . . . I am certainly sending prayers Mary's way. I am looking forward to seeing pictures of your pond. It will be so relaxing for you when finished. Take care.

Hugs . . . Sandy

—MOONIE   March 03, 2010

Prayers for your friends!

Without Further Ado & Much Fanfare!

Thursday, March 04, 2010

First thanks to all you who offered their prayers for my friends Mary & Jim. I spoke to Mary via Skype today and so far so good. Again Thank you! A Drum roll if you please!!!!!!!!!! The old pond area, waterfall removed and relandscaped, not by me others in the house. Will be used for water plants and raising up our baby Koi that are due soon. First I have to get a male to help the preganant one.

I know you all have been waiting for the new area. Well except for getting the lighting all correct and wiring finished here it is.

Thanks for waiting and asking for the pictures, my hide away is near complete. In case you are wondering, which you have to be, where did the othjer water fall go. Well it now graces the front of the house. We also have an ornamental type pond out there.

Thank you all for beign out there for me. It is much appreciated. Now the brain is fried for the day after trying to place these pictures where they did not want to go. Thanks again! God Bless You and This Country of Ours!

joe

Posted by Joseph Potocny at 10:55AM (-08:00)

Comments

—Mary   March 05, 2010

Joe, I love the pictures . . . your gardens look so beautiful and inviting! Can you just imagine if we could sit by your pond and chat, instead of on Skype, which was fantastic by the way! And thank you and your friends for saying a wee prayer for Jim and I. I just wish our doctor would get with the program! lol Hugs Mary

—Moonie   March 05, 2010

Very nice!!! I need help with my space. My spitting turtle fountain died many moons ago and my pond just collects dead things. The sound of water is so relaxing and pleasant. I miss it.

Glad to hear your friends are better too!

—Danielle   March 05, 2010

Area looks great Joe! I need to get on my backyard . . . its an open canvas.So when are you heading back up to Petaluma? I am just in Sacramento and would love to have lunch . . . Petaluma has some good places to eat. Danielle (Bill's Daugher) The Dementia Guy

—Anonymous   March 07, 2010

Joe

I am so jealous to see sun and green grass surrounding your beautiful pond as mine is burried under snow and ice . . . must wait until May to put my fish back in and get the waterfall flowing . . . will look longingly at your pics until then

Tried Cooking Again!

Wednesday, March 10, 2010

I stopped cooking the last time I tried to broil some chicken and set it a blaze. It got done, but on the chrunchy side and a little charcoallly.

First I read my friend Marys blog, she had a great picture of a head with lettered blocks int it and telling how she had to get heres back together. I feel very slighted, she has more blocks in her head then I do, the wood peckers have gotten mine. But the two I have left crash together quite nicely.

I mad spaghetti tonignt. Used a can of Hunts Traditional, to which I added galick powder, bazil, parsley, salt, peper and sugarr. I saucted a full bulb of fresh garlic, halving each clove and added pistachio nuts to it with little salt, pepper, garlic powder and Olive Oil about 1½ teaspoons. Cooke the garlic and nuts until all the oil was absorbed, dumped it into the sauce, very unceremoniesously. Browned and well drained som hamburger and blended it in and cooked about half hour. Off course we cooked noodles to. It actually turned out. Not to bad of a day today.

We do have some good days. I want to let you know of what I feel is good, at least for me having this wonderful disease, it has given me a peace inside about dieing, which is what is happening. I am no longer afraid of it, nor worry about it. In fact I look at it as my next journey, after this crappy one is over.

God Bless You All & This Country of Ours!

joe

Posted by Joseph Potocny at 06:03PM (-08:00)

Comments

—Annie	March 10, 2010

Sounds good Joe! Can I come for dinner? :)

—kenju	March 10, 2010

Joe, you are amazing. I like the sound of your recipe. I never thought about putting pistachios in the sauce, but I bet that was good!

—JUSTAMOM	March 11, 2010

WOO HOOO GREAT JOB ON THE DINNER AND LOVE THE PICTURES . . . COME FIX UP MY BACK YARD WILL YA . . .

March 11, 2010

I'm glad you are still cooking and yes, don't worry about the pounds, you can't take them with you! Sounds delicious

What Day Is It?

Sunday, March 14, 2010

Many of you probably find that an easy question. Well around here it is asked who knows how many times each day. Then I always ask are you sure. Of course minutes later I ask all over again. My wife smiles so pleasantly and reminds me one mor time. After awhile my daughter will just say Dad it doesn't matter. I guess she is right. See to me it is always someday but I am not sure which one. If I rember I will ask from now on "Is Today, Today". hopefully it will lessen some of the frustration. But first I have to remember, now that is another story.

Oh well life goes on and I just keep doing whatever it is I do. Thanks for listening, stay well and be good to yourselves.

God Bless & Keep You & This Country of Ours!

Joe

Posted by Joseph Potocny at 09:04AM (-07:00)

Comments

—JUSTAMOM   March 14, 2010

Dont' feel bad Joe I ask teh SAME QUESTION just about everyday! IT IS TODAY SOUNDS LIKE A GREAT ANSWER, I will use it!

—karen   March 14, 2010

I forget what day it is all the time but I know you forget you ask what day it was already.Which makes is hard on you and your family. But I am glad you care what day it is and bet they are too. I think today is a good answer.

My Brain on The Move.

Tuesday, March 16, 2010

I do not know what this one will be titled, because I am not sure what is really inside of me today. I finished after quiet sometim a book called "When Can I Go Home". I was asked for what reason I am not sure to review it. The author can post my review if he wishes once I write it.

I will tell you that I think, once and awhile, that most people will miss the real hidden story of the book. Caregivers will find solice from it I am sure. But

235

what struck me is that we that live in this world of AD are still put aside as the wicked stepchild. Not that, that was necessarily done here, but seems to me it was without knowing.

See I feel that way because folks say no your ok, and I am not, I never know where or who I am going to be. I started this blog in 2006 and I am not sure why anymore. I like hearing from folks but I really wish those who read this that live in this World of ever growing darkness and confusion would write me. Feeling alone in this journey is no fun and I know I am not alone but feel that way often. It is difficut writing these things trying to keep them readable.

It upsets me, again my problem, but people write you write back and never hear from them again. I am sure that I have forgotten to answer many an email. I can only same I am sorry, here to all that I have missed.

I wonder if you know that AD is the #7 killer. I think that if they put the real reason people die, like their liver stopped because their brain forgot to tell it to work and things like that happen frequently with this disease that it would very likely be #1.

My brain is just bouncing around right now so until later, be good to yourselves.

God Bless & Keep You & This Country of Ours!

Posted by Joseph Potocny at 04:59PM (-07:00)

Comments

—SkinnyBitchFlunky   March 16, 2010

No I do not live inside your world. I once lived just outside of it with my father. I can say that my father was pist all the time about it. He wasnt happy most of time. I know that all the thoughts he had were like a jumbled up ball of confusion. My father couldnt read or write. Though it was never a strong characteristic of his. I am glad that you still have that ability. Though most of us are just on the outside of your world, we appreciate the insight you give us. We appreciate your honesty. I talk to my therapist about my dad today. His conclusion is that even though my dad is gone, I am still trying to connect with him. You help with that a bit. You help us understand our loved ones a little more. Thank You.

—Anonymous   March 17, 2010

Joe . . . I am walking your shoes . . . only a different size. I know how difficult it is to put into words what your mind is thinking and I want to let you know . . . you are correct, you are not alone. I understand. It took me 30 minutes just to write this paragraph. I enjoy reading your words that bounce out of you brain . . . keep writing . . . then I know I am not alone also. A person with dementia, Sandy

—paula   March 17, 2010

Joe, I love reading your blog. This disease has taken 2 women out of my life, and I already see the signs in my father's eyes. I am in charge of all training in the long term care center for Veterans. We have a 50 bed dementia unit. I share your insight with those I teach about dementia. I can only simulate not knowing and the frustration of your world. The nurses and CNAs that take care of our Veterans with dementia really appriciate your expression of not knowing.

—JUSTAMOM   March 18, 2010

Joe I come here and read what you write and you AMAZE ME. I am loking to change jobs to a new place for all people with AD. It is run like a HOME no schedules for eating or resting or bathing. NO mass production needed. I hope I get it because I would like to tell them in charge about how well you are able to use this little box. Have a great week. keep writing.

—rilera   March 18, 2010

Joe, I read every post and now I will reply just to let you know that I feel your frustration at this horrible disease. You give me insight into what my dear mother went through with Alzheimer's. Know that you are in my thoughts.

Robyn

Need Some Thoughts.

Saturday, March 20, 2010

I know that a number of people with AD and other forms of Dementia read my site as well as a number of care givers. I had something happen to me yesterday that has me well shall we say concerned for what might lye ahead. I need some advise if any of you have experienced this. I got up, nothing special, but I went about the day doing what I had to without any type of mental or physical interruption. My wife's computer has been giving her fits, so I spent 10.5 hours on completely rebuilding it and setting it back to where it should be will all files she lost. This all took place without skipping a heart beat. I felt completely in control and as if it were 7 or more years ago. For me I felt normal, whatever that is or was. What scares me is, what the hell does this mean and is it something that happens at times, because I wonder if a bigger slide is comming and this was a sort of last hurrah. Any insight would be helpfull. God Bless & Keep You & This Country of Ours!

Joe

Posted by Joseph Potocny at 09:50AM (-07:00)

237

Comments

—karen   March 20, 2010

I am so glad you had a good day and pray for many more for you. My mom is way more advanced than you but she does have better days than others. And I have to adjust her meds. To much meds. she is no where to be found and not enough meds. and she is upset all day. But if I can get it right she talks to me and eats good and makes sense sometimes. I do hope you are on an Alz's med. I beleive if mom had of started hers sooner she would be much less advanced. The sooner you start the Alz's meds. The slower the desease progresses. I am sure you know that. But we got it on her to late for much help. But I could see a differance. She is off the Alz's meds. now the doc. said they do no good at this point but she takes pills to calm her and pills for pain and to help her sleep. Good luck.

—paula   March 20, 2010

You are AMAZING! I am so glad you posted and I read this! Thank you!!! I do know a theory about what happened. With AD, as you know your short term memory goes away, then you recent long term . . . what is spared to a great deal are EMOTIONAL memories. Double bang for your buck if they are long ago, emotional memories. Tie that in with a bit of motor memory and there you have it. I remember you saying in the HBO project "I sat down to a computer and that was it" "I really loved it". That is emotional memory. Ever wondered why you can remember events and not people? People are facts (names, who/what they are), events have an emotion tied to them, they are not just facts. Do you have people in your life you know you should know, but have no idea of their name? A name is a fact, which AD doesn't like. How they make you feel is emotion, which AD doesn't mind to let you have. I have a video that really explans it from Heather McKay. If you/anyone are interested you can email prdrn71@hotmail.com (it may take a few days for a response, but I will respond) I can get the order information. The video is meant for "professional caregivers" in the Veteran setting, but the information amazing and really helps people understand the whole brain thing . . . Hope I helped and CONGRATULATIONS on doing what you love!

—SkinnyBitchFlunky   March 20, 2010

I have had an experience with my father that resembles this. I walked in from a long day at work and my cousin, who I paid to entertain (watch) my dad, was playing blackjack with him. I watched them both play for about 20more mins and I swear to god he was adding his cards up on his own. At this point he couldnt read or write. I think that it has to do with what was embeded in your head before you started having symptoms . . . something you did all the time.

My dad was an avid blackjack player, bowler, smoker . . . and he never forgot how to do any of those things til his heart attack. That the only conclusion I can come up with.

—Mary
March 20, 2010

Hi Joe . . . and thanks so much for the Skype call. Jim and I both enjoyed talking to you.

I totally love it when I get a "nearly normal" brain day. I've chatted with others who also get these days, and have even had two in a row. I've never experienced any major downhill slide after, so I don't think you need to worry about it. Just enjoy it to the fullest! Hugs Mary~Canada

—JUSTAMOM
March 21, 2010

Great day JOE!!! Yep I have seen it over and over again, us on the outside sept back in AMAZMENT when it happens. I am told sometimes the little wires kinda re-spark for a bit . . . ENJOY IT!!!!!!!

—rilera
March 21, 2010

Wow Joe, that is awesome! Did you use to work with computers? If so, that explains this. Things that we used to do become second nature and for some reason we hold onto those skills. My mom was an accomplished pianist and she held onto this well into the moderate phase of her ALZ. I don't think it means you are going to have a decline soon. Hang in there and keep up with your posts.

Robyn

HE/SHE — HIS/HERS

Saturday, March 27, 2010

Confusing title, well maybe. See my wife told me the other day that one of the earliest problems I had after the diagnose was made, was keeping genders straight. Apparrently then and now when I talk about her I am talking about him and so on. Maybe this is why I never had much luck dating in my early years.

The last few days I have felt kind of lost in space and not sure of what I am exactly up to or doing. But I have not met any green people lately.

Will be attempting on working on changing my blog, the look and such, hopefully I can test it somewhere to fix the mess ups. Hope to make it so that those who read it can also blog on it. Maybe open some discussions or give some of you a place to say what you need to. Will see what happens.

Time to put my brain to rest again before it attacks me.

God Bless You & Keep You & This Country of Ours!

Joe

P.S. Do not feel like I do not appreciate your emails, I have been very bad lately at answering. Starting not to even turn this beast on anymore. Posted by Joseph Potocny at 10:56AM (-07:00)

Comments

—JUSTAMOM   March 29, 2010

that is so normal . . . hope you have a good week.

The Relentless Killer Alhziemers.

Tuesday, March 30, 2010

Normally I talk about how this affects me, today I like to beg the question, "Do You Really Know How This Disease Kills?"

I suggest to many of you your real and honest answer is not really. They tell us (the know it alls), that we forget things slowly, forget to eat, bathe, etc. and then linger and die. Well I in my limited capacity suggest to you that they are chuck full of shit. Joseph forgets none of these things, that which is Joseph. What happens really is that my brain, that finally tuned sharp as a tact organ, does the fucking up.

You see when my stomache or body sends the enzymes and nerve messages to my glorious brain that I am hungry and need to eat, the damned thing no longer understands, it now speaks a second language. My bladder and intestines scream, so it listens to my ears of course they have nothing to do with those lower class forlks and well you can guess the result. As time goes on my brain no longer recognizes smells, so who needs to bathe?

Latter I die do to liver failure (the second death). Why? Well stupid upstairs answered the wrong phone call, not the one for instructions from the liver, but the bladder. Or my heart stops, why, because Mr. genious was trying to tell me my toe hurt. Get the picture. I will physically die as others because my brain will no longer under stand it's own unique coding system to keep me functioning. NOT ME, not my doing, the grey matter will be out to lunch. As the old saying goes, THE LIGHTS ARE ON, BUT NOBODY IS HOME!

What brought this to my train of thought was The Forbidden Planet, where the robot is given a command and it's electrical signals (the brain) went into turmoil and with nothing to counter act the order it would just go kaput. So goes our brain, kaput. A bunch of ramdom requests made by our organs that just confuse the hell out of it, so they all shut down and so does it. Process not compatible with life, THE END.

Simple stated yes, but it is that basic. Now all the brilliant ones can tell me how wrong I am, with their fancy words that when boiled down to their basic elements will be just kaput.

You see I grow weary with all the BS of how much more we understand and all the strides made. I say to you then "WHY ARE THEIR NO SURVIVORS?" It is simple you do not have the answers and are not even close. You study rats and mice, I am neither, you study dead brains (wow they can speak), mine is still alive, study mine and others like me, maybe then you may get some real answers. I do not mean your normal 100 or 200 particpatnt studies, try one of 10, 000 there are more than enough of us.

You all claim that about 5.5 million people (this country only) are affected by AD in this country, I submit you are wrong. I have AD and I affect, my wife, mother-in-law, five children, physc, GP, physcologist, 7 grandchildren and about 5 friends. That is a total of 22 people affected by me. Lets say that 5.5 million onlyy affect a total of 7 each, that means that 38, 500, 000 people are affected. Why are we still put on the back of the bus? I wonder what the cost in $$$$$ is, billions yearly, maybe that will catch your dead ears.

Till later take care and be kind to yourselves. My brain now hurts.

God Bless & Keep You & This Country of Ours!

Joe

Posted by Joseph Potocny at 11:59AM (-07:00)

Comments

—SkinnyBitchFlunky   March 30, 2010

I totally agree with you!

—JUSTAMOM   April 01, 2010

and you say your brain is shutting down THAT WAS PRETTY DARN GOOD JOE!!!!! hhahahaa have a great day!

—BestNeurosurgicalHospita   April 12, 2010

I do welcome of your valued blog.

Before The Lynchers Come After Me!

Wednesday, March 31, 2010

Sorry I forgot they have discovered a GENE in some families that makes them more prone to AD. What a mystery, we knew it ran in some families, great rocket scientist work that there was a gene. So I ask, what does that do for these folks? Did you discover how the gene causes AD? (Yes or probably NO) Just how will this help those to follow me and others? I know I sound skeptic, but 100+ years and nothing. Imagine HIV in 1980's, we are now working and testing a vaccine for it. I am sorry for thoses who got the disease through no fault of there own, but sharing needles, unprotected sex, etc. your choice. I and those before me and with me have not had any choice in this. I could take on cancers and heart disease, but I think most of you know how I feel and why.

#7 Reported Killer—AD. No cure, No Survivors. Only you can really help come out of the shadows and join others and beat down the doors of stigma, we are not lepoards which now can be stopped.

God Bless You & Keep You & This Country of Ours!

joe

Posted by Joseph Potocny at 11:25AM (-07:00)

Comments

—SkinnyBitchFlunky   April 01, 2010

When my father passed . . . well the day of, I had the nurse pull some blood that I drove down to UCLA to have testing done as part of the research on familial AD. My father was positive for the mutated gene. When I got that news, I started to worry and wonder what that would be like for me. Now, I just take the steps to make sure that my family doesnt go through what I had to with my father. I have long term health insurance started and I am trying to be healthy overall. But it seems to be a disclaimer whenever I get serious with someone I am dating. Maybe I should stop that . . . lol.

Guest Blogger Joe Sivak MD

Saturday, April 03, 2010

I would like to thank my friend Joe for the privilege of being asked to be a guest writer on his blog. In the big scheme of things I have known Joe for only a short time through the wonderful technology of the Internet. I started blogging about eight months ago and soon found Joe's blog. I immediately resonated with so much of the feeling and emotion and spirit with which Joe writes. I felt sort of a strange kind of kindred spirit. It is sort of that weird feeling, where you never met someone but when you connect with them, you feel that connection was always there and it is sort of timeless. You see Alzheimer's was the thing that connected us. Joe has the disease, my mother was diagnosed with the disease in 1979, when most people had not heard of it. I started a book about my journey many years ago and finally finished it this year. It is titled When

Can I Go Home? I asked Joe to read the book and tell me what he thought. I knew it would be hard, and I debated a long time. I didn't want to make Joe feel sad or mad, but his review in a way was the most important one I wanted. It was more important than if I could get Publisher's Weekly or New York Times or any high profile review. Why was that? I wanted to show that people with AD are people who count, with thoughts feelings, and a spirit. No matter how far the disease gets, there is a person. The point of Joe's blog and the point of my book is that we should never, ever cast aside any human being just because they have AD. The truth of that matter is: is that now matter how far we think we have come as a progressive, altruistic, advanced and humane society, we have a very long way to go when it comes to people living with Alzheimer's. Alzheimer's initially brought us together, but immediately after that the connection was fundamentally not about the disease, but just about two guys, Joe and me who actually share a lot of the same fundamental views and insights. And Yes, Joe has tremendous insights that we can all learn a lot from. I am a psychiatrist, but Joe didn't not hold that against me. Neither of us particularly like psychiatrists. Joe instinctively knew and knows that is just what I do professionally, sometimes in that realm I can help people and sometimes I can't, sometimes all I can do is be there as a human being yet in that pretense of a professional realm. Joe said he only read a couple books in his life, mine and Bill Cosby's Fatherhood. So I was indeed in good company! Joe knew and talked about the disease, he knows first hand better than anyone, how Alzheimer's is two deaths. The disease taking the person's mind and the physical death. Joe and I know the disease tries to take the person's spirit. some days it feels like it does, but it never really can or will. You see Joe's spirit is there and always will be. You see it in those faces in those pictures he posts, it is in those grand kids. Those faces, those smiles, when you see it in his family and grandchildren you see Joe's spirit and his goodness, and the disease never ever can or will take that away. That lives on forever, that spirit is eternal. Take a look at his pictures, it is there. You see Joe's essence. Joe asked for a picture of my mother. He posted it on his blog. Her name was Madeline. She is physically gone from the earth, but Joe knows that we never forget, and her essence lives on through her kids and grand kids, and the disease does not get to take that. People like Joe are a gift to the human race, he reminds us to never forget. In a way Joe knew the pain I still feel from my mother's disease, he sort of offered me a kind of spiritual absolution, a setting free if you will. I never really considered or expected that, but Joe knew. I hope in some way although I know it was hard fir him to get through, that in reading the book, somehow our connection set him free just a little. He knows I will never cast him or anyone with the disease aside. Joe is not an Alzheimer's victim, Joe is just a guy, a human being who happens to be living with the disease. We can all learn a lot from his writing, it should be required reading in schools. He is tough and smart, he is human. We all have a little bit of Joe in us. He will keep blogging and writing, it is not about the words it is about his essence and his spirit. He will keep loving life and hating the disease, just like me. He will love his family and his love will go on generation after generation. Thank you Joe for this honor to post on your blog. Your courage and dignity and humanness is there for everyone. Joseph J. Sivak MD

http://alzheimmers.blogspot.com http://www.niagarapress.net
http://www.facebook.com/pages/When-Can-I-Go-Home/357170603956
http://twitter.com/WhenCanIGoHome
Posted by Joseph J. Sivak MD at 07:49AM (-07:00)

Comments

—Anonymous   April 03, 2010

Hi Joe . . . and so happy that Joe has your friendship, support and experience to join him in his journey. I've talked to Joe on Skype, and we too have made a connection. This would be a very lonely journey without our online friends, who perhaps have some understanding of our daily struggles. Hugs Mary~Canada

—colleenmc   April 03, 2010

Dr. Joe (both of you), thank you for this blogsite, for today's blog, and for the love and spirit show here. My mom suffered from AD for many years but did not die from it. She eventually died from the ravages of cancer. But she suffered most from the AD, from the loss of the support of loved ones. It is hard to write these words, in part because it is so soon and in part because I am accused of making people feel 'guilty' for not being there. But, if anyone can do anything for a person with AD, I believe the most important is to be there for them and to encourage, no DEMAND, like Joe P. SHOUTS so often in his blog, that we GET TO WORK ON A CURE NOW, please, now. God Bless you Joes, God Bless Mrs. P. Thank you for this blog and I will send a picture of mom soon.

—karen   April 03, 2010

Wonderful. I am proud to say I know both of these guys because of this blogging thing and both of them have made my life alot easier. Thanks guys.

—JUSTAMOM   April 05, 2010

Can't wait to get and read this book.

—JosephPotocny   April 06, 2010

Doc,

Thanks, what I wanted, but you make me sound like superman, not even close, but your being here and my friend is of great value to me.

God Bless,

Joe

May The Lord Bless You This Day & Always!!!!

Sunday, April 04, 2010

From my family to yours a very Blessed and Happy Easter. To those of you who have entered this World of mine and do not celebrate the day, celebrate it with us for you are welcomed here. To all I extend to you my hand so that YOU KNOW, THAT YOU, NEVER HAVE TO DO THIS THING CALLED LIFE ALONE EVER AGAIN.

Well I have started inviting some folks to be guest bloggers and we will see how this works. I have tried with a 24 hour chatroom for you, that was not used, different ways of talking not taken advantage of. See This is My Blog, but You are a part of it and I would like you to share in it. Only requirement is that you deal with dementia, as a caregiver, reasearcher or one on this road of unknown journey. Thanks Dr. Joe for being first to join in.

If you wish to join me and others here, just fill out the email form at the bottom of the right hand side and send me your email address and I will send you the info. Actually Blogger will send it for me.

Well the family has descended and I have found it necessary to retreat. I can only be a jungle jim for so long and I hurt. Body is definitely not what it once was, not that it was ever much to start with. My temper is much shorter and I have a hard time controlling me, so retreating works.

I feel lost today and not quite sure what the old brain wants besides to escape and be alone somewhere.

We may He Bless You All This Day and Forever.]

God Bless & Keep You and This Country of Ours and Yours!

Joe

Posted by Joseph Potocny at 10:01AM (-07:00)

Comments

—DirtyButter April 05, 2010

Hi Joe!! It's been a long time since I took the time to stop by and see how your were doing, and for that I'm sorry. I'm glad to see you are still actively blogging and recording your thoughts. As for getting old and needing to get away from all the youthful activity of grandkids??? Believe me, that's not an AD thing, that's an age thing! LOL I hope you and your family all had a Blessed Easter.

Take care, good friend,

Rosemary

HI, I am Jaye, Just a mom.

Monday, April 05, 2010

Joe has invited me to be a guest poster on his great blog. I would like to say first I am HONORED. As someone who has come into this disease differently then most most you who read here. I am a caregiver in Memory Care at a community/facility. I had never been personally acquainted with anyone who was diagnosed with A/D. 2 years ago I got a job in the field, I was scared to death not knowing what to expect and quickly fell in love. I have been surrounded with many different stages of this horrible disease and have also learned to hate it. I am amazed with the human mind and just how much to does, and in this case does NOT do. I would like to say that those of you who keep your loved ones at home, YOU have a harder job then I do. I hope you have a large support group, it can get tough. I get to do my 8 hours and leave to go home and get on with my life, you do not. I, from the outside have watched people who I have become very close to loose to this thing. The people in charge try to tell us to not get attached, HOW can we NOT? They become my family, they depend on me to make sure they are safe, clean, secure, exercised both mentally and physically. I sometimes feel I am the only one who will sit and reassure a resident life is ok. It is heart breaking to watch my residents go from being a functioning person in their world to not being able to even eat or drink on their own. I am in no place to know about the medical terms I only know the results of them. In the last 2 years of my working with residents with A/D I have seen many different ages, genders, nationalities. This disease does not choose a certain kind. I learn what they once WERE and I am at times knocked on my butt with sadness at how not WHO they have become because of this. I see that they are still the same person on the inside almost trapped in a body that will not allow them to continue with their lives. I know it is at times very humiliating to them that I have to clean them, feed them, help them dress and even a little task of dressing is hard for them.

The stages I see are the beginning confusion, anger, fear. This is where to the outsider, these people get MEAN. All they need is a little time, slow down that is my big advice. These people have done for themselves for many years. toileted, showered, dressed, brushed their teeth everything. Who are we the outsider telling them when, how they need to be doing these things. SLOW DOWN, DONT' RUSH THEM, be careful with your words. Don't say, YOU NEED TO DO, I have found the gentle, LET'S DO THIS OR CAN WE DO THAT. works so much better. Tone and Volume play a big roll here too. I truly believe this stage is the hardest to deal with. They can be sweet as pie and in a heart beat ready to KILL you. Trick here as I see it is keep your eyes open learn the triggers or the facial expressions and KNOW when it will happen as best as you can and head it off before it gets there. Turning them around after they have gone fully into a rage is very hard to do. I do NOT like medicating them as many seem to do. Take in every smooth time you can, THIS TOO SHALL PASS.

It then seems to slips into those who float through their day. We have what we call wanders/walkers who will NOT stop for the life of themselves. The seem to not be able to sit still EVER, not even to eat. I find finger foods work well at this point. So what if they drop crumbs on the floor, they are at least eating something. There are those who seem to be going on with daily lives inside. They will go from room to room and pick up things that are not theirs and carry it to another room, setting it where they think it should belong. We find so many odd things where they should not be. Best thing to do it just smile, Does it really matter where it ended up? Frustrating but IF ya leave it long enough it just MIGHT end up back where it came from in the first place.

The end of life is the most heart wrenching of all, I choose not to even go there with this. I will only say that for me I become attached to these people and my heart breaks almost as much as their families.

So for me the caregiver who get to bow out for a time I give ALL you who keep your loved ones at home with you and care fore them 24/7. YOU are the ones with the hard job, your hard work and love is what counts most.

Thank you again Joe for asking me to post on your amazing blog. Keep up your writing for as long as you can. I will keep coming back and read. You have given me yet ANOTHER view from the inside. Posted by JUST A MOM at 08:56PM (-07:00)

Comments

—ladolceliving
April 06, 2010

Living with people who have dementia or alzheimer's disease may be trying at times. It will really test your patience specifically during the times when they throw tantrums and refuse to eat. Nevertheless, caring for your elderly parents is the best thing that you could do for them. All your hard work will pay off if you see them playing like little kids with their grandchildren. It is a kind of bitter-sweet experience. And for that, you love to take care of your elderly parents and grandparents for ever.

—JosephPotocny   April 06, 2010

Thank you Jaye, this is what I hoped for. I want the site to be rounded and not just my point of view from this side.

Joe

—SkinnyBitchFlunky   April 08, 2010

Thanks Jaye. I too found how speaking to someone in the late stages can make or break your day. My father was quite violent if I told him what to do . . . his weak point was chocolate . . . so bribery was my tool. I think I bought 10 boxes of Coco Puffs a week. Thank You for your contribution!!! This is awesome Joe!

Frustration Reigns!

Friday, April 09, 2010

This week has been a difficult week for me. Just toooooo much family and kids. Good thing I have additional meds to take or I woud not have kept things to gether. I love my family, but I am becoming less tolerant, more mouthy, angry and pissed mor easily. I have a grate deal of trouble controlling my mouth and emotions lately.

I want to thank the two who have taken the opportunity to guest blog here. I have invited several that I thought could add to the thought processes found here on both sides of the fence as it awere. But it seems that some old "friends" choose not to. Everyone has something to offer. Even if it does not agree with what is felt here. That is what this blog is about. Expressing feelings about having dementia and those careing for us. Neither side is neat and tydie, they both suck. I miss the days when I could think more clearly and express myself and do it (ego here) with little room for argument. Now I am lucky to blog at all. But no this you are all welcome even those who feel I am just an angry old fart, angry yess, old yess and I guess a fart as well.

I try to not talk about everyday things, but how this disease affects me overall. Yess some days I am on top of it others I cann't even find the stairs. I do find the walls I walk into them and excuse myself. Yes I have taken additional meds today, and am still shaking inside and my temper is border line, but the impression of my teeth in my tongue helps me keep quiet. I will be posting some emails that I have been give permis to, I ask because not everyone leaves comments.

Dr. Joe I guess the 10.00 bucks I paid you for your post paid off. Doc I really cannot walk on water, trust me, I can barely walk on the ground without it moving. But I thank you, my friend.

Well you all take care and be good to each other.

God Bless You & Keep You and This Country of Ours!

Joe

Posted by Joseph Potocny at 02:31PM (-07:00)

Comments

—JUSTAMOM   April 11, 2010

hang in there have a good week.

New Link Added

Wednesday, April 14, 2010

First let me say that if you have not tried Google Chrome, you might want to, much faster.

I have added a link to the Beijing Tiantun Puhua Hospital today. This may seem strange to you, but I figure if they can use this blog as a source for them in China, least I could do was add them to my links. They contacted me, let me say that kind of took my socks off.

I needed their contact, the last couple of days have been very uncomfortable and less then memorable and they made my day. It has been difficult to know where I have been, but I know I have not been with my family or my own brain, but that is life with AD and any dementia.

God Bless & Keep You & This Country of Ours!

joe

Posted by Joseph Potocny at 10:55AM (-07:00)

Comments

—JamieVeggie   April 17, 2010

Hi sir, I just wanted to tell you that I think it's really great that you keep this blog. My grandma has AD and she's in a Memory Care unit. I love her so much, and it's hard to accept that she has AD but you certainly have helped me see how she thinks and feels. Thank you, and I hope you have a nice week.

—karen   April 17, 2010

Congrats. China is better off now that they have meant you. Good job. Hope you have a good week.

The Gift of Alhziemer's!

Monday, April 19, 2010

Yes I know what gift? You need to have the disease to understand. See because of this blasted thing, I learned something today that I did not know, even with it starring me right in the kisser. I was reading over some emails I got because of the HBO Documenttary.

It brought people I knew from over 50 years ago back into my life. Of course they had to tell me how, when, why, etc., before the old noodle could grasp it. This may get long and run in circles, but what the hell, if I can run in them so can you.

You see I wanted most of all to be a good husband, lover, friend, father and someone the Lord would be proud to call his child. Well I feld very badly in my own mind and soul. So as I re read an email from my first girlfriend, the only one nuts enough to date me, Cheryl, I really realized how fortunate I am to have AD. You see, I have invited her to guest blog, but no response, what an asset to this site she would be. Now remember she dated me (poor lady), her mom has AD and Cheryl works for The Alz. Org. in Colorado what a wealth of help. But more than that, after we broke ups I had 16 years of a real messed up life. So you understand and I am not sure I do, she was about 5'6" 115#, brown hair, brown eyes and nicely, well very pleasant to look at, not what a memory, she sent me a picture from that time, and a Leo. I always felt comfortable with her, but life goes on and people (me) screw up alot. What does that matter to you or me, well I just described my wife of over 30 years. Now she is stuck with an AD patient and she is a Leo to, and I have asked her to post, but you know these lions the roar, but are really just pussy cats. Because of this and the special I have found that my family was my career and Mr. How Smart Am I, was not even aware of it. Cheryl and the rest of you have shown me that and

I am well pleased inside.

Still confused and not sure what I will do from moment to moment but I am having quiet an adventure, and sometimes it is pretty rotten. Just spent a week isolated to my self and not really talking to anyone, without being short and less than Kind. I find that, at least i do, just wip back without concern of what I am saying. From those I tak with that have this disease seem to do that alot to. Well enough of me for now. Be good and take care of yourselves.

God Bless You & Keep You & This Country of Ours! (The World Needs Him To)

joe

Posted by Joseph Potocny at 09:40AM (-07:00)

Comments

—JUSTAMOM	April 21, 2010

look at you getting all fancy now . . . Hope you have a great week and BE KIND TO THAT LEO we gotta stick up for each other . . . Yeah I am one too.

—SkinnyBitchFlunky	April 22, 2010

Its an interesting phenomenon when we sit and think about our past. Then we start to look at what we have now because of what we had before. Take inventory of sorts.

Thanks Joe Danielle Dementia Guy's Daughter

—ScottJudyandJackie	April 23, 2010

Joe,

I finished up with another Alzheimer's class with different students this week. They watched the HBO Alzheimer's Project and fell in love with you and your sense of humor.

They had asked about the different individuals in the documentary and if I knew how they all were doing. So, I gave them all your blog address, so hopefully they will stop by and leave you a comment.

Take care of yourself and your lovely wife.

Judy

Reading Blogs

Thursday, April 22, 2010

I spent sometime today reading some friends blogs and leaving my ever uplifting comments. But you folks that change your links, dam tell me so I can keep my list correct. I list you so others can read as well. Hopefully the remaining 6 people I have invited will have the balls to post and the others will continue.

- I would post daily if I could remember, but I start processing an entry and it starts
- one way, goes another, then turns left and winds up in the back forty, lost and me with it. Hope the changes are to you liking if not to bad, deal with it.

- Like a legal pleading now.
- Find days are slipping by quicker.
- The brain is getting bluer. Always wanted to be a blue blood, but I have obtained higher standards I am a blue brain, Ok a dumbshit.
- I was at my mens support group the other night, one of the guys there mothers has AD and wwe talk about it and he told me once that you could hardly tell, but his family insisted. He sees her every couple of months or so. Just got back and said he spent 4 hours with her and he was her brother and did not know what town they were in. He was a bit taken back. I asked is she about 4 years or so out from being labeled, he said yes and that she was on Aricipet (wonder drug, not). He asked me why and I told him the truth, she is on schedule. Also the A drug was for well toilet bowl cleaning in my opinion and many others. We hugged I cried for him and prayed for her to be set free soon. These are the real stories of AD not the commercials on TV or the movies, this is what it really does to us. Like a thief in the nite it suddenly takes what it wants when it wants.

God Bless & Keep You & This Country of Ours! (The Rest of The World Needs Help Also)

Joe

Posted by Joseph Potocny at 09:59AM (-07:00)

Comments

—Peaches   April 23, 2010

When my dad started to forget the present, I went along with it. It found it easier and better to go along with his stories and what he thought was going on rather than always correct him. Sometimes it actually was fun.

Do support groups really help? I never have gone . . .

My Husband

Thursday, April 22, 2010

Well now that I have been on the guilt trip for not blogging on his site I will explain why. Even tho I am a Leo I don't do a lot of roaring. Only when it counts like protecting my family or friends. For the most part I am a real pussycat. So you wonder how in the world I managed to survive 30 years with this man. So am I. He is a tyrant when it comes to having things his way. Always has been and probably will be till the end. But he is also a very loyal and loving friend.

He is my best friend. He would fight for me. Since we have started this trip with his medical problems it has not been easy. Lately he is stubborn, mean, forgetful and just not with the rest of us. I have asked him questions and then he walks away without answering them. Or he will say something about me nagging him and getting rid of wives that nag him. Nagging consists of asking him what he wants to do on any given day. So those of you out there taking care of a spouse or loved one just remember that we do it for love because who else is going to do it. Me, I tell him I am in it for the money now. So he should probably go back to work and earn some. It is not easy and it will only get harder. But we are in it for the long haul. For those who

can't stand up to the pressure do not feel bad. This world is not for everybody and the quality of care is more important than who gives it. Take care Lynn

I Posted by Lynn at 11:08PM (-07:00)

Comments

—Peaches   April 23, 2010

Thank You Lynn for your words. Caregiver love to ya!

—Anonymous   April 24, 2010

God bless you Lynn!

—JUSTAMOM   April 29, 2010

LOVE IT!!!!!!!! AND REMEMBER when IT DOES GET way worse we are here.

Me a Tyrant?

Saturday, April 24, 2010

Really now, such a gentle wonderfull and forgiving person as I, a Tyrant. The truth be known I can be a little, just a little over zelous at times. Ok maybe tyranical to some degree. Lynn is mostly correct in what she has written although I am not sure if I even am with them as much as they may believe.

I feel things slipping more and more away from me. Going out has almost become a big no no with me. I do not want to leave my security. On the other hand I no longer want to be in this house. I feel like I have done here what I was suppose to and I am now to move on. It is a feeling I cannot explain, it is like a driving force that pushes me to do whatever it is that I am to do. Writting and talking about it does not change it, it is there and it is real. Before in life I did not hesitate to follow it. Now I am confused and frustrated over the feeling and lately very unhappy over things. I guess this is part of this world I live in now, no longer sure of feelings, thoughts, direction or security of where I am. All I know is that I am here stuck and not knowing when to get off the bus at the correct stop.

I wonder or should I say wander within my own mind what is taking place, why, where and how do I get around this bastard that is following me and sucking my thoughts away. Who am I today, not who I was 10 years ago I think and not even sure of yesterday. Yesterday is a strange word to me, since everything happend yesterday, not last week, years ago, but just yesterday. Family and friends around to help, yes I am lucky that way I guess, but they fuckin piss me off, I feel that they hover, whether they do or not is not the point it is how I feel and it makes me feel trapped. Now if they didn's I probably would get angry that no one gave a dam. No fun in this brain these days.

God Bless & Keep You & This Country of Ours!

Joe

Posted by Joseph Potocny at 07:27PM (-07:00)

Comments

—mmoc   April 24, 2010

I just think it is wonderful that you are able to write down some of how you feel, Joe. Even though it is probably hard for you, I want you to know that it is really helpful for me and understanding my Dad who has AD and who struggles for the words to explain it. It is a mysterious thing and your honesty in writing is really appreciated. God Bless and Keep you, Margaret

—karen   April 25, 2010

I get mad when people are trying to help me care for mom to much cause they are in the way most of the time and than if the stay away I get mad cause I have to do everything my safe. It works both ways. I bet they get mad at you as much as you get mad at them. God bless.

—Carlyn   April 26, 2010

Your writing really is beautiful. Please keep it up and know that what you say matters and it is appreciated!

Messing Up

Sunday, April 25, 2010

I have been making some changes, and probably should have had someone else make them. A few things have disappeared and others moved to second page with everything else. Eventuallly I hope this will all get fixed right.

The skype call button now works after months of well disconnect. See they require you put in your correct user name, can you believe that. So finally I RTFM'd (back in my computer days that meant Read The Fucking Manual), and found I forgot a (.) period in my user name. So if you have tryed without success, it seems to be working now.

Hope to have thr rest of the mes cleaned up soon. Brain cell is getting overloaded.

God Bless You & This Country of Ours!

joe

Posted by Joseph Potocny at 11:36AM (-07:00)

Comments

—karen   April 25, 2010

I love the RTFM thing. The men in this family never do that. I am going to yell that at them next time and see if they can figure it out. I like the new look. Good luck with it.

It Is May

Sunday, May 02, 2010

Just in case you wer not aware it is May. I know the calendar and my computer tell me so and they would not lie to me. Well maybe they would cannot trust them buggers. At least my brain doesn't, it really does not anylonger link days weeks or months together, let alone years.

According to the wife I have developed my own language, not heard on this Earth is billions of years. It seems that when I cannot get out what I want to say, let alone remembber what it is, I express myself in sort of a babble type lanugaggge. She seems to understand me, I sure the hell don't, I wonder who has the problem. Her or me? Since she can remember days, what to do and what she is talking about, she has the problem, those type of people do not live in my World. What the title has to do with this is beyond my mind. Sounded good.

Well we got some new young koi, will see how they do. I have to do water changes on the ponds, and I do not want to, it is such a pain in the ass. I guess the fishes like it, but not one has given me a fin to shake and say thank you. They remind me of gov. officials take it, shove it up my butt and not even a kiss. Yes I am in a mood today, have been for awhile, never kno when they will come or go, seem to stay alot longer these days.

Take care, who knows i MAY see you soon. There that is why the title. If you believe that your brain is as blue as mine is.

God Bless & Keep You & This Country of Ours!!

joe

Posted by Joseph Potocny at 02:06PM (-07:00)

Comments

—JUSTAMOM   May 04, 2010

having a whole differant world of language is SUCH A BLESSING I should use it
sometimes, throws off the OTHER people. Have a good week Joe.

From A Friend

Wednesday, May 05, 2010

Those of u that follow me know I love jokes about my condition, most are so
true and funny. The one tha follows as many I got from a good friend who
brightens my day often. Some may get offended but to damn bad, sit and think
in through it is funny, our gov. would make this suggestion.

The phone rings and the lady of the house answers, "Hello."

"Mrs. Sanders, please" . . . "Speaking." "Mrs. Sanders, this is Doctor Jones at
Saint AgnesLaboratory. When your husband's doctor sent his biopsy to the lab
last week, a biopsy from another Mr. Sanders arrived as well." "We are now
uncertain which one belongs to your husband. Frankly, either way the results
are not too good." "What do you mean?" Mrs. Sanders asks nervously. "Well,
one of the specimens tested positive for Alzheimer's and the other one tested
positive for HIV. We can't tell which is which." "That's dreadful! Can you do the
test again?" questioned Mrs. Sanders. "Normally we can, but Medicare will only
pay for these expensive tests one time." "Well, what am I supposed to do now?"
The folks at Medicare recommend that you drop your husband off somewhere
in the middle of town. If he finds his way home, don't sleep with him."

see I would get lost.

God Bless & Keep You & This Country of Ours!!

joe

Posted by Joseph Potocny at 12:14PM (-07:00)

Comments

—Anonymous   May 06, 2010

Thanks for the laugh.

Last Night

Thursday, May 06, 2010

Last night I found myself in very difficult and not likeable sitution. It was a rough day for me as it was. We sat down for dinner and I put my food on my plate and completely froze. I had no idea what I was doing or what to do, my wife tired to help put I just told her leave me, she put my fork in my hand and it just fel from it, I was in a state of, in betweenness, between here and there. I finally started eating but with my fingers and slowly got back to where I should be. I am about 4 or so years into this and it is taking hold now as it seems to do about this time.

Now I am a beginning to become really concerned and not so humorous, but life will go on and so will I. I guess that line of no return is getting closer and sneakier about things.

Well that is it for now from: us here in Oceanside, CA.

God Bless & Keep You & This Country of Ours!

joe

Posted by Joseph Potocny at 08:48AM (-07:00)

Comments

—Peaches May 06, 2010

I find it amazing how aware you still are of these episodes. The fact that you can tell us about them is really amazing. Ok . . . on your SLIDESHOW Widget . . . I just saw a sex toy . . . huh? Also . . . its funny everytime I come to your page now my Dad's face with his tounge sticking out is huge . . . love it.

Anyhow, keep talking about it all and keep that awareness as much as you can . . . I think it means you are making your brain work more than the average person with AD. I think its good.

Hope You Enjoy

Friday, May 07, 2010

First let me apologize for what may apppear on the slideshow, it comes directly from Amazon.com, their book section. You can click on any picture and go there and then if you are an amazon customer you can go shop till your heart is content. One warning once you leave amazon, you get me again.

I have added my favorite song to the site which starts attomatically, if you do not want to list to it, just click the button on the audiopal gagett. But I do hope you enjoy it as I do.

Thanks for being there for me.

God Bless & Keep You & And This Country of Ours!

joe

PS. Hey you contributors how about it, some words please? Posted by Joseph Potocny at 07:03PM (-07:00)

Comments

—Peaches   May 07, 2010

NO NEED TO APOLOGIZE!!! I thought it was hilarious!

—JUSTAMOM   May 08, 2010

I LOVE the song Joe, and about the freezing up, HEY FORKS ARE OVER RATED ANYWAY! Have a great weekend.

—userE   May 13, 2010

Hi Joe!

Just wanted to say hello. I recently saw the documentary about alzheimers you were in on tv and your story moved me. Have a great weekend, E from Sweden! :)

—Anonymous   May 13, 2010

Hey Joe!

I saw you on the Swedish Channel 2 today! I heard you talking about your illness and I feel for you thou I am only 18 years old. I hope that you can have a wonderful life and be happy all your waken time with your loved ones. God knows you deserve it!

Greetings from Sweden!

/Jonathan

No Title

Thursday, May 13, 2010

The las few days have beeen really rotten. I have been confused, frustrated and a pure asshole. I have hurt my wife, not physically. But through being just a complete moron and ass and I cannot explain why.

I need ot openly appologize to her, just doing it directly has not been enough for me, I have to share it with another human being and my God for me to be free from it.

I am afraid this is a sign of things to come, havig real problems with conversations, remembering things, I just zone out and get really confused over stuff. It is no wonder what I did really got to Lynn, she has so much to put up with me now, not to mention the prior 30+ years. I feel myself slipping more each day, so far I can for the most part notice it, but there are days I have no idea what is what. So I leave you for now, tomorrow if wonder lust here remembers I have some emails to post, that give hope to My World that there will be otherss to watch over us as we wear the current ones out.

God Bless & Keep You & This Country of Ours!!!!

joe

Posted by Joseph Potocny at 05:54PM (-07:00)

Comments

—karen
May 14, 2010

You writing this shows how wonderful you are and how you love her and we all know she loves you. She is there with you so we know it. You still got alot left up stairs or you would not be on here. God Bless you and I am so glad to be able to say I know you. Even if it is just online.

—Elisabeth
May 14, 2010

Hi, I just wanted to leave a comment for you to let you know how insightful your blog has been for me. I currently work in a specialized care community for Alzheimer's/Dementia patients so I can relate to you and your families struggles. But reading through your blog has given me a greater understanding of what my patients are going through, and the frustrations they are feeling on a daily basis. So thank you! and God Bless.

—JUSTAMOM
May 16, 2010

STILL HERE, (((HUGS)))

—Sweden
May 16, 2010

Watching your from Sweden, getting encourge by you to really be a demtianurse. Bless you

—Stiftis   May 16, 2010

Hi Joe! I'm Elena and I'm a 23 year old nursing student from northeast of Sweden. I just saw the documentary about Alzheimers that you were in and checked in to your blog to see how you're doing. The documentary was very touching, and I feel so sorry for you and your family. I think you should know that by participating in the doc. you've contributed to my understanding of AD, and family memebers point of view. I hope you'll have a nice day today, and that a memory of someone being thankful to you lingers for a good while.

—Heather   May 16, 2010

Dear Joe

I continue to be thankful for your help in understanding what my dad went through as we lost him to AD. Although he no longer knows me when he sees me, he often talks about his daughter and has wonderful memories of our time together. Although I miss my dad terribly it is some comfort that I was able to give him memories of being loved and appreciated. I pray those memories of time with your wife and family will remain. And that you will continue to find days when you are with us all. Take care

Heather

I Applaud The Younger

Tuesday, May 18, 2010

So I am late getting to this, what the hell my fingers needed to be dusted off. What follows are a couple of emails that I want to post, one with full permission, the other not so identity will be with held from that one.

My name is Jordyn and I am twenty years old studying occupational therapy. My professor had us watch the HBO Living with Alzheimer's documentary for my class, functioning of the older adult. I just wanted to let you know that I really respect you for opening up your life to the world and writing so freely in your blogs. How great is it that people of all ages follow your blog! People from 15 years old to 100 years old are reading your story and I think that is truly amazing. Hearing you say that your life didn't matter in the great scheme of things broke my heart . . . I just wanted to let you know that your life does mean something and I hope to follow your blogs from now into the future. It's a wonderful thing you're doing. Have a great day!

Sincerely,

Jordyn

Hi Joe,

I am so excited that you e-mailed me back! I would be honored if you posted my comment. I actually just found out today that I was accepted into my Occupational Therapy program at Western Michigan University and I plan to work with older adults in my future career. I hope you are your family are doing well. I will keep you in my prayers. Thank you so much for e-mailing me back.

Sincerely,

Jordyn Bell

Hey Joe!

I saw you on the Swedish Channel 2 today! I heard you talking about your illness and I feel for you thou I am only 18 years old. I hope that you can have a wonderful life and be happy all your waken time with your loved ones. God knows you deserve it!

Greetings from Sweden! Dear Joe I continue to be thankful for your help in understanding what my dad went through as we lost him to AD. Although he no longer knows me when he sees me, he often talks about his daughter and has wonderful memories of our time together. Although I miss my dad terribly it is some comfort that I was able to give him memories of being loved and appreciated. I pray those memories of time with your wife and family will remain. And that you will continue to find days when you are with us all. Take care These are emails from younger people, those that are coming up the line to care for those that will follow me and are caring. This is what keeps me posting knowing that just maybe, just maybe, we are reaching people and someday maybe just by complete accident one of these and the others in Brazil, Sweden, Chile, Argentina, Australia and other places that have writen by accident just may find out why this disease is. I am not talking a cure or a medicine that MAY SLOW things down, but what really causes this. Then and only then will the real breakthroughs come and not before. I applaud you young folks, just for your interest not to mention the course you are setting for yourselves. I WELCOME YOU TO MY WORLD. God Bless & Keep You and This Country of Ours!

joe

PS. To my friend Dr. Joe, I am a dumb SOB, ask those who really know me, God Bless and Keep You my Friend. Posted by Joseph Potocny at 05:12PM (-07:00)

Comments

—Peaches	May 19, 2010

When I did the Alz Memory Walk here in Sacramento CA that is one thing that I intended to do . . . reach the young people. Even when I was interviewed by the News I made sure to address the young people. I even through a fundraiser that had attendance of ages 21 to 50. You're right, young people need to know what they are facing . . . I am only 30 but I faced Alzheimer's at 23 and NO ONE prepared me for it. I had to teach myself and learn the red tape with health insurance all on my own. It sucks!!!

Health Buzz: A New Way to Predict How BreastCancer Will Progress — . . .

Wednesday, May 19, 2010

Health Buzz: A New Way to Predict How Breast Cancer Will Progress—US News and World Report
Posted using ShareThis
Posted by Joseph Potocny at 07:38PM (-07:00)
Pick Disease—Is frontotemporal dementiainherited on MedicineNet
Friday, May 21, 2010

Pick Disease — Is frontotemporal dementia inherited on MedicineNet

Posted by Joseph Potocny at 06:00PM (-07:00)

Comments

—UA-communication-researc	May 22, 2010

Hello,

My name is David Keating and I am a student at the University of Arizona. I am working with Dr. Steve Rains, who is an Assistant Professor in the Department of Communication. We are conducting a study about blogging and health and would greatly appreciate it if you would complete our survey. We found your blog by conducting a general search for blogs about health. We would like to know more about your experience blogging.

Our survey takes about 20 minutes to complete. To participate, you must be (a) 18 years of age or older and (b) have made a blog entry in the past 30 days.

If you meet these requirements and would like to participate, please click the link below. The study will be conducted online and the link will take you to the first webpage of the survey.

http://www.surveygizmo.com/s/283578/blogging

[Note: You may copy and paste the address directly into your web browser (i.e., Internet Explorer) to access the study.]

If you have any questions or concerns about the study, you may contact Dr. Rains at: srains@email.arizona.edu

Thanks for your consideration!

Best Regards, David Keating

*   *   *

David Keating
Department of Communication
University of Arizona

*   *   *

Is There Sex After Dementia?

Sunday, May 23, 2010

Yes if you are a rabbit. See all other tests are done on lab mice, so if they do not have it you cannot, because according to all the people with Paper Hanging Degrees (PHDs), mice and us are very much alike. I have often wondered why I had four feet, a long tail and grey fur, how stupid of me.

OK this is a serious question. I cannot speak for anyone but myself. For quite awhile the answer was NO. It did not work and my brain did not stay with it and still does not. I am allergic to the pills, I am not having rods stuck in my pride and joy, nor having a pump put in it or on it. But guess what there are shots. They use, let me get this right, vascular dilators, and have nothing to do with your sex drive or lack of it. This is man side only, sorry ladies. You administer the shot in the right or left side of uncle willie only. Not on the top, bottom, tip, or like stupid here in a vein they burst and hurt. But when done with accurate precision there is no pain, you may sweat a lot the first couple of times, but really no pain. The bugger can remain erect for sometime, so dosage has to be adjusted. One lasted almost 10 hours, wife was worried I was not, gosh it was nice to see my old friend again. Ice packs finally killed it. Notice using spell check, want to get this one right.

So YES there is SEX after Dementia. If you want to take the steps and can remember why you have these needles and stuff in the refrigerator to begin with. Thank god my wife remembers, because I am truly getting more messed up upstairs than you know, it is taking it's toll on me, conversations suck, I loose time, I cannot get out what I want to say without my tongue getting in the way, wife has learned dementiaese, new form of speaking.

Well that is all for now, more the next time whenever that is.

God Bless & Keep You & This Country of Ours!

Joe

LEGAL CRAP: The views expressed here are the views of the poster. They are not meant in any way fashion or shape to be medical advice or suggestive in anyway as how to improve your sex life, nor do they represent any deceased or living persons (except the poster), and no animals were injured in the writing of this post. Seek medical advice before trying any sexual enhancing means and be sure you are healthy enough for sex. Had to say this or I would get sued and somebody would win possession of my Alzheimer's and FTD, the lucky SOB. Posted by Joseph Potocny at 01:29PM (-07:00)

Comments

—Peaches   May 25, 2010

GOOD FOR YOU JOE!!!

—JohnnyONeil   June 03, 2010

Wow, haha. Hey thank God for technology right? Good to hear your doing better, its great to have something exciting to look forward to.

When Happiness Leaves & Shadows Come

Tuesday, May 25, 2010

As I walk on this journey of mine, although not alone, it does not seem that way anymore.

The wife and I have tried to have discussion about what is going on with me, but that veil of secrecy that has always been around me seem to be even thicker now. It is becoming more difficult for me to express what is happening and what is inside, because frankly I am not sure what the hell is taking place. I get more lost in my own head then I do elsewhere. Out and about with people is close to being a no no.

Lynn has asked me several times what would make me happy. Each time she has asked I come up with only one answer and that is to die or cross over the line. I no longer like this on the edge shit, it is to confusing, frustrating and just gets in the way of everything. I spend to much time crying inside and I have come to dislike me a great deal. But there really is nothing I can do about that, the disease is doing its job and the meds, even increasing them is not helping. Knew this time would come, just did not want to be here for it. But since I am not the ruler of the universe, be thankful, it is not in my time but his (I wish he would hurry).

God Bless & Keep You & This Country of Ours!!!!

joe

Posted by Joseph Potocny at 03:34PM (-07:00)

Comments

—JosephJSivakMD   May 25, 2010

Hey You. I'm thinking about you right now, Joe you might not realize this today but I will remind you, a lot of people read your blog. You make people think, and you are doing a great service with for all AD victims, with this blog. On your crappy days, and I know there are a lot of them, it might not seem like much, but you are helping a lot of people. When you feel like it, stop by and post something on my blog okay? Remember everybody that reads your words, is connected to you. We are all connected by this crappy machine AD. We are all human Joe, and you bring us together. You matter and you are valued. Joe http://alzheimmers.blogspot.com

—MrsSewandSew-Karen   May 26, 2010

Hi Joe! I read all your blogs. God bless you. Please know that you are helping me to understand AD and what it does. No that is not the right word (understand) no one understands this dreaded disease. But you are opening eyes to the disease and what it does. I hope you know what I mean. Keeping you and your family in my thoughts and prayers. Karen

Pay Attention

Friday, May 28, 2010

Joe posted a few weeks ago about the fact that we have had some difficulty. He has had some issues and yes I was hurt by them. But in all fairness I guess I am to blame too. As you know he can still find his way around the computer and sometimes it gets him and others into trouble. So as a caregiver and as a spouse I am going to say that we need to ask questions when our other half is doing something that we are not sure of. We need to check the bank statements and credit card statements just to make sure there are no charges there that we do not know about. $10 here and there really add up. Also just like we do with our children we need to know who they are talking to. Whether on the phone or on the computer. So I am sure that we will have a few more arguments about how we nag and are trying to control things but, if we don't damage can be done that can not be forgiven or forgotten. Fortunately we are working on our end. So do not be surprised when he writes that I am being a nag and not liking me or others very much. We do it out of love. Pay Attention to what is going on around the person you care for. Lynn Posted by Lynn at 01:08PM (-07:00)

Comments

—kenju   May 28, 2010

Amen! and thanks for saying it. My husband doesn't have AD, but short-term memory loss can cause problems too. We need to remind our men that we get concerned out of love—if we didn't care about them—we wouldn't be a nag.

—karen   May 28, 2010

Lynn you are a wonderful person. Joe knows how lucky he is to have you. Even if he forgets sometimes. Prayers coming your way always.

—MrsSewandSew-Karen   May 29, 2010

Great post Lynn. My dad has not been diagnosed with AD or dementia but is have really bad memory problems. He needs medical help but my mom is in denial. I just nagged him on the phone today about leaving the yard and walking the neighborhood without telling my mom. He has done it twice lately and she has had to walk around until she finds him. It really scares her. He does get aggravated when we try to help him. I appreciate the info that comes from Joe's blog. Blessings, Karen

—Anonymous   May 29, 2010

mom i really wished we lived closer. i know it is hard for all of you down there and sometimes i am glad im not there cause i dont have to watch it happen, but then again i wish i could be there cause i want the kids to know their grandfather before it gets to bad . . . we love you guys

morgan

—JohnnyONeil   June 03, 2010

My boss's wife started losing her memory about 6 months before she passed away. It was hard to see how hard he runs his business and to take care of her through out the night. God bless you and stay strong cherish family first :)

—Anonymous   June 09, 2010

Oooh Lynn I know exactly what you are saying. My Mom (may she rest in God's peace)was very angry at times that we had to watch over her until she finally succumed all financial power to my older sister and myself . . . very difficult for her to realize that sometimes she was getting herself into trouble. Hang in there and God bless you and your family on your journey! XOXO Diane

—carlosorjp   June 17, 2010

Lynn,

Thank you for writing your own message here. I just checked out you post for the first time tonight (after learning about it on THE ALZHEIMERS PROJECT, a DVD I got through Netflix). You're absolutely right in comparing the way one cares for a spouse (or parent) with dementia to the way one cares for an adolescent or child. In all my years of being a caregiver, previously professionally and, now, as a son to a woman afflicted with Progressive Supranuclear Palsy, I have often had quite similar thoughts. I'd like to add that I'll never view my wife's nagging—or our mutual nagging of our children—in quite the same way! (I guess my wife really does love me!) Every comment I happen to post here I will write with both you and Joe in mind. That is, whether I have addressed my comments to you or to Joe, I have written them with the hope and realization that they may be read by both of you.

My heartfelt best,

Carlos

Expectations

Tuesday, June 01, 2010

I have been doing this blog for a number of years now. Trying to tel you what it is like on this sid of the fence. I am begining to wonder if what I am saying is getting old and has no meaning. See I belong to a group study and we have a saying, "EXPECTATIONS ARE PREMEDITATED RESENTMENTS"! I feel those resentments because I seem to get far less comments or emails. That is my proble because I am expecting something in return for my posts, really I am not entitled to any replies. This is my story with the disease and only my point of vew, such as it maybe.

I met with my shrink today and we kind of got into it and I told him you do not know what is in this world in which I live now, you are on the other side, you are one of them. I know that my progresion has been seemingly slow and I have been well contained for lack of another word. But that is only because of the brain power that I possed when this all started, I could control a lot of what was happending and hide it, I am no longer able to do that, it (AD & FTD) are doing their jobs very well now and the fox can no longer out run or manuver them. Thank goodness my friends and family are around to guide me or I would be totally lost. I do not even want to leave my house anylonger or really take part in life, I am retreating into myself where I feel safe. Whether this is part of the proscess or not I do not know, all I know is that it is happening.

Take care of yourselves.

God Bless & Keep You & This Country of Ours!

joe

Posted by Joseph Potocny at 12:14PM (-07:00)

Comments

—Anonymous   June 01, 2010

Well, I for one don't think your posts are getting old at all. Anything you write about is very interesting. I think my mother (who had alzheimer's) was also able to hide her's for year because of her intellect. Unlike you she never spoke much about what it was like, so I find your writings extremely helpful in understanding the whole process. I also have to admit I want to know what it's like so I can be on the lookout for symptoms in myself! I'm sorry you are having to go through all this. Keep writing, please. Diane

—MrsSewandSew-Karen   June 01, 2010

Joe, I agree with Diane. I also find your post very interesting. I know my Dad is going to be going down this road. I just wish he would get help. I am sorry that you are not feeling like going out of the house. I am somewhat a hermit myself-a homebody for sure. Try to stay involved Joe it is important I think!

I am glad you have Lynn and the family to guide you when you need them. Take care and please keep writing. Karen

—mmoc   June 01, 2010

Joe, I also get a lot of value out of your posts and ask you to keep writing, as long as it doesn't give you more stress. Your descriptions of how you are feeling give me an insight into how my Dad must be feeling (and encourage me to ask him how he is feeling). My Dad never talks about AD. I don't even know if he knows he has it. I think he does but it is not in his personality at the moment to talk about it. Thanks for giving him a voice. Even if you think you are not expressing yourself well, you should know that the reader can still understand, to a large extent, from the words you can get down—you are still a great writer. Thank you.

—Margaret-Jan   June 01, 2010

Hi Joe, I am brand new to your blog, after watching the HBO Alzheimer's Project episode you were in. It will take me some time to go back over what you've already written so I don't know if you're posts are getting old, but I am following you now and I hope you will keep writing. What you have to share is important, now and in the future.

—Anonymous
June 01, 2010

Joe I started reading your blog after my Mother who had Alzheimer's passed away, I was not there to be with her or help her through any part of her ordeal. I started reading your blog so I could gain a better understanding of what she must have thought and went through.

I now have a sister with Alzheimer's and was able to help her a lot after having read your blogs and the info you would give us web sites we could go to for information.

We became friends and I left many comments hoping one day to get on your blog via the comment, I felt it would be an honor I would be proud to have.

Please understand there are many reasons that people sometimes slack off I for one have Parkinson's and lately it has been doing a number on me but am slowly crawling out of the hole.

Keep writing we would be lost with out you.

Friends

D. & Gator

—Mary
June 02, 2010

Hi there Joe . . . you better keep on writing, cause I need you by my side on this journey we're on! I totally agree . . . I love staying in my safe hidey hole. But I'm refusing to let this disease win quite yet! So we go out and enjoy life for a day and then I can sit for a day or two and let my brain unscramble. Many hugs Mary

—JohnnyONeil
June 03, 2010

Hi Joe, I'm new on here also. The internet/blogs are for keeping all of us informed. Your doing a good thing! Thank you.

—Hedy
June 03, 2010

Hi Joe, I've been reading your blog for about a year now. My mother was diagnosed with AD 4 yrs ago. Without your insight, I would not have had the knowledge or courage to confront her doctors as I do. An example . . . last weekend my mother was taken to the ER for respiratory problems. When she became agitated (after 6 hrs), the response from the doctors were to sedate and restrain her to the bed. At that point, I made them release her with a perscription for antibiotics. Back in the day, I assumed doctors were the "All-Knowing". Not so anymore . . . Anything that you can share means the world to me, as my mother is no longer able to communicate. God Bless. Caregiving Daughter in San Diego

—JUSTAMOM   June 03, 2010

Please stop by and read something on my blog.

—Cheryl   June 13, 2010

Hi Joe . . . I love your blog! You still inspire me with your daily courage and fiestiness. I go back and read some of your entries again and again. It helps me reflect back to our time caring for Mom during her battle with dementia. Mom hid her symptoms for as long as she could, and only shared her feelings about what was happening to her with a great deal of prodding. Your blog helped my sister and I tremendously with a look into the bubble. (My sister and I called the place Mom went, "The Bubble") I think that you are a treasure because of your ability and willingness to share of your experiences . . . Please keep up the good work Joe.

Lots of Love, Cheryl (Arlene's Daughter)

—seniorcare   July 26, 2010

Joe Nice Blog! I will stop by and visit. Well thought out.

A Call For Volunteers!!!!!!

Saturday, June 12, 2010

Hello, I hope you all had a great holiday weekend! I wanted to get in touch to let you know about an Alzheimer's Disease research study and invite you to share this with Living With Alzheimer's blog readers. Have you or a loved one ever experienced what it is like to be unable to recall things which were once so simple to remember? If so, you may know how devastating the effects of Alzheimer's disease (AD) can be. An estimated 5.3 million people in the United States have Alzheimer's, and every 70 seconds another person develops this disease! I am contacting you today on behalf of the Alzheimer's Disease Cooperative Study (ADCS) to raise awareness about AD and to encourage otherwise healthy adults with early complaints of memory problems to participate in the Alzheimer's Disease Neuroimaging Initiative Grand Opportunity (ADNI GO). ADNI GO will build on the unprecedented momentum and success of the Alzheimer's Disease Neuroimaging Initiative (ADNI), a landmark study to find more sensitive and accurate methods to detect AD at earlier stages and track its progress through biomarkers. By being able to recognize changes in the brain, scientists hope to treat memory loss and other symptoms of AD before they appear, but the only way to recognize what these changes are and learn more about who is at risk is through the participation of volunteers. "We cannot end this terrible disease unless we know more about it," says Dr. Paul Aisen, M.D., director of the Alzheimer's Disease Cooperative Study (ADCS). "That is where the amazing volunteers, their friends and their families can make the difference in our success." Dr. Maya Angelou—the eminent poet, author, educator, historian and professor at Wake Forest University—is working with researchers to ask you and your loved ones to be part of the ADNI GO study that may help bring us one step closer to finding a cure. Click here to hear from Dr. Maya Angelou. If you, a friend, or a family member is experiencing early signs of memory loss, you may be eligible to participate in this groundbreaking ADNI GO study. Please visit *http://adcs.org/Studies/ImagineADNI.aspx* or call the Alzheimer's Disease Education and Referral Center at 1-800-438-4380 for more information on study sites in your area. I invite you to share this information with your blog readers to help shed light on this devastating disease, and encourage participation in ADNI GO. Thank you for your time and please feel free to get in touch with any questions. Sincerely, Diana Diana Bakowski i-Blitz Interactive Powered by WestGlen 1430 Broadway, New York, NY 10018 dbakowski@westglen.com 212.704.9134 Posted by Joseph Potocny at 06:32PM (-07:00)

Comments

—June	June 16, 2010

Hi Joe,

long time reader, you are expressing your thoughts very well, and your blog is very good! My Mom doesn't realize at all what is happening to her. Occasionally, usually sundowning, sees people or things outside that are not there.

Keep posting, please! will look up the maya angelou project . . .

thanks again! June :) Hi Lynn !

Monday, June 14, 2010

Today I am not clear ast to what i want to say. It is becoming difficult for me to keeep my thoughts in order, as if they ever were. I am becoming more distant from my family, I feel very trapped by everything. We went to the Birch Aquarium, I think it is called, in San Diego on Friday, it was fun, but to tell the truth I was not really part of being there, although the lady at the sharks was interesting, but you know my wife, she would not let me bring her home. I am having more diffficulties with talking to, seems to come out sideways, good thing those around me have a clue to what I am saying, because I don't. I have been watching and noticing all the things now that they say will slow down your getting AD and all the things that cause it. It just leads me to believe even more so that these people are morons and have no idea what they are doing. In most cases giving people false hope and bullshit answers. Kind of sounds like are President and Congress. What the hell most of them went to the same schools anyhow. Well I am rambling, getting good at this. Also have changed the site again and probably will still more, gives me something to do and screw up at the same time. Well bye for now.

God Bless & Keep You & This Country of Ours!!!!

joe

Posted by Joseph Potocny at 01:43PM (-07:00)

Comments

—karen | June 14, 2010

You are right on all counts. Happy Flag Day!!!

—karen | June 14, 2010

I love you new design and I meant you are right about them not knowing what they are talking about. You are great.

—MadamMoonchild | June 14, 2010

Sorry to hear that you are having a bad go. But just know that your honesty is helping someone going through and feeling the same things. I can't imagine how horrible it is to lost your independence and your memory. I am rooting for you.

—MrsSewandSew-Karen | June 15, 2010

LOL to the comment you made about the President and the Congress. I like what you are doing with your site. Have a good week! Karen

—JUSTAMOM | June 15, 2010

Just keep writing I will be here . . .

—carlosorjp | June 17, 2010

Joe,

I just found out about your Blog on the show, The Alzheimer's Project. I have worked as a caregiver for people with Alzheimer's and other conditions. Now I care for my mom, who does not have Alzheimer's Disease, but the disease she has—which is like Parkinson's—comes with some dementia. I am also trying to get into a PhD program for neuroscience, hoping someday to help people with Alzheimer's in my own way, by doing research. I recently earned my Bachelor's degree in psychology (although I started out in computers, your area of interest and passion). I also noticed that you created this

272

post on June 14, which was my birthday. I turned 41. I wish you and all who love you the most solace and peace and understanding you can find in the midst of this cruel affliction.

My heartfelt best,

Carlos Jon Paul George

(You can call me "JOPOGO")

Happy Father's Day

Sunday, June 20, 2010

To all you dads, grandpa's and uncles a happy fathers day. Oh by the way one to you rascals that may not be sure if you are. To our father's in harms way our troops a very special day to you my friends.

This hopefully will be the first of two posts today. My eldest has gone to the hospital already this am to have what should turn out to be our eight grandchild. She did it once on mother's day so why not. BBQs were planned for both these occassions.

A special prayer for those in the gulf, May God Grant You Peace and Show you the Way. Amen.

More later.

God Bless & Keep You & This Country of Ours!

joe

Posted by Joseph Potocny at 08:03AM (-07:00)

It Happened

Sunday, June 20, 2010

at 2:37pm today my eight grandchild was born. April weighed in at 7lbs 6oz and 18" long. My daughter followed my orders and called while April was coming out. So there you have it, HAPPY FATHER'S DAY. Posted by Joseph Potocny at 02:43PM (-07:00)

Comments

—rilera

June 20, 2010

Congratulations on becoming a grandpa for the 8th time!

—MrsSewandSew-Karen   June 21, 2010

Congrats Joe. What a wonderful Father's Day you must have had! Take care, Karen

Me & April

Monday, June 21, 2010

Gramps & April

There you have it, the good looking one is in the blanket, the old fart well we all know who that is. Want to share some of the good with you also. Number eight and not counting.

God Bless All, joe Posted by Joseph Potocny at 02:11PM (-07:00)

Comments

—MrsSewandSew-Karen   June 21, 2010

She is a beauty. Congrats again Joe. Blessings, Karen

—JUSTAMOM   June 21, 2010

YOU LOOK GREAT GRANDPA!!!!!!!!! OH and tha tbaby is just soooo sweet too

—Anonymous   June 22, 2010

Wow—she really came with a full head of hair! Reminds me of my youngest. What a darling picture of the two of you. Congratulations, Gramps. Diane

—Anonymous   June 23, 2010

What a wonderful, beautiful blessing. A new life. Keep being brave, grandpa. This little one will find great inspiration in your fight . . . in the man you are . . . grandpa . . . the legacy you leave . . . your courage in the face of this disease. You inspire us all. A caregiver . . .

—Peaches   June 27, 2010

Congrats!

What do I see in the future?

Thursday, June 24, 2010

My shrink has sent me back to my pshycologist, for help especially since his dad died from AD and he was the first to garee with me on what was taking place in my so called mind. We have been meeting for a couple of weeks again. Known each other close to 6 years. As we sat and looked at each other, he asked why I was back and I told him. We talked to kind of catch up to current things. He asked me, "When I look to the future, what do I see?" My reply after starring for a few moments maybe longer was, "Darkness". I told him for me I see no future, for when you slice it all up and smooth it all out there is nothing there for me. Just to keep loosing what abilities I have left and then crossing over the line. What is on the other side of the line, I told him I do not know for I have no idea who or what I will be, except that it will not be me. Maybe I will be lucky and pass on before that time comes. See I look at us in this world of Dementia, as throw aways, really, how many families are able to withstand the constant care they need to give us as we move forward with this disease. It definitely has got tear at them to a point of not being able to handle things. Then they have there families and their lives and all that stuff. So put Mom or Dad or Gramps or Grams in home that can clean them up and do the things they cannot handle. Throw aways that is what we are. Never mind the years that we put into raising them and helping and nuturing and getting their asses out of trouble, that does not matter that was our job not theirs. Will I get shit for this post, YES, do I care NO, because the truth is what it is. I am becoming more distant to family and friends. My "friends" no longer email me except for those stupid forwards, some are funny. I am not part of their world and I guess they do not know how to talk to me anymore. Even those that I know that have a parent with AD and work for Alz. Org. Bitter I guess, you see I now see my world closing in and not as broad as it once was. I have my moments, but more and more they are lessening, shopping is nearly unbearable for me now. I fear leaving home because I might get lost even though I have to be taken everywhere. Take care and be good to yourselves.

God Bless & Keep You & This Country of Ours!

joe

Posted by Joseph Potocny at 11:33AM (-07:00)

Comments

—JUSTAMOM June 24, 2010

Joe I LOVE your honesty. I hope you will ALWAYS KNOW those around you DO LOVE YOU and ALWAYS WILL keep you tucked warm in their hearts. I Pray the fears in your heart do not haunt you and you can grasp a piece of JOY every hour, ok at least once a DAY. IF time comes where your family NEED to place you in a new home I HOPE they find one like the one I work at now. It is HOME for 53 residents with MANY EXTENDED FAMILY MEMBERS. They are NOT throw away's. for ME they ARE my daily JOY, they give me reason to laugh when I feel like crying. They give me LOVE when I feel unlovable. Hope you have a CALM weekend and keep writing from the heart as long as you can. Chin up and take life one breath at a time.

—Lynn June 24, 2010

Just so you remember at least for now that we do not consider you or anybody else a throw away. Your family is not like that. And there may come a day that we have a few problems with you and would like to put you out the door but it is not going to happen. I wish there were a few more days with sunlight in them for you. Hold my hand when it gets dark.

—MrsSewandSew-Karen June 26, 2010

Joe, This is a brutally honest post. I had a friend that had AD. Now my dad is just beginning this journey. It saddens me that you feel like a throw away. I never felt that my friend, my dad, or you Joe are a throw away. Here's hoping you feel better about this soon. I will take special care to try to make my Dad not feel this way. Thank you for sharing this feeling . . . making us all aware. Blessings to you, Karen

—Brangane June 26, 2010

Joe, I have read your blog for a year and feel humble that I am allowed to. The world would be a darker place without you. Blessings.

—Peaches June 27, 2010

So this post made me so sad . . . It made me think of my decision to place my father in a home. I did feel like I was throwing him away. I procrastinated the decision by going to different facilities in my area . . . 60 of them, and walking right out with the idea that they were not good enough for him. Part of it came down to money and the fact that with my paycheck and his paycheck (retirement) we would barely be able to afford to live. So after tears and holes in the wall, I decided that if I put him in a home near my house I could afford to live and have less work hours so I could see him everyday. I did see him everyday . . . morning and night. I guess when it comes down to it I have to remind myself that I did everything in my power to provide the best I could for my dad. I gave him shelter, clothes, food and most of all I gave him love. I have to remind myself that I am not like the others who just drop off their loved one at the home and return only on holidays. I was there everyday and I gave up a lot to be that kind of daughter . . . the kind that didnt give up on him. If I had a million dollars . . . I would of been the one to clean my father, feed him, walk him around in his chair. I would have if the healthcare system didnt make it so damn impossible (expensive) to care for our loved ones. I refuse to believe that I threw away my father.

Thank you for your honesty Joe.

My Forum

Monday, June 28, 2010

This is my forum to tell you how I feel and for you to talk back to me. It has always been my goal to make this not just about me, but about those that travel my journey before and after me. For you that care for us to tell how you feel. For those who contribute to leave posts on their take and views. I personally feel that my time to the line is close and I am having difficulty battling that. While I fight it, I know inside and have accepted the fact the fight is lost, but I am an honory bastard and just have to fight for the sake of it, win or loose does not matter, I just will not give this disease the satisfaction it wants. It is going to have to stomp on me and its shoes are getting heavier. Sometimes my posts are less than kind, but this is not a kind disease and I am trying to make people think about us in this world as real people not someone in a looking glass. This is my only forum to do that in. I feel caged and somewhat worthless at this point and that feeling will probbably woresen as time goes on. Well so much for now.

God Bless & Keep You & This Country of Ours!

joe

Posted by Joseph Potocny at 02:10PM (-07:00)

Comments

—MrsSewandSew-Karen	June 29, 2010

Thank you for your post. Your information is so helpful. I am grateful for your honesty. God bless you and your family Joe. karen

—MadamMoonchild   June 29, 2010

One of the things I appreciate about your blogs is the fact you are pissed off about it. I would be pissed off too. This disease robs one of their independence. I can't even fathom how extremely frustrating it must be. I appreciate you sharing and just know that others will benefit from the unfortunate card you have been dealt.

Peace be with you

—Deb   June 30, 2010

Joe, Thank you for sharing your feelings and experiences. You have no idea how much you are helping other families going through similar experiences.

My husband was diagnosed in 2007 but that explained what had been going on for the previous few years. He refuses to acknowledge that there is a problem and insists that other people's actions are the problem. I read your postings to try to gain insight into what he is going through, to help me understand him and find ways to try to help him.

My husband withdrew from everyone and everything back in 2005. His only desire is to sit in the same room day after day with the TV and have me sit there too.

The hardest thing for me is that I feel I have lost my best friend and companion as we can no longer carry on a conversation without great frustration setting in. So we exist together. This disease is not something he is going through but something WE are going through.

I am feeling so alone and isolated but your postings help me through our journey, wherever it may lead.

God bless you AND your family!! Keep up the good work with your postings and remember, your sharing is such a tremendous assistance to a lot of us you may never know.

—Heather   July 01, 2010

I am not sure that this will help but maybe it will. The hardest time for my dad was when he was aware of what he was losing and where he was going. He is at a point now that he seems comfortable where he is, in a world of his brain's making. The hard part now is for us—his family—because he is not where we are. Although he still knows my sister, my mother and my children I am lost to him. That doesn't mean he isn't glad for me to visit and take him out in the gardens or for a soda and candy at the cafe but I am no longer his daughter just someone nice who spent some time with him. Before, when he had some idea as to what was happening he would cry and yell and tell me how sorry he was. He was scared of going places and frightened at times for reasons unknown. Now he has places to go(he was leaving for England last week) and people to catch up with(memories of people long lost) that he somehow gathers comfort from.

How does this help—I'm not sure other than to say I perceive my father at peace now, the struggle and anger is mine.

Alone

Wednesday, June 30, 2010

For those of you that read the comments and those that are taking care of anybody with this damn disease you understand what Deb is talking about. Our lives take on a new direction. Not only are those with the disease withdrawn but so are the family members and the caregivers. We are withdrawn from society because we can't get them to go out or hold a conversation anymore. So yes we sit and watch tv shows and do things that we do not really want to do because it is what they want to do and it is hard. Try to keep doing normal things for you. If only it is to get out to the grocery store, or have lunch with a friend. We have lost our best freinds. And we will lose them again. Conversations are hard because they either do not want to talk or they can't get the right words out. We play charades alot. Joe will want to say something and usually starts ok but he ends up pointing or grimacing and I can usually figure out what it is he wants. As with everything else it too will go down the drain. Joe started this to let everybody that wanted to, realize what was happening inside a victims head, understand what they were going through. I am glad that he has helped. Posted by Lynn at 01:38PM (-07:00)

Comments

—paula   July 01, 2010

I love both of your willingness to share. As a family member, that lost an aunt when she was 65 (diagnosed at 55), and now I watch my dad to see if he is "normally" forgetful, or if he is forgetting, I love reading and knowing that this disease is thought so much as a memory diseas, but we all forget that this is a LANGUAGE disease also. As a nurse I work to teach and care for those Veterans who are dying of this disease. I watch Joe on the Alzhiemer's Project several times a month, read this blog, and we all must understand that this is a loosing process. Language and the ablitiy to communicate are lost and nothing is there to replace it. The stress and demand on the caregivers are tremendous. I can assure you that people who end up in Long Term Care are not forgotten, but some of the most cared for people in LTC, we become their family, because we didn't know them before the disease it is easy to love who they have become, not miss who they were.

—karen   July 03, 2010

Alone says it all.

—Peaches   July 05, 2010

Lynn, I cared for my father for 6 years and the conversation and the activities were like an adult reversing to a child . . . like Benjamin Button. I found that the moments of tenderness with my father when he would be affectionate with me was his way of talking to me. It was interesting that while no one could read his body language or understand what he was saying I did. The nursing staff and my family relied on me as their translator. Its funny how close we are to our loved ones that we can do this. I am glad you are posting on here as well.

—theadamos   July 10, 2010

We are now in the midst of taking care of our father although our mother does most of it, because in his words, she is everything to him. But it is now at the point where he is just very abusive verbally and always argumentative. Comes up with stories that have never happened and won't believe us either way if we agree or disagree. It is a sad world when as people get older and have this horrible, horrible disease that there is no way for a family to get help without going into debt or losing all of their money that they worked so hard for. I hope someday(but never in my dad's lifetime) that this happens. Thanks for listening. I pray for all families that someday there is a cure.

And You Say I am NOT NAGGED!!!

Monday, July 05, 2010

attacked from all angles

First let me wish you all a belated 4th of July!! You know it is difficult when everyone is watching what you are doing constantly. OH of course the wife does not watch over me or nag, not the kids either, THEY have trained the fricken bird and cat to do their dirty work. I am surprised they have not given the fish feet and artificial living tanks so that they can come and spy as well. It has gotten so that I have no privacy under constant surveliance like a member of the KGB, well they won't catch me, my brain cell is working out a plan. As soon as it lets me know what the hell it is then I can do something about this invasion.

Seriously they need to watch me, I do some of the dumbest things, besides not letting the wall get out of my way before I walk into it. There are times I really do not know what the hell I am doiing or what I am talking about. This is geetting more difficult as time goes on and it is suppose to, but it sure plays hell with what i want to do, which I do not know what that is to start with. Yes there has been joy this year two new grandchildren, my new koi pond, which I rarely sit by anymore, actually two ponds. all have mosiquto fish in them, cute little devils they are and do they populate.

Well I guess I have bitched enough, well maybe not, but at least I remembered most of what I wanted to say in this post, which in and of itself is something. My physcologist would say that I am still in there somewhere, but the question is where. He has been seeing me and been my friend for a number of years now, his father died from this damned disease, so he knows from where my anger and confusion and thoughts come from.

God Bless & Keep You & This Country of Ours!!

joe

PS: I can go anywhere I want, that is what I am told, but here is the kicker I have to be taken there, real freedom, right!

Posted by Joseph Potocny at 10:19AM (-07:00)

Comments

—Anonymous   July 05, 2010

And we will keep nagging at you too. Love the Monty and Gertrude

---

—diningroomtables   July 05, 2010

Wow your blog is outstanding. This is one of a kind. I never see any blog like this. I love your topic. The photo of cat and bird is so cute. Thanks for sharing.

—MrsSewandSew-Karen   July 06, 2010

Hi Joe, Hope you and Lynn had a Happy 4th. Mine is a belated wish also. Cute pic of the bird and cat! Take care, Karlee

Home Care News > Guide to Living withDementia: Are You Asking t . . .

Tuesday, July 06, 2010

Home Care News > Guide to Living with Dementia: Are You Asking the Right Questions? You may enjoy this article by clicking on the above link. I have added the base site to my links, Home Watch Caregivers. God Bless, Joe Posted by Joseph Potocny at 12:29PM (-07:00)

A Prior Post if You Will. With Added Comment.

Saturday, July 10, 2010

A Warrior's Lament: (by j.v. potocny)

I kneel before thee Upon bended knee My battle axe rusts upon a tree The Steed that served me well Now runs free and frail He served us both with grace and might Let him rest well each night There is no deadly mace That you can see before my face Gone is my shield which I cannot hold All that is before you is my sword and face I have stood tall in all battles With You I have won and battles song sung Many with scars some with none Since a child I have fought the fight Now I wish for it to end this night My strength is dried up and gone No longer does exist that fierce warrior in me I long to face only Thee This battle I am in is lost and so am I So before You I am on bended knee Prostrate would I lay But this body is to broken and brittle this day So I lay before you all I have left Worn, beaten, yearning, to you I give my soul No longer in the dust of battle let me roam I await You and Your Hand to take me in your time I pray Thee take ME HOME In Your Name Amen.

This more reflects my wishs of today and my feelings. I no longer like it here. I no longer communicate with those around me well. Most of the time I am in my own little world and do not want to be bothered by anyone. My wife has noticed more and more that I am not with those around me. This is not a friendly world it rather sucks. Things I once enjoyed are a chore, getting things done takes it seems like years to me. It feels at times like my brain is being crushed or squeezed down. It is not a headache but a sensation of being pushed out and away. God Bless & Keep You & This Country of Ours!

Joe

Posted by Joseph Potocny at 12:10PM (-07:00)

Tuesday, July 13, 2010

I greet you this day not really knowing why. It seems that the days are starting to have little meaning anymore. I try to keep a sense of humor about things, but there is nothing humorous about what is happening to me or those around me. I find myself staring off into space or just at nothign these days nore amd more. Things seem to mean little anymore to me and I just do not know how to handle these feeelings and moods. Things keep slipping farther and farther away from me.

I have tried to make this blog as time has gone by a place for meeting and exchangin thoughts and felings on dementia in general. I gave the site a chat room for a year that I paaid for open 24/7 for whoever wanted to talk not just to me but to others a failure. I opened a direct chat line to communicate whichcost me over$80 a month so we could talk, 5 people, a failure. I invited over 25 people to blog here because of their involvement with dementia, that has been a failure, I even set up Yahoo Messenger for instant chatting that too went down the tubes, I even have tried skype without any success. Comments I have gotten, emails I have gotten, but I guess my expectations (premeditated resentments) should not have been. I have removed all of the about except comments and email.

I am trying to give u articles as I find them that maybe of interest. I have a feeling that will be of no avail. Bitter yes I am, angry and pissed, yes, at those who come and cannot even take time to comment yes, but most of all at ME, for especting and planning and most of all trying to plan the outcome.This fricken disease plays a lot of games with your head and sometimes I am not even sure of what I am writting, minutes from now I will forget and I guess for me that is ok. Keeping my angry under anytype of control is getting difficult, increase in meds is not helping, well so much for my bitching, like most things it will get me nowhere fast.

God Bless & Keep You & This Country of Ours!!!!

joe

Posted by Joseph Potocny at 01:16PM (-07:00)

Comments

Hi Joe, I am sorry I am late commenting. I LOVE coming and beign able to get an insight of this thing from your inside view. I think the guest spot for me was one of a first lettign peopel know MY side of it. BUT my side of it is the same day after day, I have several people in my care and they are at differant stages of this thing. I HATE IT I truly live the same day after day, so really feel I have nothing to add. I DO love being able to come and hear YOUR side. I truly believe it has helped me with my care for my people. Keep your chin up and know you ARE loved out here.

Alzheimer's Facts and Figures

Thursday, July 15, 2010

Alzheimer's Facts and Figures Here is an article I received from Alzheimer's Org. One fact in it is not correct, they show AD as the 7th leading cause of death, it has just been upgraded to the 6th leading cause of death. Enjoy, Joe Posted by Joseph Potocny at 07:07PM (-07:00)

Home Care News > Caring for Parents withDementia and Alzheimer' . . .

Friday, July 16, 2010

Home Care News > Caring for Parents with Dementia and Alzheimer's: If I had Only Known Then What I know Now! This is the 2nd in a series from Homewatch Caregivers. Enjoy. Let me know if the articles I have been posting are of help. God Bless, Joe Posted by Joseph Potocny at 07:22PM (-07:00)

Comments

Joe, Hope this finds you hanging in there the best that you can. Thank you posting these links . . . it helps me out in my classroom. Gives me new information to teach my students. In fact, all of your posts help me with my students in attempting to have them understand what it is like for the person who suffers from this nasty disease.

Thank you again for giving us all an insight to what you and your family are going thru!! Judy

—MonicaScott   August 13, 2010

Very interesting reading . . . I have my 79 and 83 year old in-laws living with me. Both have dementia, I thank God that I don't have to deal with some of the heartbreaks that I have read about. But it is difficult on a daily basis and I assume it will only get worse.

My poor husband is having a very difficult time seeing his father become a child. His mother is such a nervous nelly that she runs around like a chicken without a head. She is so afraid of doing the wrong thing that she seems to make it worse for herself. She gets angry with her husband when he forgets things and people.

They have been with us 3 years now and we both wonder how much more we can take.

They are both very healthy and we find ourselves resending the fact that they could live another 5 or 10 years.

Thank you for listening.

Monica in NJ

Home Care News > Home Care Plan: Summertime Activities for Early . . .

Saturday, July 17, 2010

Home Care News > Home Care Plan: Summertime Activities for Early Stage Alzheimer's or Dementia Posted by Joseph Potocny at 08:42AM (-07:00)

Comments

—Eva   July 22, 2010

Thank you so much for this link. I am an activity director in a long-term care facility and I work with people with AD every day. I learned about your blog from the HBO documentary, and it really helps caregivers to see things from thr perspective of those with AD. We usually meet our patients when they are in the later stages, when they no longer realize that they have AD, and do not get the opportunity to know them in the early stages. I think your blog is a must-read for anyone caring for those with AD, and I will pass it on to all the caregivers I know.

Just When You Thought—

Friday, July 23, 2010

For the last couple weeks I have been considering not posting any longer since ther did not seem to be any response to anything I posted. Especially yelling at you my extended family for not using the tools given to you. I guesss as we move forward I will become less tolerant and more bitchy. My wife will probably say I have already made it ther. I know I am more withdrawn and really don't care much about things, even my KOI ponds. The book here "When Can I Go Home?", i got to read before it came out. See Dr. Joe is a friend of mine, even though he is a Phsyciahtrist, i cann't speel, that does not make him bad. It is a pretty good book for caregivers to read I think.

Here is why I asked so many of you to become posters on this blog: Message = Just found your blog and it is great. It might be a good help for me to understand my husband. He does not talk much about what he feels and when he does he yells. I try to listen but how do I get him to talk without being so mean? He has alzheimer's and was only diagnosed a few years ago but it seems that he is slipping more these days. I hope your troubles are few. You look like a fun guy. Forget the last sentence. I get a great deal of emails from people like this lady. I can only answer from my side. She needs help fro you guys, you can see she is drowning in a sea she does not know how to swim in. Please POST and help her. This is part of my reason for not wanting to continue to post. I feel that we as a family are failing people like this lady. My emotions control me now rather than the other way around. Even if you do the same thing each day I am sure you do something different, maybe a minute that can help someone. I do the same thing each day, become more forgetful, angry, frustrated, pissed, fingers hurt typing all of this, my brain wanders while I am tyring to post. If you want to be a guest blogger on my blog, send me your email address and why and I will email you the link. Postings have to be all related to Dementia in anyform or caregibing to Dementia patients. God Bless & Keep You & This Country of Ours (Help The World Too)!!

joe

Posted by Joseph Potocny at 01:22PM (-07:00)

Comments

—SeniorCare | July 26, 2010

Joe, don't get discourage. I think your blogs are very informative.

—Peaches | July 26, 2010

Joe,

Because of your blog I have found other people's blogs that relate to AD. I have got to their sites and posted there for them. When I post to your site it is for you. I may not be able to post everyday but I make it a point to visit your site at least once a week. So even if we do not post to your site in response to others it doesnt mean we arent reaching out to them all the time . . . at least for me, I am posting to their site.

Again, it is because of your blog that I have met via blogger others like me and others like my dad.

You blog made a difference to me and I dont think I am the only one.

talking it out

Saturday, July 24, 2010

Joe just told me about the lady in the previous post. So here's to helping her at least dog paddle. Joe does not talk alot about how he is feeling anymore and as he puts it I nag. It is not so much nagging but wanting in to his thoughts so I can understand what he is thinking and how he is feeling. Yes I know he does not know what he is thinking alot of the times but when he does it is really good. So I am relegated to asking only once a say certain questions such as "what's on your brain?" To which the answer is usually mud, eh, or I forget. I have to ask specifically about how he is feeling to a body part. If I ask in general I can only ask once a day. So if I know his fingers hurt or his head hurts I ask specific questions. I also have learned how to ask the same question in different ways but he is catching on. So he will ask me if I have already asked that for the day. And don't be afraid to say hey it's not my fault I am here for you but let me in once in a while. I need to know how he is feeling so that I am prepared to help with either just holding his hand or letting him be on his own. Even though they have this problem going on in their heads they still need alone time too. Hope this helps a little. Lynn
Posted by Lynn at 12:31PM (-07:00)

Comments

—Peaches   July 26, 2010

When I would take my dad to the Dr's Office or the ER it was so difficult for him because they would ask him questions and he would get confused so of course he looks at me and I have to break down the question for him one by one. My father suffered from depression through out the time he was suffering from AD. I tried in everyway to make him laugh once a day. Whether it be silly faces or taking him to pizza and pinball games. When I stepped away from my problems and just focused on making him smile and laugh it relieved my stress. I went along with what he wanted to do. Eventually after the steal gate to his emotions came down I would tell him how I really loved him and I want to give him the best like he wanted to do for me. Then it seemed to help him past the anger and be able to tap into the soft emotional side of his and we could talk about how he felt. We as caregivers really do have to be mind readers and therapists it seems. My dad's birthday was yesterday and I remember how making that last birthday the best one and how he smiled and laughed. So I say hang in there and take breaks from your caregiving life so you dont become resentful and it allows the time to let go of the fight you just had . . . because they have already forgotten about it so we need to as well.

—Anonymous   July 27, 2010

Hi there Lynn & Joe. You two sound like such a perfect couple. I'm sorry to say that I am not feeling that way about my husband and I. My spouse is 17 years older than me. He was diagnosed about the same time as Joe and yes, he seems to be experiencing relatively the same stages that Joe is going through. But I must confess, I am not feeling like the pleasant, let me make you feel better caregiver right now. The TV can only be on one of the two channels he chooses, Fox News or the Weather Channel and he doesn't even watch them. He, like you Joe, stares off into space. I try to strike up any type of conversation by commenting about what they have just shown on TV but he wasn't watching it and has no idea what they were talking about. Then he gets angry with me because he is confused about my comments. Lately, he is always crankey and YELLING at me and our extended family (5 children, 6 grandchildren) so they don't seem to come around anymore. I do go to work part time but he is insistant that I not leave him for more than a few hours at a time and demands that I not go anywhere away from him for any type of enjoyment. He doesn't even want me to go shopping to get things that we need, only to the grocery store a half mile away. He makes me feel guilty that he is afraid he will die alone and that I must be with him at all times. And I don't mean just at our home, he insists I be in the same room with him ALL the time. People say to me that I should get out and do things for myself. I agree. But the reality of life is that other people don't include you when they know you have to be home with your spouse all the time. They don't want to be the cause of his anger either. So here I sit feeling so all alone in the same room as him. I provide his meals, cut his hair, do the grocery shopping, take care of our expenses and accounts, pick up his prescriptions, do his laundry and clean up after him. He refuses to go ANYWHERE. Will not leave the house and wants me to do the same. I do understand that what he is going through is very difficult. But there is never any expression of gratitude or even acknowledgement that this is difficult for me to go through also. He used to tell me every night when we went to bed that he loved me, but even that has gone. Now I only seem to be the object of his anger and frustration. But all the same, I will keep on keeping on. I won't give up, but it does help to have an outlet to release my feelings, even if it is to someone I have never met and never will.

Joe, please give Lynn a hug and let her know how much you love and appreciate her. Sounds like you have a real piece of gold to hang on to through this journey we all pass through. My love to you both.

—karen   July 27, 2010

God bless you both. I do Love reading Joes post. And yours lynn. I hope he starts up posting again if he can

The very Fabric of This Blog

Friday, July 30, 2010

Anonymous has left a new comment on your post "talking it out":

Hi there Lynn & Joe. You two sound like such a perfect couple. I'm sorry to say that I am not feeling that way about my husband and I. My spouse is 17 years older than me. He was diagnosed about the same time as Joe and yes, he seems to be experiencing relatively the same stages that Joe is going through. But I must confess, I am not feeling like the pleasant, let me make you feel better caregiver right now. The TV can only be on one of the two channels he chooses, Fox News or the Weather Channel and he doesn't even watch them. He, like you Joe, stares off into space. I try to strike up any type of conversation by commenting about what they have just shown on TV but he wasn't watching it and has no idea what they were talking about. Then he gets angry with me because he is confused about my comments. Lately, he is always crankey and YELLING at me and our extended family (5 children, 6 grandchildren) so they don't seem to come around anymore. I do go to work part time but he is insistant that I not leave him for more than a few hours at a time and demands that I not go anywhere away from him for any type of enjoyment. He doesn't even want me to go shopping to get things that we need, only to the grocery store a half mile away. He makes me feel guilty that he is afraid he will die alone and that I must be with him at all times. And I don't mean just at our home, he insists I be in the same room with him ALL the time. People say to me that I should get out and do things for myself. I agree. But the reality of life is that other people don't include you when they know you have to be home with your spouse all the time. They don't want to be the cause of his anger either. So here I sit feeling so all alone in the same room as him. I provide his meals, cut his hair, do the grocery shopping, take care of our expenses and accounts, pick up his prescriptions, do his laundry and clean up after him. He refuses to go ANYWHERE. Will not leave the house and wants me to do the same. I do understand that what he is going through is very difficult. But there is never any expression of gratitude or even acknowledgement that this is difficult for me to go through also. He used to tell me every night when we went to bed that he loved me, but even that has gone. Now I only seem to be the object of his anger and frustration. But all the same, I will keep on keeping on. I won't give up, but it does help to have an outlet to release my feelings, even if it is to someone I have never met and never will.

Joe, please give Lynn a hug and let her know how much you love and appreciate her. Sounds like you have a real piece of gold to hang on to through this journey we all pass through. My love to you both.

The above is a comment shared on this blog in respose to a posting by my wife Lynn, who I am 16 years older than. This lady is suffering just as Lynn is, I have become very combative, pig headed, a dick, paranoid and more withdrawn. I have asked many of you to be guest bloggers for the above very reason. I cannot tell you how many 100's of emails I have received just like the above comment. See all I can respond to these people is that I am sorry for your mate and you, but it is only going to get worse, a lot of comfort right, wrong, but it is the truth. I ask again that you help with posting. See even if you do the same thing everyday, you still do something a little different and that little difference could help someone like this lady. Me i love and appreciate your words of encouragement, but really they are gone as soon as I read them. You see I know that I will not get better only worse and it is doing that quite well. I am on a journey to keep an appointment with mental collapse and physical death that is the reality of it. It sucks, i hate how i feel, i do not like my distrust and disgust with others, but my emotions are no longer mine, I even do not feel bad anymore when I am a real pain in the ass or hurt feelings, my brain says tough crap to you. I hear and see things now that are not there, i do not even know when I am being talked to. Sex keeps rolling in my brain but the old pecker does not help out and I even say who the hell caaares to taht. I am getting like my good friend Dr. Joe Savick, making a 42 paragraph post. Thanks for listening shit has hjust built up in me and while I am thinking of it I am making this post.

God Bless & Keep You & This Country of Ours.

Joe

Posted by Joseph Potocny at 11:09AM (-07:00)

Comments

—JUSTAMOM   July 31, 2010

JOe!!!! I love this post and YES this would be the PERFECT REASON FOR YOUR BLOG. Sorry I am just now catching up on posts . . . My oldest daughter and grand baby have moved in with me. Hang in there and keep on keepin on my friend.

—Heather   August 03, 2010

I read your blog and comment when I can. For me you have given insight to what happened (and continues to happen) to my dad. I don't really have a connection to the caregiving side because that was done by my mom and it seems there are so few that are children of AD patients that aren't caregivers that I feel out of place. I continue to struggle with losing my dad(and to a certain part my mom) but still having him here physically. I have become lost to him and that is probably the hardest part. So many try to make a happy ending for this story but for now I don't see one. Reading how you and Lynn are facing this challenge and reading others responses does help pull me through. It is this group of people that truly understand how much this sucks even if we are trying to put on our happy face. Thanks once again for letting us inside. It is a difficult task but one you have taken on and by doing so given so much to so many.

—Anonymous   August 05, 2010

Good Morning!

It's me, Anonymous. I have to write as Anonymous as my husband would absolutely flip if he knew I was posting anything. He is a very private person and for the first four or five years was in total denial that there was anything happening with him. He now will at least comment about his mind being so foggy that he can't think straight but don't dare say that he has AD. I suspect that a lot of people who read this site and would like to comment are probably going through similar experiences.

I wanted to share with you and the readers that when I wrote last, I was so down and depressed, with tears dropping down my cheeks as I typed, but I was angry and needed someone to talk to, someone who might understand how I was feeling. Life is strange, but you have no idea what a release it was for me and I felt so much better after I spelled it all out. In the past I attended an AD support group but found it of no assistance. People seem to want to tell you what you should and shouldn't be doing to cope with what you are dealing with. I, like others can read about all these things.

Anonymously, we can all be brave enough to talk about our innermost thoughts and true feelings. God bless you Joe for having the courage to share your innermost thoughts and feeling so openly with all the world. As you can see from the lack of people responding, the rest of us do not have the courage you display. Maybe you can't always tap into the knowledge you once had but you certainly do display the wisdom that you have attained, even during such a difficult time.

To Heather,

I appreciate hearing your comments. Out of our five children and their spouses, I have one daughter-in-law who sometimes talks with me regarding her feelings of how this has effected our family relations. It does really help me to know that I am not the only family member recognizing the changes in our lives and it gives me the opportunity to share my feelings and observations and to remind them that even though life may be different now, I am so greatful that I still have him with me, still able to hug him, kiss him, know he is beside me at night. Yes, we have all lost the lives we once considered our normal, but life is continually changing and physically we do still have our families. The challenge as I see it is how we continue adapting to our circumstances. Please continue to share your feelings as I think you can be of so much help for me and others to understand some of the challenges our children may be experiencing.

I must admit, this is the only site I have ever found that really says it like it is, and I for one really appreciate the honesty I find here.

Love to you ALL.

Thursday, August 05, 2010

I think that Anonymous has hit it right on the head. There are times that I want to wring the old guys neck. I love him and always will but he can be such a pill that it he is hard to take. But then he would dearly love for all of us to take a hike and not come back because we bug him. Two way street. I have not wanted to write on the blog because I am a private person and Joe has put us out here. So I guess that in the long run if it helps one of you out there, so be it. I understand the not happy caretaker thing. Joe and I have had a few problems lately and I have walked out of the house a few times and I probably will a few more before this is over. I have promised him that I will let him know when I am leaving now because the last time I left for 20 min. he left and we did not know where he was for an hour until the park rangers found him. I was even on the phone with the police. Scary times. Our kids say things will get better but I feel that things will only get different. Better will be when we do not have any more worries or fights. I cry alot too. You really are not as alone as you think. I have not coped with this as well as it seems. I am learning though that there are others out here that feel as I do and I guess that is what this blog is all about. Please keep reading and posting when you can or care too. Our stories are so close, Joe hates to go out and I wait for him to decide what he wants to do, we tell each other that we love each other when we are awake to do so. Forget it at night. I do believe that he is grateful that I am around, but I do not expect him to say it. Just holding hands sometimes is

enough. Take care and enjoy those moments when he is truly with you. Lynn
Posted by Lynn at 10:46AM (-07:00)

Comments

—Mandy   August 08, 2010

I just want to say that I am finding all this talk back and forth very helpful. My
spouse has ad and he can be a real pain at times. I feel like I am reading my life
story between some of these posts. I find that sometimes I just need to leave
him alone and walk away from the situation before one of us blows up and it
is usually him. we both know it will not get better but just a glimpse of who he
was before is a precious moment. Thanks for listening and being there.

Asking for Help & New Link Added.

Friday, August 06, 2010

I have added a new link, Nursing Home Abuse, for those of you that may have
problems with a nursing home or need help in finding and how to look for one.
Do hope that this will be of help.

I am glad to see the comments of help going back and forth, this will help you
I think and hope. This is what this blog has been waiting for. Out of the avg of
179 people that visit each day, I think some of you have great wisdom to offer
each other. For me, getting better is not taking place, getting worse is and will
till it kills me.

You all know I just love the medical profession and researchers with great and
profound moranity. I got a mailer the other day, Alhzeimers cured and the
cause, medical book supposedly. AD caused by lack of insulin in other words
diabetes of the brain. The gist is that extra insulin can halt or even reverse the
damage. A lot of quacks out there, amazing that this one dr. has found this
out and has not shared it with the medical community but is with the world.
I think I will go have to cokes so the caffine stops my AD.

I need some help or at least to know if any one with AD out there or caregivers
have noticed this happening: For a cpl of months now I have been experienncing
pain in the brain, this is not a headache or migrane as one knows them to
be. It is like someone with really big hands is reachin inside my skull and just
squeezing the hell out of my one brain cell, trying to make it smaller. This can
last for hours to days, even longer once it is gone I notice that more of me is
gone. I guess the details I follow because of my employment was in the field
of computers and data gathering and details, still with me to a degree. Have
talke to my shrink and pyhsycologist about this and get a dumb look. So you
folks my family if you have any info on this I sure would like to know about it,

I feel alone enough now without being the only one with this bull shit. Posted by Joseph Potocny at 12:40PM (-07:00)

Comments

—MrsSewandSew-Karen	August 06, 2010

Joe, Thanks for putting yourself out here and being so honest. I am diabetic and at 57 notice some decline in my memory. My new goal is to control my glucose better, to eat correctly, and exercise daily. Thank you for inspiring me to fight back even though I do not have AD (only diabetes). I know totally different diseases but you inspired me! Take care. Karen Ps. Thanks for the new link.

—Peaches	August 10, 2010

Here are 2 sites that I found quite helpful when searching for my father

    CalQualityCare
    MediCare

Joe, My father had quite the headache everyday. Though it was hard to communicate with him on how he felt, I did see that it affected him about half the day. Doctor told me to give him some Ibuprophen or Asprin. The doc told me that it was either he was dehydrated or he just couldnt tolerate the heat so much. I think it was the dehydration since my dad had his own A/C and it was alway 65°F in the house.

—Annie	August 13, 2010

Joe,

If Mom ever experienced what you describe she didn't have the words to express it. As her caregiver, I did notice that she got more agitated/restless whenever a weather front moved through. I don't know if it was pain, but changes in air pressure definitely changed her behavior. Have you noticed if weather changes coincide with your brain pain?

Brains or Trains

Monday, August 16, 2010

I wonder sometimes if I have any brains left or if they are just trains runnnning in a circle. Things to me seem to be getting fuzzier each day. I forget mor of what I am going to do each day. Wife is up North visiting daughter and kids, I just could not take going after her 50th a week or so ago. I found 32 good reasonss to commit homicide that day, way too much noise, movement, people, just a real grate on my brain, nerves and patience.

I am glad to see the going back and forth in comments and Lynn's posting. We got one the other day that we discussed and both of us for diffferent reasons. She could understand the people resenting the fact that the parents who are becoming a problem and like me, living another 5 or more years. Lynn feels that way about me at times and we both think it is normal and good to express it. You need time away from us guys to help yourselves. See I look at it that I may have to put up with those arround me hovering, checking, watching ever annoying me even for another year. I wish they would just disappear at times. I think both sides feel this way, have to, we with Dementia are really a handfull, I think worse than trying to raise baby tripplets. See have the time I do not know what I want or what I am doing, just like a kid.

I want to say welcome to all of you that visit my blog. From Russia, US, Canada, Latvia, China, Brazil, Austrailia, etc., it boggles my brain cell. Thank you all for visiting. I hope to be adding new resources to the list on the side soon for you all.

God Bless & Keep You and This Country of Ours (and the World)!!!!!

joe

Posted by Joseph Potocny at 06:40PM (-07:00)

Comments

—MrsSewandSew-Karen   August 16, 2010

Hang in there Joe. Ya, I hate to say this but even without demetia we need time away from our mates. It is good to hear from both sides (caregiver & demetia patient) how you both feel. Take care and be good while Lynn is away! . . . lol. Karen

—RumanaAkter   August 18, 2010

Looking for recipes? You've come to the right place. The Year of the Cookie has many free recipes—all created, tested, reviewed.

The Year of the Cookie

—Peaches   August 18, 2010

In the end I was just happy that my father was out of pain. Yes, there were times I would think of him passing sooner rather than later. But then I have some tender moments with him that I would of missed out on. The time we have with each other is the time we have. We cant question it. Just embrace it.

—Margaret   August 19, 2010

Hello Joe, Found your blog after seeing the HBO special in my alzheimers group. I want to thank you for sharing so much of your life. My mother has alzheimers and she does not believe anything is wrong. Your posts allow me to see what she is going through. I have read most of your posts now . . . I have read your words and have felt your thoughts. You are a remarkable person . . . allowing others to learn from what you are experiencing. You are a true warrior in the battle of alzheimers. I will keep you and your family in my thoughts and prayers. GOD BLESS YOU AND YOUR FAMILY! I will keep reading your blogs so keep writing when you can. Hang in there my friend . . . there are people out here who appreciate your efforts so much! Big Hugs! Margaret

You Are Needed!!!!!!!!!!!

Wednesday, August 18, 2010

—Original Message—Subject: Thanks for Taking Action! Date: Wed, 18 Aug 2010 15:55:15—0500 (CDT) From: Brendan Burns, Alzheimer's Association Reply-To: Brendan Burns, Alzheimer's Association Organization: Alzheimer's Association To: jolynn1@cox.net

Joseph, Thanks for taking action! We need your help to gather more petition signatures. Please take a moment to forward the message below to your family and friends. It's quick, it's easy and it will only take a few moments to make a big difference. Thank you, Brendan Burns

Subject Line: It's Time for a Breakthrough Dear friends, Alzheimer's disease steals the future from millions of Americans. It robs spouses of their companions and children of their parents and grandparents; it erodes the health and financial resources of caregivers. I just signed a petition calling on Congress to make Alzheimer's disease a national priority. Will you add your voice? *http:// www.alz.org/petition* Your signature will be delivered to Congress on September 21, 2010 World Alzheimer's Day. Together, we can make Alzheimer's a national priority. Posted by Joseph Potocny at 04:31PM (-07:00)

Comments

—Anonymous   August 20, 2010

Thank you for this info . . . I signed and will be sending it to all my friends. Shannon

—Anonymous   August 24, 2010

Hello Joe,

I just found your blog. My mother has alzheimers and your blog has allowed me to see inside her world. Thank you so much. You are a true warrior in the battle of alzheimers . . . information is knowledge and your willingness to share your feelings will help many . . . take care my friend . . . you and your family are in our thoughts and prayers . . . GOD BLESS YOU AND YOUR FAMILY!! Thank you again!!!! Margaret

Par Boiled Fanny

Wednesday, August 25, 2010

Yes yours truly master of home repairs and as dense as a tree was at it again today. One needs to know that me and ladders do not belong in the same universe, I get on one and by the time I reach the second step on it I am 30 pounds lighter. Today we started on clean the outside of the house, redoing the pation and th driveway. Well do to my immense brain power I got on the roof to wash down the roof and upstairs portion of the house. Well sitting on the roof was a bit on the hot side. Did you know that when you spray down a roof that the sun has been beating down on the water turns to steam, well I do now. As this small river came rushing down the roof towards my secure spot, it reached my butt, yess my backside, and it cooked it. I felt like I was sitting ing boiling water, guess what DAH i was. I am fighting this disease the best I can, but the longer we go down the road, the more I find out what I do not know that I thought I knew, before I found out that I did not have the first idea about it.

Lately when I get up I am not able to finish crossing that bridge from sleep to being fully awake. I was talking with my ologist this week and he asked if I felt like I was is a fog. Well the answer is yes, the above is proof of that.Things are just not clear to me any more and I stop more in the middle of things then I did before and wind up doing something else. Each day I decide to write on here and say I should write things down before I post so I remeber what it is that I want to say. GREAT IDEA, problem is I sit down to do it and forget what it was I was going to do, welcome to dreamland.

Well I need to stand right now so you all be good to yourselves and THANK You for helping me win the new award posted on our blog. This is your victory as well.

God Bless & Keep You & This Country of Ours!!!!

joe

Posted by Joseph Potocny at 03:55PM (-07:00)

Comments

—karen   August 25, 2010

Congrats on the award and sorry for your cooked bottom. Thanks for the info because I am always on my roof sweeping off pine needles so now I know not to use the water hose to wash off the pine needles. Stay cool.

—Margaret   August 27, 2010

Hello Joe,

Thanks for the HOT tip on the roof . . . I think my husband would have done the same thing . . . Hang in there . . . I appreciate your thoughts and words . . . God Bless you and your family . . . and yes I am going to VOTE along with you! Big HUGS! A new person to your blog and I check in all the time to see if you are blogging . . . Margaret

—Heather   August 29, 2010

At least you didn't need the fire department. One day my mom made the comment that the gutters needed cleaning. She then went to the store and returned to find my dad sitting on the roof. When she asked him what he was doing there he said he didn't know. When she told him to come down he said he had been trying but just couldn't get his feet to do what he wanted them to. Well poor mom was in no position to climb up and get him so the next best thing was the fire department. Once they got my dad down he let them know he would have figured it out sooner or later. My mom hid the ladder after that and was MUCH more careful about comments she made around him. Here's to a cooler bottom

—Adirondackcountrygal   September 05, 2010

Joe I stop in the middle of doing something and go do something else all the time and I do not have Alzheimers. Which reminds me I was about to put the laundry in the dryer and got distracted and it still is sitting in the washer . . .

About the parboiling

Monday, August 30, 2010

First of all let me tell everyone that I was totally against him going on the roof. I have been doing the roof projects for a long time now and I could not stop him. I asked him why he felt he needed to do it and the response was He needed to prove to himself that he was still able to do things like this. So we put on his tennis shoes for better grip and tucked in his pants legs and boy did he look ducky. And he did not go up very high just a couple of feet and as the water came down the roof he remembered that the roof was warm and so was his behind. I guess what the point of all this is, is even though they have this coming on they want to feel useful around the house and that they need to feel wanted and needed. Joe still does things around the house. He has his daily routine, feed the fish, bird and take out the recyclable stuff piled up on the counter. He has taken over doing the towels once a week and heaven help us if we interfere. (He takes them out of the dryer and puts them on so he can warm up). So if your loved one or patient can do some chores around the house let them as long as they do not pose a danger to themselves or others. I am sure there are some things they can do such as feeding animals or folding laundry. You will figure it out. But the roof is probably a bad idea. Joe won't be going up there again. Take care Lynn Posted by Lynn at 01:51PM (-07:00)

Comments

—Anonymous   August 31, 2010

Good morning Lynn and Joe. I can certainly relate to this situation. Unfortunately, memory is not the only effect of this disease but also logic, reasoning, and EGO are noticably effected. We have one and a half acres of lawn which we have a good sized tractor for mowing. My husband refuses to allow me to mow with the tractor and always says that I wouldn't be able to handle it. The truth is I used to do the mowing with the tractor but he claims that he doesn't remember that I ever did. The truth has come out that he really feels it is the one thing he still does and doesn't want me taking over it. We have fought and fought over this over recent years now and I can't seem to win. His abilities to maneuver and control the tractor are noticably impared but I still cannot get him to concede to allow me to do the mowing. He is aware that he has problems with doing the mowing and procrastinates just as long as he possibly can. The best plan that I have come up with is to use the hand mower to cut the two areas that are potentially dangerous with the tractor. When I first started doing this he even continued to take the tractor over the same areas that I had already mowed just because he resented the idea that I felt it was something he could no longer do. I just can't seem to get across to him that just having him safe and uninjured by my side day after day is so much more important to me than him proving to himself that he can still do certain things. I think we could all benefit from hearing from others who have faced these challenges and how they were able to successfully navigate through these types of situations. Thank God Joe's experience was his parboiled fanny and not a fall from the roof! I pray that my husband's experience will only be damage to his tractor and not to his body. May God bless us and guide us through our journey of life, whatever it brings our way!

This Comment Deserves Posting Status

Tuesday, August 31, 2010

The following comment deserves to be used as a post. This is what I have tried to get others that were invited as posters to do. I share my side, you share yours.

Anonymous has left a new comment on your post "About the parboiling":

Good morning Lynn and Joe. I can certainly relate to this situation. Unfortunately, memory is not the only effect of this disease but also logic, reasoning, and EGO are noticably effected. We have one and a half acres of lawn which we have a good sized tractor for mowing. My husband refuses to allow me to mow with the tractor and always says that I wouldn't be able to handle it. The truth is I used to do the mowing with the tractor but he claims that he doesn't remember that I ever did. The truth has come out that he really feels it is the one thing he still does and doesn't want me taking over it. We have fought and fought over this over recent years now and I can't seem to win. His abilities to maneuver and control the tractor are noticably impared but I still cannot get him to concede to allow me to do the mowing. He is aware that he has problems with doing the mowing and procrastinates just as long as he possibly can. The best plan that I have come up with is to use the hand mower to cut the two areas that are potentially dangerous with the tractor. When I first started doing this he even continued to take the tractor over the same areas that I had already mowed just because he resented the idea that I felt it was something he could no longer do. I just can't seem to get across to him that just having him safe and uninjured by my side day after day is so much more important to me than him proving to himself that he can still do certain things. I think we could all benefit from hearing from others who have faced these challenges and how they were able to successfully navigate through these types of situations. Thank God Joe's experience was his parboiled fanny and not a fall from the roof! I pray that my husband's experience will only be damage to his tractor and not to his body. May God bless us and guide us through our journey of life, whatever it brings our way!

Posted by Anonymous to Living with Alzhiemers' at 6:50 AM

God Bless & Keep You & This Country of Ours!!!

joe

Posted by Joseph Potocny at 02:17PM (-07:00)

Comments

I can so identify. My husband still uses the riding mower to mow. He has taken out the well water to the house by mowing too close to plumbing even before his dementia was a factor. Now we have little posts so he won't do that.

He still loves to escort me places and even drives with a GPS. I let him do what he can do now.

Carol http://plantcityladyandfriends.blogspot.com/

My mom never drove but she use take off walking and we would find her on the neighbors porchs sitting in there lawn chairs. Thank goodness she did not go far. We were at a buffet once and we would take her to the table and than go get hers and our food but one time she decided to leave. We found her walking the mall. Needless to say it was time for someone to keep and eye on her 24/7.

Waking Up What Is It?

Sunday, September 05, 2010

I have come to belive that waking up is not all that it is cracked up to be. It seems that I never seem to wake up completely anymore. I more or less remain is a state of awakeness if that is a word, if not it is now. I just never seem to quite get with it anymore. I am becoming much more testier and argumentative, wow I think I spelled that right. Time is more jumbled now then ever before and I have more difficult in getting things out and what the hell i do no t know what i whant to say here.

I no longer enjoy being downstairs in my home, only outside in the front or back or upstairs, i do not know what it is, i am very uncomfortable now. We just spent I do not remember how much when remodeling downstairs the way we wanted it and I do not want to be down there now. I do not understand me anymore. Lynn wants me to talk to her and I cannot even talk to myself. Hell I always talked to myself, I was the only one that had the answers I wanted to hear now I cann't think of them.

Well take care for now.

God Bless & Keep You & This Country of Ours!!!!

joe

Posted by Joseph Potocny at 12:14PM (-07:00)

Comments

<u>—NewKidontheBlogg</u>   September 05, 2010

Joe, I love how you can express your feelings and experiences. You help me understand my husband. He needs to have coffee and think about a new day when he wakes up. I don't think we should change much about our house so he can be comfortable. I am learning from you. Thanks so much.

<u>—Mary</u>   September 06, 2010

Hi Joe: I know I'm happiest when the space around me isn't too busy. If there is too much 'stuff' I seem to get more agitated. Almost like its all too much for my brain to process these days I guess. Hugs to you Joe Mary

<u>—Anonymous</u>   September 08, 2010

Last winter I moved our portable fireplace to the other side of the room as my husband was always complaining of being cold. I thought he would really appreciate having the warmth of the fireplace closer to him. He kept complaining that he liked it where it was and wouldn't I put it back. I thought that he would eventually get used to it's new location. After three weeks of his continual complaining about it being moved, I gave in and moved it back to it's original location. My husband has his own personal space in our family room that is HIS space with several things that are special to him. It may look cluttered and out of place but it is his comfort zone and everyone knows that it is HIS space so don't mess with it. I can't say that I understand the importance of things staying the same but I do recognize the uncomfortable situation it creates for him. I wonder what the effect is for a person with AD who has to move to a different home? Do they eventually become comfortable with their new surroundings and after approximately what period of time? Would love to hear from others with AD who have experienced this. I sure hope you are able to create a JOE space in your newly remodeled downstairs where you will once again find your comfort zone.

<u>—karen</u>   September 08, 2010

You still write great. I understand everything you write and it helps me out alot. Sorry you don't like downstairs. But just stay were you are happy. That is all that matters.

Needing Space

Wednesday, September 08, 2010

Just so all of you understand, we remodeled a few years ago. Things were in an uproar then and we have not done any remodeling in the house lately. We just painted the patio outside and have been working on his ponds for the last year. So where there was at one time alot of things going on it has died down alot. Joe has even mentioned that it seems that we have come to a standstill on doing things around here. It is just recently that he has mentioned that he is not comfortable in the downstairs of the house. He will go up to watch tv at 8 at night and stay awake until 2 or 3. I do not know what is going on with this new emotion. He has his space at the ponds but in the house it is the sanctuary of our room that he seems to be the most comfortable. It is completely opposite of what he used to do. Joe would love to change things. We would paint or move stuff and then it was time to start over again. The house always needed to change and so did he. Not so anymore. Joe would like to do stuff but then when it comes time to do it he backs off. The same for going out. He has a hard time just going out with me to the store. Part if the problem is physically being able to walk without to much problem and the other is the fact that there are so many people around. We were in the store a while back and I let him go down one aisle looking for something and when he walked sown the aisle that I was in he looks right at me and continued on, he came back to the aisle and said I know you. Little scary. So I have to not let him go because even though he seems ok when we are together it is the what happens when we are not together that is scary. But try and tell him that. It comes back down to them wanting to prove that they can still do things the old way. So once again it is good luck with who you have. I do believe that change is not a good thing with these guys and that the more stable and calm things are the better. Take care Lynn Posted by Joseph Potocny at 02:15PM (-07:00)

Comments

—NewKidontheBlogg   September 08, 2010

I have read to keep things the way they are. With short-term memory you can't be changing things!

The store situation sure was scary for you.

—MadamMoonchild   September 09, 2010

I sometimes wish I could add something substantial to your posts but I can't. I just know that everything you guys are both going through must be terribly difficult. Bless you both.

As The Present Fades
Tuesday, September 14, 2010

I am still amazed at this point that I can still converse with you and tell you how things are going in my journey or battle if you will. In the beginning and still now i am prepared for the mental walkings and goings but I was never prepaired for the physical problems. Walking with a swagger, actually kind of a stumble and hunched, feeling icky most of the time, getting exttermely upset around people and sweaty like a pig, shaking like i do, not able to hold things all the time, just not ready for this crap.

I find my world in fading in and out now. I recognize family and people and suddenly they start to become someone else. Same person standing there but my brain seems to switch off and step back and say who the fuck is that. I am finding this to be happening more and more, I feel like i am fading away from Joe and going somewhere and I cannot stop it anylonger. I really wish I would hear from others in this world of mine and what they are going through and how they feel. It is really a lonely place, yes I have people around me that care and help, not the same, they are not here with me, in my reality such as it is.

I must go now my mind is confused and i am getting very angry.

God Bless You & This Country of Ours!

joe

Posted by Joseph Potocny at 12:36PM (-07:00)

Comments

—Adirondackcountrygal   September 14, 2010

Joe I am so sorry to hear that you are having such a difficult time. I will be praying for you.

—NewKidontheBlogg   September 14, 2010

Thanks so much for explaining so well how it is for you. I am sorry that you are experiencing confusion and trouble walking. May the LORD sustain you each day and give you things to enjoy.

Carol http://plantcityladyandfriends.blogspot.com/

—Anonymous   September 16, 2010

Hi Joe,

Thank you for sharing how you are feeling and experiencing. Unfortunately, I doubt that there are many others out there with your condition that have the courage to admit what they are experiencing. I know my husband when asked how he is will only say "About the same as always". I know him well enough to know that he would not verbally express any experiences such as you have described but would try to ignore it and pretend to himself that it didn't happen. He continues to live in denial of his condition. His defense seems to be to try to sleep as much as he can. Yes, I do notice his posture and gait just as you describe but not the shaking. He is not currently displaying signs of anger. It is his compulsions that are so noticable (checking the door three times to be sure it is locked, even when he watches me lock it and several other things).

I am really sorry to hear you say that you feel so alone inside and wish there were some way you could help us to figure out a way to reach you. But then, isn't that the magic answer everyone who has a loved one with AD looking for, how do we truly connect with them?

Thank you for really helping us to understand what you are feeling and thinking, and thank you for your courage to share!!!

—Anonymous   September 28, 2010

Dear Joe,

Thank you so much for posting what is happening inside your mind and being. My mom has AZ too. She too is quite intelligent, but has not been able to communicate what is going on internally at all. Your courage and wisdom is amazing. Very inspiring for me.

Your wife is very inspiring too. Thanks again. A fan

You Know My Love for Studies

Saturday, September 18, 2010

Here is a link about possible preventive things against Alzheimer's:

http://www.newsmaxhealth.com/headline_health/breakthroughs_ Alzheimers/2010/09/17/3 50866.html?s=al&promo_code=AC7C-1

You be the judge of this. I think you will know my demented thoughts on this. The gene one only covers to my understanding maybe 5% of people who get AD. I would really like to know how they determine that the one's that did not get AD, would not have gotten it anyway. Stats can mean what you want them to.

God Bless & Keep You & This Country of Ours!

joe

Posted by Joseph Potocny at 02:22PM (-07:00)

Comments

—JUSTAMOM   September 20, 2010

still around just really busy these days.

What is in YOUR Refrigerator?

Tuesday, September 21, 2010

A few years ago we had the kitcehn remodeled. New Honey Oak Cabinets, with black nobs with dark cherry wood centers, the walls in a chocolate color, and a Brazilian Cherry Hardwood Floor, Black Stove & Microwave and a Black & Stainless Steel Dishwasher. Then there sat6 are very old but working fine White Refrigerator. So for years you know who has been bitching for one to match, yes me. Well we just purchased a new one. Reasons, much more energy efficient then are 15 year old one, quieter, it has crushed ice a must for me, but most importantly it is BLACK and matches the decor. Happy am I, yes, except for opening it.

You see the last one the bottom drawers were solid and you could not see what was in them. This one they are CLEAR and you see everything. So what you say, well let me tell you there are creatures in those bins. I open the door and they stare at me, I know they want me. I cannot look at them, sill y yess, but that is how my brain reacts to them.Lynn just says Joe, get over yourself and deal with it. Not so simple, things like this are creeping into my life now and I can only wonder what lies ahead. The part of my brain that still understands logic laughs at me, but there is that growing part that sees and witnesses strange things and seems to have more control. The stuff in thre drawers seems to have eyes and moves when I look at it, not anyone else, just me and that is what really counts is how I feel about it.Well I guess I will just have to outfit myself for hunting when I go to the refrig that way I am prepaired for any attack.

Thank you all for being here for me.

God Bless & Keep You & This Country of Ours!!

joe

PS: PLEASE NOTE IN MEMORY OF PHOTOS NOW HAVE THEIR OWN PAGE!!!!!!!!
Posted by Joseph Potocny at 12:05PM (-07:00)

Comments

<hr>

—Anonymous   September 24, 2010

I have an idea. Maybe you could cover the front of the drawer so it would look solid and not so scary.Perhaps use some construction paper. I don't have an account so I must remain anon.

<hr>

—Adirondackcountrygal   September 24, 2010

Just don't shoot the refrigerator Joe!

<hr>

—Annie September 26, 2010

<hr>

I have creatures living in my refrigerator bins too; a mouldering cucumber, a half-eaten head of now wilted lettuce. I was going to suggest the same thing as Anon. Cover up the bins so you can't see in. At night, Mom would always wonder who those people are out there. She was seeing our reflections in the window. I soon learned to cover the windows at night so she wouldn't worry. Do whatever you have to do to make yourself comfortable.

It is what it is

Friday, September 24, 2010

I have been trying to think how to say this . . . I am angry. I am royally ticked off at this disease. I am ticked that I do not have the man that I married anymore. Yes I understand that I am not the same person that he married and that we all change. That is how it is supposed to be, but this is different. They lose themselves and we lose them. I got my haircut over the weekend and Joe has asked me twice now if I got my haircut. I can't take my frustration out on the guy who cuts me off on the road, I can't yell at the broad who runs the stop signs in our neighborhood, (well I can but it does not do any good), there is no one to lay the blame on when Joe is sitting and wondering where he is or who he is talking to. I try not to get frustrated with him when he is in a foul mood because he does not know what is going on. I can't yell at him because he does not always understand why I am angry because he doesn't know that he is aggravating me because he who used to make snap decisions now can't decide what he wants to have for lunch. He takes naps at the drop of a hat and leaves right in the middle of a conversation. Not physically but mentally. We were talking about some stuff the other day and he asked if I was disappointed about something and my response was not disappointed but I have to learn to understand that it is what it is. Our lives are all about that now. When you come to grips with the fact that this is what we have to deal with it does bring a little peace. Not alot but just a little. And there will still be those times that I may lose my patience but I need to remember that "It is what it is". Lynn Posted by Joseph Potocny at 05:28PM (-07:00)

Comments

—Adirondackcountrygal

September 24, 2010

Lynn, you are doing good, your feelings are normal. Are there any support groups in your area?

—NewKidontheBlogg

September 24, 2010

It's hard to not take things personally. I think about my husband's Alzheimer's—that were the situation reversed, I know he would be my faithful caregiver and that is my privilege to be his caregiver now. Like the song says on your blog, "You raise me up to be more than I can be . . . You raise me up walk on stormy seas." May the Lord sustain you. Carol

I Can Take Directions???????

Tuesday, September 28, 2010

I was told do not shoot the refrigerator. Last hunting trip it was still alive and well. I just look straight in and not at the botoom creatures. They call but I do not listen I just hear them, kind of like your kids do.

Went and saw my shrink today and we changed meds again, or actually I did. Told him the last stuff he gave me I think it was lats month was at the hazardous waste dump. It ripped my system apart. Back on the old stuff, feeling fine, except have to get the old poop train back on track and the fund dissolver as well.

having fun refinishing a cedar chest, of course my friened Bobby had to sand the thing, otherwise it would have had mountain ranges and gorges in it. He did a beautiful job on the sanding. Yess my staining and varnishing shills are excellent except the stuff makes me loopy, just what I need.

To all of you who visit here and leave your comments, I deeply appreciate them. You who claim to have nothing to say, I say bull, HELLO works well. Nothing important to add, the fact that you stop by, say hello or whatever is important to me and the rest of this world family we have created.So do not be shy.

God Bless & Keep You & This Country of Ours!!!!!

joe

Posted by Joseph Potocny at 04:58PM (-07:00)

Comments

—MadamMoonchild

September 28, 2010

Glad to see you are in a better mood and the new meds are working! :-)

—Brangane   September 29, 2010

Hi Joe, glad to hear that you are back on the meds that suit you more. I look forward to seeing photos of your wood stained chest.

:)

—Carol   September 29, 2010

Joe, I have been reading your posts for awhile but struggle with leaving comments to anyone. It means a lot to me to see your posts and how you and your wife are doing. My mom who has AD will be moving in with us this weekend. She fought to stay on her own but she knew the time had come to have the help of family with her. It has become a struggle for her to do the little things now.

—NewKidontheBlogg   September 29, 2010

Joe,

Love this project and the music, "you raise me up to more than I can be". Will you post a picture when you finish?

Glad you meds are better. My husband also does well with coconut oil in his food.

Cordially, Carol http://plantcityladyandfriends.blogspot.com/

—MrsSewandSew-Karen   September 29, 2010

Hi Joe, Glad to see a post from you. You sounds more positive on these meds. Was worried about you on you last few post. You and Lynn take care. Many blessings, Karen

—sandy   September 29, 2010

I'd like to say hi too, and that I really enjoy reading your posts. I think it's wonderful that you share your perspective and your life and are so open about your struggles. I don't have much to contribute other than thanks for sharing!

Yes Two Days in a Row.

Wednesday, September 29, 2010

Well I am not going to tell you why today, but will tomorrow.

I am having a fairly good day today, so I am going to enjoy it and share it with you.

Good Day.

God Bless & Keep You & This Country of Ours!!!!

joe

Posted by Joseph Potocny at 03:05PM (-07:00)

Comments

—MrsSewandSew-Karen   September 29, 2010

Oh the suspense! LOL! Glad you are having a good day! Blessings, Karen

—Annie   September 30, 2010

Hurray for the good days! Enjoy.

TO BE CONTINUED —

Thursday, September 30, 2010

Well I am back today. Hope you all are well. My day is a bit foggy and slow, but that is how things go. It is cool and rainy here, rain part very unusual for us, but welcomed.

Now tehn since you have wiated with great anticipation, pounding hearts and sweaty palms here is what is going on. First can you guess why the title to this post? Bet your wrong.

Living With Alzhiemer's (A Conversation if You Will), is in the process of being published. All of you have made this possible and have contributed in one way or another to it. Hopefully it will be out before xmas 2355, you know how slow and forgetful I can get. The Book as it is called, is not a novel or such, it is our conversation we have had over the last 4 years I think. Completely unedited and to the point. Yes it is this blog in print, comments and all, except the side materials as they appear.

So to you all Thank You, for your support, caring, sharing and just being there as I make this journey.

God Bless & Keep You & This Country of Ours!

joe

Posted by Joseph Potocny at 01:20PM (-07:00)

Comments

—MrsSewandSew-Karen   September 30, 2010

Woo hoo!!!! Congrats Joe that is great! You will be helping so many people. Glad this is happening for you!!! Blessings, Karen

—JUSTAMOM   October 01, 2010

THAT IS THE BEST NEWS EVER!!!!!! I think the world needs to see just what this does to people . . . have a great weekend!

RESOURCES

Lewy Body Organization *http://www.lewybodydementia.org/*

Alzheimer's Organization
http://www.alz.org/index.asp

Picks or Frontal Temporal Lobe Dementia
http://www.mayoclinic.com/health/frontotemporal-dementia/DS00874

Government Clinical Trials
http://www.ClinicalTrials.gov

Alzheimer Research Forum
http://www.alzforum.org

Well Spouse Association
http://www.wellspouse.org

These are but a small selection of those resources that are available.

My blog and many others help to tell this story of the #6 Killer of Adults in America.
http://living-with-alzhiemers.blogspot.com/

Edwards Brothers,Incl
Thorofare, NJ 08086
09 November, 2010
BA2010314